The Rationality of Feeling

The Falmer Press Library on Aesthetic Education

Series Editor: Dr Peter Abbs, University of Sussex, UK

Setting the Frame

LIVING POWERS:
The Arts in Education
Edited by Peter Abbs (1987)

A IS FOR AESTHETIC:
Essays on Creative and
Aesthetic Education
Peter Abbs (1988)

THE SYMBOLIC ORDER:
A Contemporary Reader on the
Arts Debate
Edited by Peter Abbs (1989)

THE RATIONALITY OF
FEELING:
Understanding the Arts in Education
David Best

The Individual Studies

FILM AND TELEVISION IN
EDUCATION:
An Aesthetic Approach to the
Moving Image
Robert Watson

LITERATURE IN
EDUCATION:
Encounter and Experience
Edwin Webb

DANCE AS EDUCATION:
Towards a National Dance Culture
Peter Brinson

THE VISUAL ARTS IN
EDUCATION
Rod Taylor

MUSIC EDUCATION IN
THEORY AND PRACTICE
Charles Plummeridge

THE ARTS IN THE PRIMARY
SCHOOL
Glennis Andrews and Rod Taylor

EDUCATION IN DRAMA:
Casting the Dramatic Curriculum
David Hornbrook

Work of Reference

KEY CONCEPTS:
A Guide to Aesthetics, Criticism and the Arts in Education
Trevor Pateman

THE FALMER PRESS LIBRARY OF AESTHETIC EDUCATION

The Rationality of Feeling:
Understanding The Arts in Education

David Best

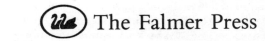 The Falmer Press

(A member of the Taylor & Francis Group)
London • Washington, DC

UK   The Falmer Press, 4 John St, London WC1N 2ET
USA   The Falmer Press, Taylor & Francis Inc., 1900 Frost Road, Suite 101, Bristol, PA 19007

First published in 1992

A catalogue record for this book is available from the British Library

ISBN 0 75070 056 4
ISBN 0 75070 057 2 (pbk)

Library of Congress Cataloging-in-Publication Data are available on request

Typeset in 9.5/11pt Bembo by
Graphicraft Typesetters Ltd., Hong Kong.

Printed in Great Britain by Burgess Science Press, Basingstoke on paper which has a specified pH value on final paper manufacture of not less than 7.5 and is therefore 'acid free'.

Cover illustration
"Be silent, steadfast and forbearing" from *The Magic Flute*, a series of etchings, reproduced by kind permission of the artist, Lynne Gibson.

Contents

To
Jennifer Ann
and
Philip

Preface

The Rationality of Feeling, a major re-working of David Best's earlier volume *Feeling & Reason in the Arts*, forms the final volume in the philosophical frame of the Library on Aesthetic Education. The new emphatic title can be seen as relating to the main concerns of the library — for in *Living Powers*, the first volume in the series, it was claimed that all the arts are cognitive, that they are vehicles for understanding and learning and that, for this very reason, they must lie at the heart of any coherent curriculum.[1] This is the great theme of David Best's book. In practical terms, it means that the arts teacher's primary task is to develop the artistic understanding and creativity of the student through a profound initiation into the relevant culture. It is neither possible nor desirable to begin with zero or 'to make it new'. As David Best puts it:

> The development of individuality in the arts as in other areas of human life, logically depends upon the learning of an objective, disciplined structure of thought and action in that only such a structure can provide the ground on which to stand and which can make sense of the notion of progress. It makes no sense to suggest that one can stand on and move forward from, *nothing*.

Exactly so. And yet so many versions of Modernism and Progressivism, versions of what David Best would characterize as rank subjectivism, insisted on beginning *nowhere* and established that *tabula rasa* classroom which beginning nowhere, was doomed to end there, in a radical state of cultural dispossession.

In this book, David Best lucidly delineates and further extends much of what has been argued or presupposed in the individual studies of the library. In particular, I would stress the following five positions as the key unifying tenets:

1   The need to expand the current conception of rationality to include the arts. Here David Best's notion of *interpretative reason* — a reasoning which may not be able to come up with absolute truths, but is always able to offer *arguments* for its working conclusions — is particularly valuable.
2   The need to end the destructive pseudo-dialectic between scientism and subjectivism, where science is seen as yielding public truth and art merely private states of feeling. As Best points out, this dichotomy is still deep

in our culture and has had poisonous consequences, particularly on the teaching of the arts and their still marginal position in the National Curriculum.

3   The need to envisage the arts in the context of cultural and historical communities, as public conversations across the ages. For in the words of D.W. Winnicot, quoted in the earlier volume *A is for Aesthetic*: 'It is not possible to be original except on a basis of tradition'.

4   The need to understand that the notion of freedom in the arts must always be a freedom *within* a defined cultural field and not as freedom from all restraints, conventions and codes. In this respect, the quotation from J.R. Bambrough (used by David Best in chapter 5) is both precise and eloquent:

> In every sphere of enquiry the learner may come to question what he has been taught, but when he does so, he is appealing to what has been taught as well as against what he has been taught

In the arts it is always a matter of working within and against the cultural continuum as defined by earlier volumes in the library.

5   The need to recognise the place of accountability and objective criteria by which to evaluate creative work in the arts. Interpretation is not a matter of private and arbitrary response; it is, rather, a matter of public judgment which draws upon reason; it can offer coherent argument and adduce evidence and can, in turn, be questioned, tested by counter arguments and propositions.

The reader will see how these positions, developed here with telling examples and logical acumen, relate to the previous volumes. But, he will also discern some real differences. The reader will notice, for example, how David Best is critical of the Kantian tradition of aesthetics, of the notion that the arts form a generic community[2] and of the assumption that the words aesthetic and artistic have a logical connection and affinity.

A preface is clearly not the place to engage with these important and animating differences. But two points must be made. The first is that the reader, concerned with exploring the nature of these differences, would do well to refer back to earlier volumes in the series and particularly to Trevor Pateman's *Key Concepts*. Here the entries under *Aesthetic/Aesthetics, Aesthetic Intelligence* and *Arts in Education: the Idea of a Generic Arts Community* will be of help. The second point is that it is absolutely fitting that in the final philosophical volume differences of conception emerge, for this will serve to keep the whole project self-questioning and articulate. It is almost certain that some of the critical issues raised by David Best in *The Rationality of Feeling* will determine the debate in the coming decade; it is also likely that other major issues will emerge of which, at the moment, we are hardly aware. That is often the paradoxical nature of development; *that the excluded returns and claims primacy.*

What is of the greatest importance now is that the value of the arts and their place in the curriculum is increasingly recognized. David Best gives us cogent, powerful reasons for seeing the arts as agents of learning, of understanding, of development. And it is precisely this, and its intimate and necessary relationship

to the effective teaching of the arts, that needs to be grasped not only by educationists and arts teachers, but by the whole of the society, not least politicians
and policy makers. It is this radical broadening of understanding that we are all
committed to and that this book will do so much to promote.

Peter Abbs
Centre for Language, Literature and the Arts in Education
University of Sussex
February 1992

Notes

1 See particularly pp. 52–55 of *Living Powers: the Arts in Education* edited Peter Abbs,
   Falmer Press (1987).
2 For a further account of David Best's argument against the arts as a generic
   community see 'Feast as a Dog's Dinner' in *Times Higher Education Supplement* (31st
   January 1992) and 'Generic Arts: an Expedient Myth' in *The Journal of Art and Design*,
   Volume No 1 (1992).

Acknowledgments

It is impossible to name all those who have been kind enough to contribute in some way to my work in general, and in particular to the writing of this book. I offer my warmest thanks to all those, in various countries, who have done me the honour of inviting me to address conferences, and to speak at universities and colleges, as a consequence of which many stimulating points have arisen in discussion. I have also been privileged to be invited to contribute to seminars and in-service courses for teachers, whose perceptive comments I greatly value.

I am grateful to many friends in the National Society for Education in Art and Design, and especially to its General Secretary, John Steers, for his unfailing courtesy, thoughtfulness and support, especially during the long bad times. Similarly, I am greatly indebted to David Davis, for his constant encouragement and support. My thanks, too, to Graham McFee for the serious and keen interest he has taken in my work, over many years, even when he has disagreed.

My graduate students on the summer course which I taught at the University of Victoria, in Canada, in 1990, contributed stimulating discussions. I am also indebted, for the interest shown in my work, to numerous other people in several countries. In particular I must mention the enthusiasm for my work shown by many in Western Canada generally, especially in Alberta, and also by many in Norway. I have formed a great affection and respect for both countries, and I earnestly hope that the very congenial contacts which we have formed will become closer, and will continue indefinitely.

My thanks are due to the Dean of the Birmingham Institute of Art and Design, Professor Eddie Price, for allowing me the opportunity to write this book, and to those colleagues who have shown interest in my work. I am also grateful to friends in the University College of Ripon and York St John for their continued interest in my work over several years.

I am greatly indebted to Jennifer Bird for her consistent support and encouragement, especially during the period when I struggled alone through an apparently endless bleak desert. I am grateful, too, for her help in meticulously checking the manuscript.

My greatest debt academically is owed to my friend David Cockburn, of the Philosophy Department of St David's University College, Lampeter, for his considerable help with the earlier version of this book, for exciting and illuminating discussions of some of the complex problems involved, and for so generously giving his time and incisive expertise to offer valuable suggestions which have greatly improved some aspects of this revised version. I am also indebted to him for the enrichment I have gained from our continuing and wide-ranging discussions of philosophical and other serious issues over several years.

Most of all, I am indebted to Lesley Lyon for her keen interest in my work, for her selfless support and encouragement, and for her remarkably dedicated, painstaking care with the word-processing, to which she gave many hours of her own, unpaid, time. Nothing was too much trouble. She also gave her help and support in countless other ways. I only hope that the work of the author is even half as good.

Introduction

The most important aim of this book is to provide the strongest possible support for the arts, and especially the arts in education, at a time when alarmingly narrow conceptions of education, and therefore of human possibilities, are being imposed and accepted. For anyone who gains enrichment from the arts, the threat of depriving young people of artistic experience is of the utmost gravity.

Let me emphasise that the educational potential of the arts should certainly not be limited to the formal educational system. Perhaps their most important characteristic is what can be learned in and through the arts, throughout our lives.

There are strikingly contradictory attitudes about the arts. On the one hand, as we know to our cost, in our society they are commonly regarded as peripheral, expendable, of no great importance in education, and certainly not serious candidates for priority, as, for instance, are mathematics and the sciences. It is widely assumed that the arts are merely for entertainment or enjoyment, from which nothing of significance can be learned.

Yet, on the other hand, the powerful possibilities of learning from the arts are clearly and significantly, if implicitly, recognised in the nervousness about the arts exhibited by authoritarian régimes of right and left. It is all too common for artists to be censored, banned, imprisoned, even tortured and executed. Why are they so worried, if there is nothing of significance to be learned from the arts? Mathematics and the sciences, usually assumed to be more important, do not normally make such régimes nervous. This point is highly significant in two ways:

(a) It will always remind us, when we feel dispirited by the general dismissive regard for them, that what can be learned from the arts is of the *utmost* importance, for education and society generally.

(b) It points starkly to the crucial importance of the main theme of this book, which is to show unquestionably that artistic experience is as *fully cognitive and rational*, and as fully involves *learning and understanding*, as *any* subject in the curriculum, including the so-called 'core' subjects of mathematics and the sciences. That clearly is the case if, as I have indicated by example, there are such powerful and humanly important possibilities of learning in and from the arts. For the notion of learning, in this sense, and thus of education, necessarily implies cognition, rationality and understanding.

This book is a considerably revised and extended version of *Feeling and Reason in the Arts* (1985). It provides, to most arts educators, a revolutionary philosophical approach to, and foundation for, the arts in education. It rejects traditional and still almost universally unquestioned assumptions about the arts, such as, primarily, that artistic experience, whether of the artist, spectator or audience, is either purely subjective, or answerable to mysterious metaphysical realms. These are often assumed to be the *only* possible alternatives. But since few people these days explicitly refer, in their attempts to justify artistic experience, to, for instance, metaphysical forms of feeling, my main target will be the subjectivist doctrine, which is still rife. However, I shall sometimes mention the metaphysical, since it often runs into subjectivism. For instance, in some versions it is claimed that one is supposed to know about the presence or absence, or the quantity, of a vaguely postulated metaphysical 'aesthetic' quality, by a purely subjective process of 'intuition'.

Such widely prevalent assumptions carry the inevitable consequence that there could be no legitimate place for the arts in education. It is remarkable that these subjectivist preconceptions have persisted so long. For to base the case for the arts, and the arts in education, on such untenable notions amounts to denying that *any reason* can be given for particular artistic understanding and experience, or for the value of the arts. How can one intelligibly justify the case for the arts on an appeal to supposed purely 'inner' occult mental processes which, in terms of the theory itself, are totally *outside* any possibility of reason or verification? Nothing intelligible whatsoever can be said for the arts on this basis. Yet astonishingly, this kind of obscure and self-defeating attempt to support the arts is still dominant. Appeal is made to the subjectivist/metaphysical doctrine, as the supposed ultimate grounds of justification for the arts, by the great majority of arts educators, under the unquestioned influence of traditional philosophers such as Kant, Cassirer, Suzanne Langer, and Louis Arnaud Reid. It is the influence of that conception which led one philosopher to characterise aesthetics as 'the natural home of rapturous and soporific effusion'. It will be a main aim of this book to expose that whole tradition of pervasively influential thought as fundamentally mistaken, and the source of most of the currently self-defeating attempts to offer support for the arts. Until its fatal flaws have been exposed, and a new framework for the arts provided, there is no hope of providing the rigorous and sound support for which there is such an urgent need.

The central issue discussed in this book is crucial to arts education. For, as I shall show, those most influential in arts education continue to propound, explicitly or implicitly, subjectivist views which in fact destroy the case for the arts in education. In this sense most theoretical, and even some practical, proponents of the arts in education are their own worst enemies. It is vital that the arguments offered for the value of the arts should avoid this obvious self-contradiction, and that the case for the arts in education should be thoroughly sound, especially in these times when economic expediency puts them under severe threat.

It is important to be clear, though, that there is nothing automatic about the contribution of the arts. If, as I have indicated, the arts can have powerful social and educational influence, then we should recognise that they can be a force for encouraging destructive as well as constructive attitudes. This aspect of the arts reveals the immense and unavoidable responsibility of teachers. There may be considerable dangers if teachers use harmful material and approaches. Moreover, some art is cliché-ridden and trivial, and thus serves merely to confirm the trivial conceptions and feelings which are so prevalent in society; such art does nothing to open for students the greater integrity of deeper, more discriminating, more truthful understandings of and attitudes to life. Much art falls into the category of what George Eliot referred to as 'small tinklings and smearings'. Given the close relationship of the arts to the deepest aspects and aspirations of humanity, this means that, in an important sense, degenerate or trivial art may be partly constitutive of degenerate or trivial human beings.

There is no escape from this responsibility. Some subjectivists regard it as a moral obligation to try to avoid making decisions about the kind of art which is learned and taught. But this aspiration makes no sense. To do *nothing* is inevitably to have incurred a moral responsibility. For students may have gained greater enrichment if something *positive* had been done. If the arts are indeed important to human development, then every arts teacher should recognize this unavoidable responsibility. Indeed, she or he should welcome it — for it is an inevitable consequence of the deep and vital human importance of the arts.

In short, the educational and artistic values of the arts depend upon the particular works of art concerned, and how they are taught. There can be no substitute for sincerely committed, high quality, highly educated teachers. Given such teachers, the potential of the arts in education is immense, yet too often misunderstood, and greatly undervalued.

The subjectivist doctrine (even, often, a dogma) presents a seriously misguided, but usually unquestioningly accepted, picture of an autonomous individual self which is independent of the surrounding culture. This is what Ryle (1949) has famously called a 'ghost in a machine' — a supposedly gaseous self-contained entity. Modern versions, which at first sight seem to avoid the intractable problems of subjectivism, but which on examination will be shown to be equally untenable, locate this deeply confused notion of the autonomous thinking self in the brain. The most fundamental misconception here is that of regarding the individual, his thoughts and experiences, as *independent of a cultural context*. This subjectivist conception is what Kerr (1986) has aptly called a 'mentalist/individualist' picture of the self, and it is just as fundamentally misconceived, whether regarded as a ghost in a machine, or as a collection of brain-processes. This book is a sustained exposure of the philosophical confusions and educational damage created by subjectivism in some of its most important but varied guises. With guidance, which I hope to provide, and practice, this subjectivist doctrine may easily be identified in the work of most arts educators, such as the currently influential Elliot Eisner, and even in the few who deny it, such as Louis Arnaud Reid, whose work continues to influence thinking about the arts in education.

Experience suggests that resistance, and even hostility, will be considerable, because artists and arts educators are normally so deeply infected with the subjectivist conception that they are unable to think outside it. They are so thoroughly impregnated with it as to be oblivious of it, thus they are unable or unwilling to consider it objectively, and recognise its fatal deficiencies. It is paradoxical that arts people, from whom one might have expected the greatest open-mindedness, imagination and adventurousness in their thinking, are among the most rigidly conservative in their adherence to the subjectivist doctrine which destroys their own case.

Jan Michl, in one of my audiences in Oslo, observed that the whole status of the arts, in most Western countries, is almost universally assumed to *rest* on this unintelligible subjectivist/metaphysical conception. I am indebted to him for a perceptive insight. Subjectivist mystification ('rapturous and soporific effusion') has been the refuge of the arts. To remove this false prop may well initially leave the arts dizzily groping for support until fresh arguments have been understood and thoroughly assimilated. So one can sympathise with the resistance and defensive hostility. But I cannot over-emphasise that the traditional prop is thoroughly and dangerously misguided. So far from providing a solid foundation, it continues seriously to distort and depreciate the immense human potentialities of the arts, in education and in society more widely. It is partly through a recognition of the incoherence of, and educational damage done by, the traditional doctrine of subjectivism, that the advantages of the fresh conception which I am offering can be fully appreciated.

It will already be clear that 'pure' philosophical questions are inseparable from the fundamental questions for the arts in education. Arguments for the educational values of the arts arise from a careful examination of the character of the arts. Thus it is hoped that, although my primary concern is to offer the strongest possible support for the arts in education and society generally, this book will also be a useful introduction to philosophy of the arts.

The most fundamental questions in the philosophy of the arts cannot be considered in isolation from other central areas of philosophy. Many of the deep misconceptions in traditional philosophy of the arts arise from a failure to appreciate the inextricable relationship with other aspects of philosophy. Yet, as will become obvious, one cannot consider, even remotely adequately, philosophy of the arts independently of philosophy of mind, and of language, to name but two major areas which are inseparable from an examination of the character of the arts, and thus of their significant contribution to education, and to human life.

Because of these complexities, in writing a book of this kind one is always walking a tightrope. As I have said, my main aim is to provide solid support for the arts in education, since they are under considerable pressure, and, tragically, most of the theoretical work in this area is very weak, confused, and even self-contradictory. It still too often consists in rhetorical appeals to a mystical subjectivist romanticism, which often even implies a *rejection* of carefully considered reasons for the importance of the arts. So the arguments need to be clear to arts educators who may have no or very little acquaintance with philosophy.

Yet, to offer sound support for the arts does entail going deep, not exclusively, if that makes sense, into the character of the arts, but into what we shall see are inseparably related areas. Thus the arguments cannot be simple. Indeed, it is precisely the attempt to provide simple answers to the complex questions involved which has led to the confusions of several influential arts theorists. In the arts, as in most areas of philosophy, simple answers are almost invariably false answers — and sometimes not only false but extremely damaging educationally.

I hope that I have managed to walk that tightrope with some success, although, as I know to my cost, there will be philosophers who will complain that I have not gone deeply enough, and there will be arts educators who will complain that the arguments are too deep and complex. Nevertheless, since my main aim is to offer maximum support for the arts in education, in order to make my arguments more accessible to arts educators, in this version I have leaned more in their direction. Consequently, in some respects, greater clarity for arts educators may be achieved at the cost of some philosophical oversimplification.

It seems to me to be an enterprise well worth undertaking if one is committed to the vital importance of the arts in education, and concerned about the general weakness of the arguments for them. Indeed, the very difficulty to which I refer is *itself* an indication of the deep human significance of the arts — which needs to be emphasised in this utilitarian and materialistic age. For it indicates how fundamental the arts can be to human life, conception, consciousness, that there can be no simple answers, and that there is such a profound interconnection with the other central areas of philosophy.

When I was an undergraduate at Cambridge, one of my teachers once remarked that it is impossible to write an article on philosophy of the arts since the issues are so deep, complex and wide-ranging that it would always require a whole book. I have learned increasingly how perceptive he was. But in fact he understated the case, for, in my view, it is impossible even to write a normal book — to be adequate it would have to be a very large book, incorporating, for example, philosophy of mind, language, science, religion, moral philosophy etc. Since that would be more than a lifetime's occupation, and since arts educators, for whom this book is mainly intended, would, justifiably, never even attempt to read such a vast tome, I shall have to skate over the surface of several complex areas, and merely indicate others.

My central concern can be stated simply: if artistic judgements cannot be rationally, objectively justified there can be no place for the arts in education. Yet, since it is a vital characteristic of artistic judgments that they are often, and importantly, expressions of individual feeling and value, this seems to imply that they are purely subjective. This creates a problem about how they can be justified, in which case there is also a problem about how the arts can be justified in education. It will be very clear how important this issue is in view of the current entirely justifiable demand that all aspects of education should be assessable and accountable. But it should be emphasized that, even for anyone not directly concerned with education, the fundamental questions which centre on this problem are unavoidable if one wishes to reflect seriously on the nature of the arts, and their relation to society.

The main aim of a sermon, priests sometimes say, is to comfort the disturbed and disturb the comfortable. That is also one of my main aims. I hope to comfort those who are seriously disturbed by the generally dismissive regard in which the arts are currently held in education — a philistine attitude which, sadly and paradoxically, is confirmed, rather than opposed, by the almost universally weak and self-defeating attempts to 'support' the arts. I offer instead at least an outline of a strong in-depth case for the value and educational significance of the arts. I hope to disturb the comfortably complacent circle of arts educators who, despite good intentions, have been smugly repeating self-defeating subjectivist clichés for decades, without reflecting *seriously* about whether they make sense, and what are their implications for education. Those who really are serious in their commitment to the arts will, I hope, welcome the disturbance, even though it may be very uncomfortable radically to reappraise long-held dogmas and slogans which have never previously been rigorously examined objectively.

The confusions and self-contradictions are relatively easy to recognise, but only if one can escape from the mistily rose-coloured spectacles of subjectivism, and consider the central questions for the arts in a fresh, objective light. For the depth of the difficulty is that it lies on the surface. That is, we have been effectively conditioned, by the traditional and prevalent doctrine, into believing that the meaning of a work of art, in some mysterious way lies *behind* it, or is to be found *away* from it, in a subjective or metaphysical realm. What I am saying, by contrast, is, in a sense, much more obvious. For, to put it briefly, my thesis is that its meaning is to be found *in the work of art itself*. This reflects, of course, precisely what most of us *do*, all the time, in our involvement with the arts. To justify our judgments and feelings about a work of art we give reasons which refer *not* to unintelligibly mysterious subjective mental events, but to objective features of the work itself. The great difficulty, which I certainly do not underestimate, is that of overcoming the pervasive subjectivist doctrine which denies and prevents our recognising this obvious fact of normal artistic experience. Thus, from the initial discomfort of having to reconsider long-held, unquestioned assumptions, there will emerge, I submit, a far more soundly based comfort.

Chapter 1

The Rationality of Feeling

This chapter is pivotal for the argument of the whole book. It examines the most widely accepted and convincing of the many guises of the subjectivist conception, and one which has probably been the source of greater and more pervasive confusion than any other. I refer to the misguided assumption that emotional feelings in general, and the kinds of feeling most centrally involved in the creation and appreciation of the arts, are purely subjective.

Chapter 1 will, I hope, provide readers with at least a clear outline of the central features of the thesis of the whole book. The filling out of this outline, in later chapters, may require more careful, reflective thought. But they will, I hope, be more readily comprehensible if this chapter is clearly understood. Moreover, I hope that Chapter 1 will convince readers at the outset just how revolutionary and crucial for arts education is the whole thesis of this book, perhaps especially at this critical time when the arts are under such threat. A largely contributory factor to that threat, and to the prevalent dismissive regard for the arts, is precisely the subjective conception of feeling which is so very commonly assumed and proposed as central to artistic experience. Ironically, it is that conception which is most commonly adduced in *support* of the arts in education, yet it is that very conception which *destroys* the case for the arts as genuinely educational.

Consider the following quotation, about the arts in higher education, from an editorial in *The Times Higher Education Supplement* a few years ago:

> It is thought that such subjects do not need to be taken seriously, since it is stated quite explicitly that creativity is an inspirational and even anarchic activity rather than a cognitive and disciplined process. As a result, the arts are often regarded as of low academic content, and hopelessly subjective . . .

How have the arts reached this position in Western societies? By far the most influential source of this dismissive intellectual regard — even contempt — for the arts, is the traditional subjectivist doctrine, and especially that aspect of it which is the principal concern of this chapter. It is one of the reasons why some arts subjects in schools are regarded as the province of those students who are not very intelligent. These wounds to the intellectual regard for the arts are largely self-inflicted, by those arts educators, for instance, who insist that the arts are essentially a matter of subjective feeling, *rather than* cognition or reason. The three major stages of the argument of this chapter are to show that:

1 *Artistic feelings necessarily involve understanding* or cognition: they are expressions of certain kinds of understanding. An artistic feeling is identified and its character determined by its direction on to an object; the feeling cannot be identified independently of a certain interpretation, conception or understanding of an art object.
2 *Interpretative reasoning*, of the kind discussed more fully in Chapter 3, is of central importance, and not only in the arts, for giving *understanding and evaluation*.
3 Thus, *reasoning can change understanding*, and with it, *feeling*. It is in this sense that artistic feeling, like emotional feelings generally, is rational in kind, in that it is *answerable to reason*: it is always, in principle, open to the possibility of change, as a consequence of reflection, or of reasons offered by someone else for a different conception of the object, and therefore a different feeling.

It is crucial to recognise that I am emphatically *not* arguing that, on the one hand, feeling, and on the other hand, reason/understanding, are very closely related, or interdependent. To put the point in *that* way would be a version of the subjectivism which I am exposing as radically confused and educationally disastrous. On the contrary, artistic feelings are *rational and cognitive in character*. There are not *two* things, but only *one*, rational/cognitive feeling. This shows that the arts can be as fully educational, because they as fully involve rationality and understanding, as any other area of the curriculum. Moreover, because of the vital human possibilities of the kinds of learning involved in the arts, there is a strong case for arguing that the arts should be in the centre of the curriculum, but only if we reject subjectivist conceptions of feeling.

The Dangers of Subjectivism

It is impossible to learn anything in the arts. The arts are just a matter of having a non-cognitive experience.

Is this a typical statement by one of the many these days who regard the arts as unnecessary frills in education — one of the enemies of the arts in education? On the contrary, this is precisely what teachers of the arts, arts educators, and theorists of arts education say, and have been saying for years. That is, as their attempt to support the case for the arts in education, many arts educators are continuing to insist that the arts, by their very *nature*, cannot involve *learning* at all.

In case it be thought that I exaggerate, let me cite an influential arts educator in the UK, who has stated explicitly that teachers who see drama in terms of learning are distorting the nature of the art form. I have every reason to believe that he holds similar views about the other arts. However, I do not want to pick on any individual in particular, because the conception to which I am drawing attention is widely prevalent, although it is far more usually an implicit consequence of what arts educators say and write than stated explicitly.

Subjective Feeling

The root of the trouble is the largely unquestioned conviction that the creation and appreciation of the arts is a matter of subjective feeling, in the sense of a 'direct' 'inner' subjective feeling, 'untainted' by cognition, understanding or rationality. Hence, Robert Witkin (1980) wrote that in order to achieve this 'pure' feeling for art, one needs to erase all memories. The idea seems to be that cognition, understanding and memory will prejudice and limit the capacity for direct feeling-response; that they will prevent pure artistic feelings. Yet the *opposite* is true. Only if we recognise the crucial place of understanding and cognition can we give an intelligible account of education in the arts; and only in that way can we see how individual freedom is possible. Yet even to question the central place of subjectivism often raises such immediate hostility that arts educators cannot really listen to the rest of one's argument.

The Myth

The misconception I am criticising, and which must be rejected if we are to have any hope of providing an educational justification for the arts, is based on, or part of, the common assumption that there is necessarily an opposition between, on the one hand, feeling, creativity and individuality, and on the other hand, cognition and reason. For instance, it is frequently said that the arts are a matter of feeling, not of reason or cognition. This is part of the subjectivist Myth of the human mind as consisting in two distinct realms — the Cognitive/Rational realm, and the Affective/Creative realm. It is of the utmost importance to recognise the manifestations of this Myth, because it is one of the most plausible, yet most damaging, persistent and pervasive, of the various guises of the subjectivist/metaphysical doctrine. Moreover, not only is it disastrous for the educational credentials of the arts, but it expresses a complete distortion of the character of other disciplines, such as the sciences.

For example, in the influential Gulbenkian Report, *The Arts in Schools* (1982), in the chapter which is supposed to offer the philosophical foundation for the rest of the Report, the authors define the area of the curriculum with which they are concerned, i.e. the arts, as 'the aesthetic and creative'. This not only confuses and conflates the aesthetic and the artistic — an issue which we shall consider in Chapter 12 — but mistakenly implies that creativity is *exclusively* the province of the arts. (The Gulbenkian Report also sometimes denies this, but it is so confused and self-contradictory about creativity that it is impossible to be clear what it does mean.) This common mistake seems to stem from the Myth, mentioned above, of distinct mental faculties. Yet if, for instance, the development of creative attitudes is not central to the teaching of mathematics and the sciences — and regrettably often it is not — that is an indictment of the educational policy. Creativity is not in a closed mental box, along with the arts. It can and should apply to *every* area of the curriculum (and even to personal relationships). In some schools science-learning is far more creative than arts-learning. The Myth connives at an attitude to education *in general* which ought to be dead and buried. Both arts and sciences require creativity and imagination.

There are numerous other examples. For instance, a discussion document of the Scottish Committee on Expressive Arts in the Primary School (1984) states: 'The main curricular emphasis is still upon *cognitive* learning, with other areas — physical, emotional, affective — coming off second best. We maintain that a better balance should be found . . .' This clearly implies that whereas the sciences and mathematics are cognitive, the emotional and affective areas, such as, primarily, the arts, are *not* cognitive. Again, the assumption is that the arts involve feeling, as *opposed* to cognition and reason.

The Myth often underlies talk of a *balanced* curriculum. The suggestion is that the cognitive, rational faculty of the human mind is well catered for in, for instance, mathematics and the sciences, but in order to achieve balance we need to give more time to the non-cognitive, affective, emotional faculty, by giving greater emphasis to the arts. But again, formulating the argument in this way is disastrous in the damage it does to the case for the arts in education.

I certainly agree that there should be a better balance achieved, by giving greater opportunity for the arts. However, *this* kind of argument, common though it be, is self-defeating, in that it *destroys* the case for the arts. For how can it be seriously claimed that the arts should have a central place in the curriculum if those who are supposed to be supporting the arts themselves insist that there is no place for learning and education in the arts? And let us be quite clear that that is the inevitable consequence of denying the place of cognition and rationality. My point is that in rightly insisting on the importance of feeling in the arts, we must *not* be denying the importance of reason and cognition.

This confused Myth is sometimes given a pseudo-scientific dress by reference to the different functions of brain hemispheres. It is said that one hemisphere is concerned with the affective/creative, the other with the rational/cognitive. The 'balance' argument is then formulated in terms of developing each hemisphere equally, i.e. it is argued that the current and traditional emphasis in education is to develop the rational/cognitive hemisphere, at the expense of the creative/affective hemisphere. But without even considering the philosophical confusion involved in this way of thinking, I hope that, on reflection, one can see immediately how utterly bizarre it is as an *educational* justification for the arts. It would be on a par with arguing that a justification for painting in the curriculum is that holding paint brushes develops arm muscles. (The misguided attempt to justify the arts in education by reference to functions of the brain is further discussed later in the chapter.)

Let us return to the main argument. It is, as we have seen, an expression of the Myth of the Separate Faculties that the arts are a matter of feeling, not of reason or cognition. It is important to recognise clearly that in that case there could be no grounds for the notion of education in and through the arts. For *how can there be education if understanding or cognition have no place?*

The most that could be claimed taking this subjectivist view is that emotional feelings can be *induced*, as in the case of sensations such as pain. This is an inevitable consequence of insisting that the arts are concerned solely with *experience*, not understanding or rationality. Moreover, this subjectivist conception cannot give sense to the crucial notions of individual freedom, and integrity of feeling, which are, or can be, such significant contributions of the arts. It can no more allow for freedom than can the feeling induced by hitting one's finger with a hammer. Yet that is how the subjectivist construes emotions, as induced effects on a passive recipient. This assumption of the essentially passive nature of emotions runs deep in empiricist philosophy, and is still prevalent in psychology and arts education. It is certainly manifest in the assumption that artistic creation and appreciation are matters of feeling not of cognition, and thus that the arts consist in having non-rational, non-cognitive experiences, as opposed to progressively developing understanding. There can be no freedom, no individual artistic development, no *education*, on this subjectivist basis, but only something like conditioned responses.

There clearly has to be a far richer relationship between the person and the work of art, between one's emotion and the work, to make sense of education in the arts, and to make sense of the idea of progressive achievement of individual freedom. Let me emphasise again that this is not in the least to deny the importance of *feeling* in the arts. It is to point out that we need a much richer conception of what an emotional experience *is* than is offered by the oversimple, severely limiting, and ultimately unintelligible, subjectivist account.

Feeling

Can such a conception be provided, which will allow in the fullest sense for a rational, cognitive content of emotional experience? That is, can a conception be provided which can show that the commonly assumed antithesis between feeling and reason is fundamentally misconceived? It certainly can be provided, and indeed, it will be shown that it is a serious *distortion* to regard the emotions and artistic feelings as non-rational, non-cognitive experiences. Let me emphasise that I am *not* arguing even for the *close* relation of feeling and reason, but rather that artistic feelings are *rational in kind*. It is an instance of what I sometimes call the disease of the dichotomous mind that my arguing for the crucial rationality of involvement with the arts so frequently provokes the hostile reaction that I ignore feelings. Because the Myth is so commonly held, I shall have to pursue much of my argument in terms of it. But let me repeat that my argument is for the essentially rational character of emotional experience of the arts.

In order to bring out fully the strength of this argument, and the dangerous weakness of the subjectivist Myth, both philosophically and educationally, let us approach the issue from another direction. According to the subjectivist, an emotion is a purely private 'inner' mental event which may emerge in various ways. Wordsworth captures this notion aptly: 'All good poetry is the spontaneous overflow of powerful feelings.' According to this view, an emotion wells up inside and overflows into artistic expression. One might refer to this version of subjectivism as the 'Hydraulic Theory' of the Emotions whereby emotions well up, burst out, and are dammed up or released by opening floodgates etc.

There are at least two major mistakes involved in the Hydraulic Theory. First, it fails to recognise that there is a logical connection between the emotion and its object. Second, according to this view, no understanding is necessary in order to have emotional feelings. Let us consider both these points together, since they are really impossible to separate. Why do I imply that there has to be a logical connection between an emotion and its object? It is fairly generally recognised in philosophy these days that a central feature of emotions is that they are directed onto objects of certain kinds — one is afraid of X, angry at Y, joyful about Z. But the object has to be understood in a certain way. For example, since I am afraid of snakes, my feeling will be very different if I take an object under my desk to be a rope from what it would be if I take it to be a snake. There is a logical relation between my feeling, and my understanding or cognition of the object. It would make no sense to suppose that I could experience that kind of fear — of snakes — if I take the object to be a rope. If I believe it to be a snake I shall want to get away from it rapidly. It would make sense to suppose that I could experience that kind of feeling — fear of snakes — only if I believe it to be a snake. That is, it makes no sense to suppose that one could normally have a certain kind of emotional feeling about a wholly inappropriate object. Yet, the subjectivist Hydraulic account construes the feeling as an 'inner' event, which can be characterized entirely independently of any external circumstances. On this basis, it would have to make sense for normal people to be terrified of ordinary currant buns. But if one understands it *as* an ordinary currant bun, if one has that conception or cognition of it, then no sense can be made of being terrified of it.

It can be seen, then, that the subjectivist view is based upon a radically oversimple conception of emotional feeling. The subjectivist construes emotions on the model of sensations. Since it is true that certain kinds of understanding or cognition are not relevant to sensations such as pain, the subjectivist assumes, wrongly, that the same is true of emotional feeling. Yet it is important to recognise that it is precisely the crucial role of *cognition* which *distinguishes* emotion-feelings from sensation-feelings. For instance, if someone were to poke me with what I believe to be a soft rubber stick, which is in fact a sharp nail, I shall have the feeling of pain — *whatever* my cognition. By contrast, if I believe an object to be a snake which is in fact a rope, I shall be afraid of it. That is, in the case of emotional feelings *understanding or cognition is all-important*. The significance of this point to the philosophical basis of the arts in education cannot be over-emphasised. To underline it again, *an emotional feeling necessarily involves cognition or understanding* of the object of that feeling. The object has to be understood as threatening or harmful in some way in order to make sense of the notion of one's feeling afraid of it. In the case of emotions the feeling is *determined* by and inseparable from cognition.

Gavin Bolton, in his splendid book *Drama as Education* (1984) writes 'aesthetic meanings are *felt* rather than comprehended' (p. 147). He then rightly insists that perhaps the major contribution of drama in education is to do with bringing about a change in a participant's *understanding* of the world (p. 148). It is clear evidence of the difficulty of extricating oneself from the Myth of the Two Realms that even so thoughtful and perceptive a writer as Gavin Bolton can fall into self-contradiction on two successive pages. His main emphasis is, rightly (and ahead of many other arts educators), on the crucial changes in understanding (i.e. cognition, conception) which can be brought about by an involvement with the arts. Yet he feels so uneasy about what he takes to be the necessary consequence of that view, namely a repudiation of feeling, that he unhappily includes that too. Thus, in effect, he asserts both that the arts are essentially a matter of feeling *rather than* comprehension, and that the arts are essentially a matter of *changing* our comprehension. With respect, I would suggest that he certainly does not need to disown understanding while emphasizing feeling. He can, and should, have *both*. It is only the underlying and unrecognised power of the pervasive and pernicious Myth, based on an over-simple conception of mind, which makes him feel so uneasy about the supposedly inevitable choice between feeling, and reason/cogni-tion, that he includes both at the cost of self-contradiction. But he is not forced to a choice, or to self-contradiction in rightly wanting both. On the contrary, the kinds of feeling which are the province of the arts are given *only* by under-standing, cognition and rationality. They are not possible for a creature incapable of such cognition. A more coherent philosophy of mind greatly strengthens Bolton's case — and in general, the case for the arts in education.

King Lear, in mental torment, buffeted, cold, and drenched while wandering without shelter in the violent storm on the heath, is brought to a sharp realization of an aspect of life of which he had never been aware in his days of power:

> Poor naked wretches, whereso'er you are,
> That bide the pelting of this pitiless storm,
> How shall your houseless heads and unfed sides,
> Your looped and window'd raggedness, defend you
> From seasons such as these? O! I have ta'en
> Too little care of this. Take physic, Pomp,
> Expose thyself to feel what wretches feel . . .

Was it Lear's feeling which changed his understanding, or his new under-standing which changed his feeling? To put the point in either way is misleading. The example reveals not that there are two distinct but closely related mental states here, but an essential characteristic of what it is for a person to experience emotional feelings. It would make no sense to attribute to Lear that feeling without his characterizing the object of his feeling in the way he does. Thus it is clearer to say that Lear's emotional feeling is an expression of his changed understanding.

It can already be seen what a big step forward this is towards an account which will give a sound philosophical basis for the claim that the arts are in the fullest sense educational. For, by contrast with subjectivism, it can be seen that the feelings involved in the arts are necessarily cognitive in kind.

The notion of feeling will be much more fully explored later in the book, and especially in Chapter 8. But even this outline should be sufficient to vindicate my claim that the subjectivist conception is a grossly oversimple caricature of emo-tional feelings. More important, I hope that it has vindicated my claim that a philosophical basis *can* be provided which will allow for the cognitive character of feeling.

Reason

There is another important source of subjectivism. The subjectivist who assumes the Myth of the antithesis between Feeling and Reason has a distorted and oversimple conception not only of feeling, but also of reason. I hope I have already said enough to show clearly what is wrong with the subjectivist account of feeling. But the subjectivist also believes that reasons are limited to the kinds of deductive and inductive reasons which are commonly used in mathematics, symbolic logic, and the sciences. This is to fail to recognise that crucial kind of reasoning, which we shall consider more fully in Chapter 3, which I sometimes call 'interpretative reasoning'. This kind of reasoning is important in *all* areas of knowledge — not only the arts but also, for example, the sciences. I should add that it applies equally to the creation and appreciation of the arts.

If they share the common misconception that reasoning is solely deductive or inductive, then it is understandable that arts-educators want to deny the relevance of reasoning in the arts, and are confirmed in their conviction that reasoning is *inimical* to artistic feeling. For it is then reasonable to suppose, as it is widely supposed, that emotional feeling distorts reasoning, and conversely that reasoning inhibits and distorts feeling. Of course, both *can* be true. But that is certainly not necessarily the case. The most appropriate way to respond to the common conviction that reason is incompatible with feeling is to deny that the deductive and inductive are the only or even the most important kinds of reasoning. Interpretative reasoning involves, for instance, attempting to show a situation in a different light, and this may involve not only a different interpretation or conception, but also a different evaluation. It is important to recognise that, unlike the deductive reasoning typical of, for instance, syllogistic logic, interpretative reasons do not lead inexorably to universally valid conclusions. There may be sound reasons given for conflicting interpretations and evaluations, and there may be no way in which it is possible to resolve such differences. So my insistence on the central place of rationality in no way conflicts with that central and exciting characteristic, the creative ambiguity of art. But it does show how genuine reasoning can be used to open up new perspectives, new visions, fresh evaluations.

The importance of this kind of reasoning for fresh interpretations in the sciences can hardly be exaggerated. Herman Bondi, the eminent astronomer and theoretical physicist writes: 'Certain experiments that were interpreted in a particular way in their day we now interpret quite differently — but they were claimed as facts in those days.' The point, of course, is that a major change of interpretation was required to enable scientists to see in a different light the character of their investigations. There are numerous other examples one could give from the sciences. This exposes another confusion of the Myth. For the ability to use and understand interpretative reasons necessarily *involves* imagination and creativity. So it makes no sense to assume that reasoning is distinct from, or opposed to, creativity or imagination. More obvious examples of interpretative reasons can be seen in the ways in which we support our conflicting opinions on social, moral and political issues. Again, such reasoning does not necessarily lead to agreed conclusions. But neither is it necessarily ineffective. Reasons given for seeing a situation in a different perspective may lead us to change our opinions.

There is no need to offer more examples of the numerous ways in which reasons may be given for seeing, understanding, evaluating a situation in a particular way. It is obvious, on reflection, just how widespread it is. Moreover, by contrast with the assumptions of the subjectivist, such reasoning is essentially *liberating*, in that it can open fresh horizons of understanding, new ways of seeing the world. Indeed, we can now see that it is subjectivism which is so narrowly limiting, for if one takes that view, one is necessarily imprisoned in feelings and thoughts which are not open to reason. The subjectivist can give no sense to the notion of recognising the validity of different interpretations. This underlines again that it is precisely the predominant subjectivist view which is so damaging educationally. It also underlines why a revolution of thought on the philosophical foundations of the arts in education is so urgently required. Far from limiting or eradicating the possibility of differences of opinion, in the arts and in other areas of human life, the very *existence* of interpretative reasoning *depends* upon, and is an expression of, the variety of different conceptions, interpretations and opinions.

The Rationality of Feeling

There is one final step in the argument of this chapter. I have been concerned to expose as narrow, distorting and damaging to the case for the arts in education the conception of both feeling and reason assumed by the subjectivist. First, we have seen that emotional feelings are not separate from or opposed to cognition and understanding, but, on the contrary, emotional feelings are cognitive in kind, in that they are expressions of a certain understanding of their objects. Second, we have seen that reasons are not always of the kind which lead to inevitable conclusions, but that there are very important kinds of reasons which offer new interpretations and evaluations, yet which do not necessarily compel single definitive conclusions. The third step is to see how such reasons can be inseparably involved with feelings.

This third step is easy to grasp, if one has understood the first and second. For it consists in showing that the reasons which can be given for a change of interpretation and evaluation may be inseparable from a change of feeling. Let me give an example. At the beginning of Shakespeare's play, Othello takes Desdemona to be a purely virtuous woman whom he idolises and loves. It is that understanding or cognition, that way of seeing her, which identifies or determines his feeling. Iago gives him reasons for a different conception or understanding of her, as unfaithful and dishonest. Othello's changed conception of her involves a change of feeling to intense jealousy, as a result of which he kills her. Too late, Iago's wife, Emilia, gives Othello further reasons for recognising that it was Iago who was treacherous, and that Desdemona was innocent. These reasons change his conception again, and with it his feeling, to one of intense remorse. In each case, Othello's feeling cannot be separated from his understanding or conception of the object of his feeling — Desdemona. His feelings in each case can be *identified* only in terms of his cognition. That is, his feelings can be identified only in terms of his understanding his wife to be virtuous and faithful, treacherous and unfaithful, and the innocent victim of his violently unjust reaction, respectively. And, in at least two cases, it was reasoning which changed his understanding or conception, and with it his feeling. There are many such examples, from our ordinary lives, where reasoning for a change of understanding and evaluating a situation inevitably involves a change of feeling.

Education

It becomes clear that, by contrast with subjectivism, this thesis offers an account of *education*, in the fullest sense, in and through the arts, involving both feeling and rationality (although putting it that way may seem dangerously to imply that feeling and reason are independent). It shows how education of the emotions is a real possibility. This follows from the essentially rational/cognitive nature of emotional experience.

A more striking consequence of my argument is that a vast range of emotions is possible *only* for creatures capable of the relevant kinds of rationality and cognition. For example, artistic feelings are necessarily dependent upon *understanding* the relevant art forms. Although an animal may respond to art — my neighbour's dog howls at Beethoven — it is incapable of *artistic* response precisely because of its lack of understanding. Thus, contrary to subjectivism, the Myth, and the Hydraulic Theory, it is only because we are capable of *rationality* that we can *have* artistic feelings.

Of course, I am not for a moment suggesting that we always, necessarily, or even usually, reason our way to a feeling about a work of art. Neither am I in the least denying spontaneous artistic feelings. My point is that such feelings are always *answerable* to reason, in that they are always, in principle, open to the possibility of being changed by reasons given for seeing and feeling about a work in different ways. To repeat, cognition and rationality are inseparable from artistic feeling and creativity, whether spontaneous or not.

The Myth in Disguise

The Myth appears in various deceptive guises, and it is important to recognise at least the more important of them. One of the more persuasive guises has appeared recently, in an attempt to support the notion that the various art forms constitute a generic area of the curriculum. I have more fully exposed the philosophical fallacies, and educational and artistic dangers, of this supposition elsewhere (Best, 1990, and 1992). Here I want to reveal it as a disguised version of the Myth.

To recapitulate, the Myth is the assumption that the human mind consists in two distinct, inimical realms — the cognitive/rational realm, and the affective/creative realm. The adherents of this deeply ingrained Myth assume that the cognitive/rational realm is the province of the conceptual, factual, cognitive, reasoning areas of the curriculum, such as the sciences, mathematics, geography, history, whereas the affective, imaginative, sensual realm is supposed to be the province of the arts. We have already seen that this Myth is not only fundamentally misconceived philosophically, but that it grossly distorts the character of *all* areas of education and knowledge. Much more will be said about this issue as the book progresses, since it is a central theme. But, to put it very briefly, imagination, creativity, and feeling are just as important in the sciences as in the arts; and cognition, rationality, and the development of conceptual understanding are just as important in the arts as in the sciences. The notion that the arts constitute a generic area of the curriculum, *entails* that there must be a characteristic or set of characteristics which is both *common* to all the arts, and *distinct* from all other areas. No credible candidate has been proposed, and I have challenged anyone to produce one. Consider some of the commonest attempts to meet this condition. Imagination is a popular candidate, but, as we have seen, imagination is necessarily required in the sciences, as in all forms of knowledge. Einstein has said that in science, imagination is more important than knowledge. Although that usefully makes the point, it is, in fact, to misconstrue the character of the sciences. For scientific knowledge, and most obviously the advancement of scientific knowledge, necessarily requires imagination.

Another proposed candidate is that, unlike the other disciplines, the arts work essentially through the senses. But this is vacuous since every discipline works through the senses. Another, self-defeating, candidate is that a distinctive feature of the arts is that they are not concerned with conceptual understanding. It is extremely unclear what is meant by 'conceptual' here, but in the most obvious sense it is untrue, since a *principal* claim for the educational value and importance of some art forms is their potential for giving richer conceptual understanding.

However, for the purposes of this book, what I am primarily concerned to show is that attempts to support the notion of generic arts in the terms given above, amount merely to thinly disguised versions of the Myth. The Myth supposes two distinct and inimical realms, on one hand the cognitive/rational/conceptual realm, and on the other hand the feeling (including senses), imaginative, non-conceptual, non-rational realm. The latter is supposed to be the province of the arts. Enough has been said, I hope, to demonstrate unmistakably that such a supposition is not only fundamentally mistaken philosophically, but as serious a distortion of the character of the arts as it is of the sciences and other disciplines.

It is ironic that some of those who support, using the above terms, the notion of generic arts, are *also* delighted by and supportive of my argument *for* the rational and cognitive character of artistic experience. That is, they have come to recognise that *only* in this way can it be legitimately argued that the arts are genuinely educational. But they still cling to, or are trapped in, the Myth. They have not thought through their position carefully enough to recognise that to accept my position *inevitably* entails a *rejection* of the Myth, and consequently a rejection of arguments in these terms for generic arts. They cannot have it both ways: (a) to argue for generic arts in the way outlined above *is* still to be immersed in the subjectivist doctrine of the Myth: (b) the Myth is incompatible with the crucial notion of the cognitive/rational character of artistic experience: (c) to deny the cognitive/rational character of artistic experience is to deny any place in education for the arts: (d) therefore, the Myth, and this way of arguing for generic arts is a *denial of the educational possibilities of the arts.*

I have a strong suspicion that most or even all other attempts to support the misconceived, but economically expedient, notion that the arts constitute a generic area of the curriculum will be found to be merely thinly disguised versions of the Myth. We need to be very vigilant, for the Myth is one of the most persistently damaging expressions of the subjectivist doctrine, which destroys the case for the arts in education, and distorts the character of other disciplines, such as the sciences.

Scientism

It is important to make clear what I am *not* arguing for. This is important, because I have sometimes suffered from the mistaken conception that my thesis is the same as, or at least supported by, two others. Thus I want to ensure that my argument is sharply distinguished from those others.

(a) The first such thesis is part of another very prevalent myth, which I shall call 'scientism'. This consists in the assumption that all valid justification or proof *must* be of an empirical or scientific kind. In this case, it is assumed that proof of the cognitive/rational content of artistic experience must be of an empirical/scientific kind. Thus, for instance, when I was speaking at a conference in Hungary, one of my hosts politely expressed interest in what she called the 'soft' proof, by philosophical argument, which I had offered, but insisted that what was really required was *hard* evidence, from the hard sciences. What does this 'hard' evidence or proof consist in? Experiments over an extended period were conducted with different groups of children, some of whom were given experience of the arts, some of whom were not. It was found, by statistical analysis, that, in general, those groups of children who had had the artistic experience subsequently improved more in their work in science and mathematics than those who had not had the artistic experience. Since mathematics and sciences are assumed to be paradigm cases of cognitive, rational activities, this was supposed to show conclusively by 'hard' evidence of the 'hard' sciences, that the arts, too, are cognitive and rational.

So far from providing hard, conclusive proof, this kind of experimental work is *irrelevant*: it provides not even a slight indication of the cognitive/rational content of artistic experience. The most that could be claimed is that it has been shown that happenings of a certain kind improve mathematical or scientific cognitive/rational abilities. This does not indicate that the happenings *themselves* are of a cognitive/rational character. Such happenings could be the eating of certain foods or vitamins. For example, in a Third World country, where children are suffering from severe malnutrition, it is highly likely that one would, in general, find a pronounced improvement in mathematical and scientific cognitive/rational abilities among groups of children who were given good, nourishing food over a period of time. Of course that would not be 'hard evidence' that eating nourishing food is itself a cognitive/rational activity. The whole enterprise is thoroughly confused. One cannot show empirically, scientifically, that artistic experience is cognitive and rational. To do that requires a *philosophical* examination of the *character* of artistic experience.

Moreover, it is fatal to try to support the case for the cognitive character of artistic experience by *external* reference to the standards of mathematical or scientific cognition. That would be to concede the inferior status of artistic experience, namely as justified externally. What is required is what I have tried to provide, an account of artistic experience which proves that it is *necessarily*, *internally*, of a rational, cognitive kind. However, when I say that the cognition is internal, I do not, of course, mean that it is cut off from all other kinds of understanding. Far from it. It is the relation with understanding in life generally which provides one of the strongest *educational* arguments for the importance of some of the art forms. Some of the clearest and most powerful examples are from drama and literature, where a greater understanding of life issues can be and frequently *is* achieved *through* that medium.

(b) The second confusion concerns supposed support from brain-hemisphere arguments. I have already shown these to be irrelevant. But because of the increasing prevalence of this kind of proposed argument, let me add further reasons for rejecting it. Merely to show that a section of the brain is little-exercised or un-developed does *not* imply that it should be *more* exercised. What if, for instance, it were shown that to exercise a certain part of the brain increased criminal tend-encies? Surely that would be a good reason for *not* developing it. In short, it is not appeal to supposed functions of the brain, about which most of us know nothing anyway, but the *normal* justification for the *values* of the arts which is required — that is, for instance, philosophical, artistic, educational justification. At the very most, any argument for brain functions will be secondary to that, i.e. if we *already* regard an activity as valuable and it is found to be correlated with a brain function, then we might regard that brain function as worth developing. But it is the previous *philosophical* argument for the value of the activity which is fundamental.

I hinted in the Introduction to this book that locating thoughts and feelings in the brain is effectively, in practice, as untenable as locating them in a non-physical 'mind'. This whole topic, called in philosophy materialism, or the mind/brain identity theory, is a very complex and contentious issue. But we need not go into it in any depth to see that, as a supposed justification for the arts, it is completely misguided. Let us consider the question in one of its most popular forms, in relation to creativity. Once when I was talking to art educators in Finland, one of them, despite my arguments, insisted that the creative process must be a brain process. I asked her whether she was able to assess improvement in the artistic creativity of her students. She replied emphatically that she could. So I then asked whether, in that case, she brought in neuro-surgeons at regular intervals to examine her students, to see whether there had been developments in their brains.

The point, of course, is that *in effect*, in *practice*, artistic progress in creativity is assessed and evaluated by reference *not* to brains, but to what is actually *done*, and *said*, by students. To base one's case on functions of the brain makes just as little sense as to base it on subjective events in an occult, 'inner' mind. In relation to the main theme of this book, the principal similarity is that in both cases the artistic experience is confusedly, if implicitly, construed as logically *independent* of the artistic medium, and its setting in a whole cultural context.

A colleague with whom I was discussing the creative design process became bewildered by my persistent denial that thinking went on in the brain. Eventually, in exasperation, he asked: 'Well, in that case, where does *your* thinking go on then?' To which I replied: 'In my office, for instance.' That may seem like a facetious remark, but in fact it encapsulates a crucial philosophical point, which runs throughout the argument of this book, that it is a *human being* who thinks. It makes no sense to try to locate thinking in the body somewhere. A human being thinks, and those thoughts are, to a huge extent, given by a *whole cultural context* into which instinctive, primitive natural actions and responses are channelled and developed.

It is not necessary for the concerns of this book to consider in depth the major problem of identity theory or materialism (although I believe its thesis to be fundamentally mistaken). What matters for arts educators is to recognise clearly that what may be going on in the brain is *irrelevant* to assessment of the creative process and artistic progress, as our judgments and evaluations will be made solely on the basis of what our students *do and say*.

Scientism, which we shall discuss in Chapter 3, is currently one of the most popular shibboleths of our age. Briefly, it consists in the unquestioned assumption that *all* proof must be of an empirical or scientific kind, involving, for instance, experiments, testing, measurements, statistics, sociological surveys etc. Scientism is as much of an unquestionable *foundation* of thinking about knowledge, for many people, as is subjectivism about the arts for most arts educators. It amounts to the elevation of the methods and procedures of the empirical sciences to the status of a religious belief. It is as unquestionable an article of faith for many people as his belief is to a fundamentalist religious believer.

What I am criticising is the wildly exaggerated but remarkably prevalent assumption that the *only* valid kinds of proof or knowledge are those delivered by the sciences. That general assumption has led to serious confusions, and invalid scientific enquiries. In short, it is the *inappropriate* application of scientific methods which I am criticising. But that certainly should not be construed either as a rejection of the vital importance of the sciences, or as an espousal of the subjectivist/ metaphysical doctrine which it is a main aim of this book to expose as radically confused and damaging to the case for the arts. The danger of misunderstanding is that it may be assumed that to insist that the scientific approach has its limits is to espouse a 'romantic', metaphysical conception of philosophy which it is one purpose of this book to expose as unintelligible, and harmful to the academic credentials of the arts. That is, it may be assumed that my insistence that empirical investigation cannot tell us all we want to know about human experience, commits me to the contention that there are meaningful questions about it which are not objectively answerable to what is, at least in principle, perceivable, and therefore that the answers to such questions can be provided only in terms of the mystical or subjective. Nothing could be further from the truth. Winch (1958) puts the point this way:

> . . . it should not be assumed . . . that what I have to say must be ranked with those reactionary anti-scientific movements, aiming to put the clock back, which have appeared and flourished in certain quarters since science began. My only aim is to make sure that the clock is telling the right time, whatever it might prove to be. Philosophy . . . has no business to be anti-scientific: if it tries to be so it will succeed only in making itself look ridiculous. Such attacks are as distasteful and undignified as they are useless and unphilosophical. But equally, and for the same reasons, philosophy must be on its guard against the extra-scientific *pretensions* of science. Since science is one of the chief shibboleths of the present age this is bound to make the philosopher unpopular; he is likely to meet a similar reaction to that met by someone who criticizes the monarchy.

It cannot be too strongly emphasised that in rejecting the subjective as unintelligible, one is not committed to the view that the only meaningful questions are scientific. I entirely endorse the scientist's exclusive preoccupation with what can be objectively substantiated or refuted. What I am concerned to point out is that there are questions which, although they are not of the kind which can intelligibly be examined scientifically, are still fully objective. Moreover, it is important to draw attention to the fact that failure to recognise the point may lead to seriously distorted empirical conclusions.

Reason and Freedom

On the subjectivist view, I am permanently *confined* to the inner feelings I have. I can only impose them on other people, situations, works of art. Simone Weil (1968) points out how regrettably often we *invent* what other people are thinking and feeling. That is, we impose our feelings upon them because we have not developed the imaginative ability to move *outside* our own prejudices to appreciate what *they* — the *other* people — think and feel. The same is true of artistic appreciation. We need progressively to learn to enter into what is expressed in the work of art, rather than imposing our subjective feelings upon it.

I offer the deliberately provocative phrase 'the liberating emotional power of objective reasoning'. 'Objective' is by contrast with rationalisation, which consists in manipulating reasons merely to support one's subjective prejudices. It is by coming to see objectively the characteristics of other people, situations, and works of art, that we may be progressively liberated, in both understanding and feeling. No such liberation is possible with a subjectivist view, since one is then confined permanently to the feelings one has. Neither different understanding nor different reasoning can affect feelings for a subjectivist, which is precisely why he can give *no* account of the *educational* credentials of the arts.

Summary

To summarise, we need to reject the long-held subjectivist dogmas by which arts educators still continue to damage their own case. We need to recognise that subjectivist conceptions of artistic feeling are oversimple and distorting, and ultimately make no sense. We need a revolution in philosophy of arts education. We *can* argue that artistic experience is as fully rational, and as fully involves cognition or understanding, as any discipline in the curriculum, including the so-called core areas of the sciences and mathematics.

The subjectivist Myth of the supposed inevitable opposition between feeling and reason dies hard. In fact, it shows no sign yet even of having caught a terminal disease. Accountability is rightly demanded of all subjects in the curriculum these days. But accountability depends not only on what we do, but also on what we *say* about what we do, i.e. on the *justification* we offer for the arts. The common saying that the arts are a matter of subjective feeling, not of reason and cognition, is seriously damaging to the case for the arts in education. It is even more damaging that those who say it are arts educators themselves.

We need to reject subjectivism, and to insist that artistic *feeling* is itself *cognitive* and open to objective justification. That is why, in relation to the arts, in this book I am offering a proof of the *rationality of feeling*.

Chapter 2

Natural Response and Action

The principal intention of this chapter is to show that, in the most fundamental sense, the meaning of the arts, as of language, is rooted in human actions and responses, and cultural practices. To some that may seem obvious, yet to others perplexingly radical. For it is opposed to a whole tradition of philosophy of the arts which is still the unquestioned — almost, in effect, unquestionable — foundation of most current thinking about the arts and the arts in education. That tradition, derived from Descartes, Kant, Cassirer, and Langer, is based upon resort to supposed 'inner' occult mental processes. An important aim of this book in general is to expose the unintelligibility of the most important consequences of that tradition. But a more important aim is to outline a new, much sounder account of artistic meaning which also reveals the arts as potentially far more powerful and influential in human lives than can be the case on the traditional view. Thus this new account has educational implications of great importance.

The kinds of theories or assumptions to which I refer regard artistic meaning in general as founded, for instance, and very commonly, on symbolism. The confusion is exacerbated by the widespread conflation of the aesthetic and the artistic, with the assumption that the aesthetic is the generic notion. For then it is often contended, or implicitly assumed, that the essential and distinctive 'aesthetic' quality is an immanent form, instantiated in the work of art, but emanating from a metaphysical Form — rather like a Platonic universal, or Kantian noumenon. This is the tradition of the still-influential Cassirer and Suzanne Langer, whose metaphysical 'forms of feeling' are similar to Platonic universals. Louis Arnaud Reid, although latterly opposed to Suzanne Langer in detail, still shared her most fundamental metaphysical assumptions, as is clear from the ultimate dependence of both upon intuition. I am not, of course, in the least denying the importance of intuition, and not only in the arts. The deep and serious misconception to which I refer is that of regarding what Suzanne Langer calls 'the *basic* intellectual act of intuition' as the *ultimate* foundation of meaning, whether artistic or linguistic. For that is to say that meaning is a subjective, 'inner' private process, which, as we shall see, is an unintelligible supposition. Intuition cannot be the ultimate basis of meaning. On the contrary, the intelligibility of the notion of intuition is given by its answerability to public, social practices, such as language and the arts. (For a further discussion of intuition please see an earlier book [Best, 1974, especially Section J].)

The insuperable difficulties involved in assuming occult 'inner' mental processes, or in postulating unintelligible metaphysical forms, can be avoided, and an intelligible account provided, by recognising that artistic and linguistic meaning is rooted in natural, instinctive human actions and reactions. Subsequently, although not clearly separable from the former, such meaning is rooted in the cultural practices which surround children, and which they take in rather as they breathe the surrounding air.

Resort to subjectivism is largely a consequence of basic philosophical confusions, such as the definitional fallacy (that meaning is given by definition); the essentialist fallacy (that where the same term refers to various instances there must be some underlying common and distinctive essence); and the pervasive misconception that it is the main function of linguistic expressions to *name objects*, including supposed 'inner' occult mental processes. (This last has its equally pervasive counterpart in the misconceived notion that works of art in general stand for, symbolise, represent, or picture, objects or private mental states. See my earlier book [Best, 1974] for a discussion of these questions.) Rather than engaging in extensive examination of these influential and widespread fallacies, which permeate the subjectivist theories and assumptions which still infect most contemporary arts debate, I shall concentrate mainly on my positive thesis. But it is necessary to some extent to reveal what I am opposing and how the approach which I outline is so radically different.

I mention this influential subjectivist/metaphysical tradition in which current thinking about the arts is embedded in order to alert readers to the fact that it may well be the conceptual framework within which their own thinking about the arts is confined. Thus, to grasp the new conception I am proposing may not be easy — yet it is not difficult. It is, however, very difficult to escape from the confines of the traditional subjectivist conception in order to evaluate objectively its validity, since at present it constitutes the limits of one's ability to think about the fundamental questions. Yet, in an important sense, the radically different philosophical account which I am offering is much *easier* to understand than resort to the supposition of mystical 'inner' mental processes. The great difficulty is to escape from what one might loosely call indoctrinated preconceptions in order to reflect on the situation objectively. To put the point paradoxically, the depth of the difficulty is to recognise that the answer lies on the surface. We do not need, even if it made sense, to delve into inaccessible mental processes. The difficulty is to recognise the significance of what lies clearly in view. To achieve that, one needs to escape the grip of assumptions which are so deeply held that they do not appear to be assumptions at all. They appear to be just obvious and unquestionable points of departure. It should be emphasised, perhaps, at this point that my rejection of the subjectivist tradition does not in the least imply an espousal of behaviourist or quasi-behaviourist conceptions, which are equally untenable, as I shall show later.

Underlying the subjectivist conception is a very widespread, deeply held conviction about the character of the individual self. Again, this is too deeply held to be called even an assumption, so it will be very difficult for most readers to escape from its grip both sufficiently to evaluate the arguments against it, unintelligible though it be, and sufficiently to evaluate the account offered here. These issues will permeate the book. To characterise briefly this subjectivist notion of the self, I cannot do better than quote Kerr (1986), who writes of 'the picture of the self-conscious and self-reliant, self-transparent and all-responsible individual which Descartes and Kant between them imposed upon modern philosophy' (p. 5). This conception permeates the work of contemporary arts educators. The picture of the self which I am offering in this book derives from the later work of Wittgenstein, and is aptly captured in Hölderlin's phrase, quoted by Kerr 'the conversation which we are' (p. 115). That is, it is the common human way of acting and responding, set in the context of cultural practices, which is the foundation of the self, not some supposed subjective 'inner' spirit or mentality. That is, the self is a *responsive* agent, acting and reacting in vital connection with other human beings in society. But this difficult (because of tenacious preconceptions) notion will, I hope, become clearer as the book progresses.

However, to pre-empt any possible misconceptions, let me emphasise immediately my conviction of the vital importance of individuality. My rejection of subjectivism is because it can make *no sense* of individuality, at a time when that vitally human attribute is under threat from narrow, conformist approaches to thought and feeling generally, and to education in particular. The great danger of current trends is the submerging of individual potential in a wash of unthinking, unfeeling cliché and imposed norms.

Natural Action and Response

What is the underlying explanation of or justification for artistic experience? Where do we find the foundations of the arts?

Part of the enterprise of this book is to reject the preconception of much recent philosophy that reasoning is of a rigidly narrow character. The traditional tendency in philosophy is to intellectualize in the wrong direction. With respect to the arts, a damaging consequence is the depreciation of the importance both of reason and of feeling. Yet, for instance, it is important to recognise that although I criticize the subjectivist, this is not because he is wrong to insist on the central place of feeling in the arts, but because he misconstrues its character. For far too long it has been an unquestioned assumption that feeling is quite different from, and even inimical to, rationality and cognition. This notion is enshrined in some psychological theory, in terms of the supposed affective and cognitive divisions of the human mind. As already stated a main theme of this book is to expose the fundamental and damaging confusions inherent in such deeply ingrained assumptions. For to insist, as do many arts educators, that the arts are a matter of feeling *rather* than reason; to insist that cognitive/conceptual matters are the sole province of the sciences, mathematics etc. and are outside the province of the arts, *is* to insist that there is *no* place in education for the arts. For how can there be learning and education if there is no place for the increase of knowledge, no place for personal development through the giving and recognition of the validity of reasons?

As we saw in the previous chapter, we are not faced with an insuperable problem of trying to explain how non-rational, non-cognitive activities can be a legitimate part of education; we do not have to abandon hope of justification and consign the arts to the hopelessly subjective; we do not have the insuperable problem of trying somehow to bring together irreconcilable human faculties. To reiterate, we must and can insist that artistic experience *is* of a rational, cognitive character; that artistic feeling *is* cognitive, rational feeling. Consequently, the arts are at least as fully educational as any other aspect of the curriculum. It should, however, be emphasised that this conception does not in the least imply any *diminution* of the importance of artistic feeling. A major problem here, which will be discussed in Chapter 3, is a very common misunderstanding of the character of reasoning, which is so often assumed to be inimical to feeling. Indeed, a main aim of this chapter is to show that, in an important sense, reason is ultimately rooted in natural response, which may well be a response of feeling.

Fundamental to my argument is an emphasis on the natural ways of acting and responding which underlie the concepts of the arts. The emphasis is necessary in order to avoid the misapprehensions (a) that to argue for justification in this sphere implies that responses to the arts are ultimately justified by reason, and (b) that one reasons one's way to feeling about the arts. There is some truth in those misapprehensions, as we shall see, but in a more fundamental sense, on the contrary, it is the natural instinctive actions and response which underlie and give sense to the reasons. At a more sophisticated stage there is a more complex relationship between primitive response and reason, in that reasons can confer new possibilities of feeling, and whole dimensions of feeling are possible only for those with rational understanding. Thus to contend that the immediate, natural response is primary is certainly not to depreciate the place of reason, but rather to provide an account of what ultimately gives sense to reason.

It might seem that to argue that it is the natural response, rather than rationality, which is fundamental is to concede to subjectivism. But the point I am making applies to rationality in general, and not only to that in the arts. Where the arts are said to be subjective, this is usually assumed to be by contrast with disciplines such as the sciences where judgements are rationally justifiable. That is, if the source of subjectivism is the dependence of what we call 'reason' in the arts on this fundamental natural response, then that is not what I am repudiating, since such dependence is the substratum of all reasoning. As Kerr (1986) puts it: 'It is amazingly easy to believe that the alternative to behaving "thoughtlessly" is behaving with the full panoply of reasoning, reflecting and conscious deciding' (p. 12).

Wittgenstein writes (1967) '. . . the way of behaving is pre-linguistic: . . . a language game is based on it, . . . it is the prototype of a way of thinking and not the result of thinking' (§541). Perhaps I can approach the point in this way. Language is the pre-condition of rationality, in that only creatures capable of using language could be capable of giving and understanding reasons (see Bennett 1964). Yet language itself could not have been constructed as a result of reasons. It is often assumed (e.g. by Eisner, see Chapter 8) that man invented language in order to communicate. Yet this assumption which is a classic and prevalent expression of the subjectivist doctrine of the totally independent, mentalist/individualist conception of the self, is unintelligible, since in order to create language there would already have to be a language in which its ideas could be formulated. In this respect language is significantly different from a game.

Wittgenstein (1958, §7 *et seq*) uses the term 'language game' to refer to the various related areas of discourse which together constitute a whole language. Although the term is useful in some respects, it may also be misleading. It is possible to invent an entirely new game and even, if one will allow Esperanto in this sense to be a language, a new language. But even if a language could be invented, it would make no sense to suppose that *language* could be invented, since it would have to be presupposed to formulate the ideas and structure of the new one. Similarly, Wittgenstein's insistence that language is spoken according to certain rules may also give a misleading impression, for one could not learn to use language by following certain rules, as one could learn to play chess from a rule book, since the rules have to be formulated *in language*. The rules of grammar and logic are not prior to, but codify or describe in summary form, the ways in which language is used. That is, it is not that linguistic usage depends upon the rules of grammar and logic, but the converse, that the rules depend upon the linguistic usage. That is why grammatical rules and the logic of language cannot be exact. Thus what gives sense to the notion of a reason *is* the usage; there can be no external rational justification of the usage.

Wittgenstein (1980) 'Did we *invent* human speech? No more than we invented walking on two legs' (vol. II, 4.3.5). Language has evolved, is a development from, primitive, instinctive, natural responses and actions. Reasoning, in its various forms, has the same roots.

What justifies our having the concepts we have? It was generally assumed that the traditional quest of the philosopher was to find those bedrock propositions which are unquestionably true, and on which the whole edifice of knowledge and rationality can be securely built. Yet, although my brief sketch here is obviously inadequate as a discussion of one of the most complex issues in philosophy, it is sufficient, I hope, to indicate that this is a self-defeating quest, in that of any bedrock proposition it can also be asked how *it* can be justified.

To illustrate the point by reference to language again, it is for this reason that in his later philosophy Wittgenstein presents a very different approach, and suggests that language is a development from, sometimes replacing, various ways in which human beings instinctively act and respond. Language itself is a network of forms of behaviour, but it is underlain by pre-linguistic behaviour. It is important to recognize (a) that the natural responses and ways of behaving are the roots of the arts, language and rationality, and (b) that the arts, language and rationality enormously *extend* and diversify the possibilities of feeling, responding and behaving. The latter point will be discussed at greater length in later chapters. Here I want to concentrate on the former.

The evolution from pre-linguistic to linguistic behaviour consists in the learning of *different* behaviour. For example, verbal expressions of pain replace the primitive reactions of crying out, rubbing the injury, and so on, and they are just as immediate; they are not based on any reasoning. The same is true of our responses to other people in pain. We simply respond immediately, whether verbally or not, without making hypotheses or assumptions as to what might be occurring in the supposedly 'private' recesses of their minds. It is in this way that verbal expressions of pain are underlain by and are extensions of natural behaviour and responses. At this level we cannot intelligibly speak of knowledge and justification, but simply of ways of behaving and responding.

There are two levels of response and behaviour to which I shall refer as 'natural'. At the deeper level are the responses which are instinctive, and to which appeal must be made for any learning to be possible. A clear illustration is the philosophical problem of induction. This is the problem of what justifies our confidence that when in the past one event has been regularly correlated with another, such a correlation will continue in the future. The expectation that such correlations will continue is, of course, fundamental to all the sciences. Yet the problem, which has puzzled many philosophers, is that of finding or providing a rational justification for induction. For instance, the sun has risen every morning of recorded history, but how does that justify our confidence that it will rise tomorrow? There is nothing contradictory about saying that however frequently it has risen in the past it may not rise tomorrow. Of course, it may be possible to give cosmological or other reasons, citing *other* correlations, which justify our confidence that the sun will rise tomorrow, but clearly these are equally inductively derived. To put the question another way, particular inductive statements may be justified by reference to others, but what justifies our confidence in any such statements? The oddity of the question becomes apparent when we notice that any 'justification' of the statement that induction can, or cannot, be relied upon would *itself* require an appeal to induction. In short, it makes no sense to suppose that there can be an underlying reason which justifies our confidence in induction in general. Yet this does not imply, as some philosophers have concluded, that our confidence in induction is irrational, and that no inductive statement can be justified. What it shows is that the reasons given *within* the practice of induction, to justify *particular* inductive judgements, cannot themselves be justified in some more fundamental, external sense. The standards of what counts as a valid inductive reason are not justifiable in that sense, but are rooted in the instinctive expectation, revealed in immediate ways of acting and responding, that things will continue in the future as they have in the past. Unless there were something which humans just *do* — some innate, instinctive response — there would be nothing to which learning could appeal, nothing on which a reason could get a grip. A good inductive reason is one which cites a frequent correlation, and it counts as good only by implicit reference to our innate expectation that such regularities will continue.

This deeper level, then, is concerned with the grounds for, or underlying grasp which gives sense to, knowledge. The roots of knowledge are the immediate, primitive reactions to situations: a form of knowledge is derived ultimately from a certain kind of *interest* in the world. For example, the concept of causality, which is central to the sciences, is rooted in certain immediate, instinctive responses to situations. Wittgenstein (1976) writes:

> *We react to the cause.* Calling something 'the cause' is like pointing and saying: 'He's to blame'. We instinctively get rid of the cause if we don't want the effect. We instinctively look from what has been hit to what has hit it. (p. 410)

It is important to recognise that the concept of causality does not precede, is not logically prior to, these reactions: it is rather that the instinctive reactions are the roots of, are inseparably involved in, the formation of the concepts.

At the other level are those responses and actions which are learned in the sense not so much of being the result of explicit teaching as of being *assimilated* by growing up in and emulating the practices of a social environment. Examples are learning to wave goodbye, smiling as a greeting, nodding in agreement or approval, and various other gestures and facial expressions which a child assimilates as the norms of behaviour. These underlie language as they are underlain by the instinctive responses which are the roots of reason, knowledge and under-standing.

The distinction can be illustrated by means of an example. An experiment was carried out in which a psychologist claimed to have taught rats how to discriminate colours. The rats were released at one end of a cage, and there was food at the other end. The floor between them was covered in coloured squares whose positions were periodically changed, and every time a rat crossed or touched a red square it received an electric shock. It learned to avoid the red squares. But did it, as was claimed, learn to discriminate red? Clearly not, since unless it could *already* discriminate colours (or some other factor which differentiated the squares) it could not have learned which squares to avoid. The possibility of learning depended upon an innate capacity to recognise differences; without such a natural ability the learning would have had nothing on which to obtain a grip, as it were. In general, the possibility of learning by conditioned response depends on un-hesitating behavioural response to regularities, in this case electric shocks corre-lated with going on to red squares. That behavioural response could not itself be learned, but, on the contrary, is the *precondition* of learning.

With respect to the arts, the underlying instinctive responses on which the possibility of learning and of grasping the concepts of the arts depends would be, for instance, swaying to rhythm, reacting to sounds, colours and shapes. Without such innate propensities there would be nothing to which learning at the higher level could appeal. Although the distinction between the instinctive and the learned levels is important, I shall use the term 'natural' to refer to the responses and behaviour of both, since it is sometimes difficult to distinguish them, and since what is of greatest significance to my thesis is to recognize that such *non*-rational ways of behaving and responding are the roots of the concept of art; that they give sense to the *reasons* used in discussion of the arts.

Traditionally, philosophers have sought the foundations which it was sup-posed there must be to justify our concepts. Wittgenstein rejects this foundationist picture, that is, the notion that our concepts need, or can coherently have, under-lying *justifications*. Instead, he points to the way in which concept-formation is a development from instinctive behaviour and response, and then from being brought up in the ways of acting and responding of a particular community.

Consequently, so far from man's being able to create language, there is an important sense in which *language and the arts create man*. For the natural actions and responses, and the linguistic and artistic forms which develop from them, give man his conception of life — a conception which is expressed not just in forms of words, but ultimately in ways of living, and in possibilities of *being*. Thus, contrary to the unintelligible, but very common assumption of a 'subjective' inner, private world, to adapt Kerr (1986, p. 97), there is no world, for me or anyone else, other than the world which language, the arts, and other public practices give us. It is a world which we have in common: the predicament of private worlds is an illusion.

There are various loosely related sets of human activities, and one should look not for an underlying justification of each, but rather at what counts as justification *within* each. There is no intelligible room for a question of whether it is rational to engage in them. This position will be qualified in Chapter 13, since the arts, the rest of life, and language are interdependent, and I do not wish to suggest that what is expressed in the arts cannot be criticized or justified, for instance, in terms of the validity of what it says about life. Indeed, a great advantage of recognizing that artistic meaning has its roots in natural reactions and cultural practices is that it emphasises from the outset the inseparability of art and life. The arts are rooted in the *shared human life* of a culture, not in supposed individually isolated subjective mental events.

At this fundamental level, we learn to create and respond to the arts in the same way. A child grows up in an environment where there are social and cultural responses to the arts in which he learns to join. It would make no sense to speak of reasons for responses at this level. By analogy, one learns to play chess according to certain rules, and certain moves *within* the game may be illegitimate, but it would make no sense to suggest that the rules themselves could be illegitimate, since illegitimacy is determined by failure to conform with the rules. An activity may be legal or illegal, but it would make no sense to ask whether a law were legal.

A child simply learns to act and respond in ways which constitute the beginnings of a grasp of what is involved in engaging in artistic activities. That the possibility of reasoning depends upon this more fundamental level of simply learning how to respond can be shown by means of an example. Imagine someone who came from a country where there was no activity of drama, or anything like it, watching Shakespeare's *King Lear* several times. He comes to realize that the actors do not really die, and that members of the audience know this. Yet the latter, every night, are profoundly moved emotionally by what they see. And what they see is, according to his conception, someone who just pretends, every night, to die — and they *know* he is merely pretending. Hence, he concludes, their emotional response is simply irrational, for how could they, if they were rational, be moved by a situation which they know to be false?

It is important to notice that it would be impossible to give a rational justification for why people respond in this way. The foreigner may be told and may accept that most people in our society respond in similar ways to situations which they know to be not real life ones, taking place, moreover, in the obviously 'artificial' environment of a stage, in a theatre. But he could not engage in such an activity, and respond appropriately himself, and the crucial point here is to recognize that this inability to respond would not reflect a failure of *rationality* on his part. The reasons we offer to him cannot connect with anything which would allow him to respond. Admittedly this is a rather odd example. For instance, I said that the foreigner knows what pretending is — yet this has *some* relation to the convention of drama. Moreover, it may be hard to imagine a society in which there are no activities at all which bear any relation to the ways in which children act out situations in our society.

The roots of concepts and the reasons which express them are, then, ways of acting and responding which have been absorbed as the norms of the way of life of a society. Training may be involved here, but such training needs something on which to work, by which I mean that a child must already share attitudes and responses with us if the training is to be possible at all. There are many related activities which are part of the roots of the concept of art, such as 'make-believe', imagining being Red Indians or nurses, forms of representation in painting and drawing, nursery rhymes, being told stories, responding to and making rhythm, clapping games, responding to simple tunes. (That *training* is involved at this level does not, of course, imply that it is appropriate at other levels of education. But, as we have seen, a precondition of being able to engage in rational discourse is to have grasped, *without rational justification*, what counts as rationality.)

Margaret Wootton, in an unpublished work, has written of her experience of teaching several years ago in Kenya:

> The students were shown a number of pictures, the idea being to get them talking. As the lesson progressed it became clear that they had never seen a representational painting before and were quite unable to pick out what was in the picture or see any resemblance between the pictures and the people, landscapes and objects that had been painted. There was no tradition of painting and drawing in the tribe in this way — they had painted masks and their own faces, and had a strong tradition of wood-carving.

Unless someone could grasp what it is to respond to something *as a sketch of a person*, it would be of no use attempting to give him reasons for seeing a resemblance, and *therefore* for responding to it as a representation. He would be unable to comprehend how pencil lines on a piece of paper could possibly be *like* a human being, and reasons could make no appeal to what comes within his understanding. The reasons given for the attribution of resemblance are *internal to*, and cannot be used to explain, representation.

A similar example is the imaginary one of a people who find black-and-white photographs grotesque. By contrast with us, they see the miniature black and white images as a repugnantly distorted representation of human beings. No reasons, *external* to the concept, could be given to show them that such judgments are inappropriate, and that a photograph can be an accurate representation of a human being. There could be no separate external step of reasoning. To grasp the kind of resemblance or representation involved here, which could give the possibility of appropriate judgements, would be to grasp the concept of photography.

This raises a serious objection to the prevalent assumption that artistic meaning can be explained by a general theory of symbolism. For while of course there can be symbolism in art, it cannot be what explains or gives meaning to the arts, in some sense which is *external* to them, since an understanding of the arts is a precondition of recognizing the symbolism. Any such attempt to provide an external explanation of the creation of the arts is misguided, since it has to presuppose in the explanation what it purports to explain. When an art form is in existence, symbolic meanings can be expressed in it, but it would make no sense to suppose that the arts were created in order to express symbolic meanings. Understanding the arts, in the sense of being able to *engage* in them, presupposes roots in non-rational feelings, responses, or attitudes. Understanding the arts, in the sense of being able to *articulate* artistic experience, presupposes, at least to some extent, understanding in the former sense.

That artistic understanding is rooted in natural response does *not* imply that there are no criteria for the appropriateness of responses to particular works of art; that is to say, it does not imply that there are no limits to the kinds of feeling or attitude which an individual may appropriately have. Strawson (1968, pp. 71–96) distinguishes between the *reactive* attitude which we normally have to other human beings and the *detached* attitude. The reactive attitude consists in the ways we act and respond to other people, for example, in our moral expectations, in holding them responsible for their actions as well as feeling responsible to them, in our natural responses of sympathy, and so on, by contrast to our attitude to animals or inanimate objects. Although this is the norm, it could change to a detached attitude, if, for instance, someone were to become insane. In certain cases of insanity, indeed, the person *could* no longer be an object of the normal reactive attitude appropriate to a human being, and could be regarded only as a subject for treatment. There is a role for choice of attitude, but it is a limited possibility. One could not simply adopt a reactive attitude to an insane person, although there are exceptional circumstances in which one may adopt a detached attitude to normal people. One might, for instance, see people as rather like helpless machines, scurrying about aimlessly on predetermined tracks, and one might imagine a rather horrifying play or film presenting such a perspective on human concerns and activities. But this attitude could not be adopted permanently and for all people. It is significant that such a play or film would be *disturbing*, and such a response would be because these are normal human beings being represented. That is, such a response would be parasitic upon the normal reactive attitude. There are criteria for the appropriateness of attitudes and, except in unusual circumstances, the suggestion that one might adopt the detached attitude to normal people would make no sense. The reactive attitude is an essential part of understanding other people and living in a society, and it gives sense to the notion of reasons in relation to them.

Swift, in *A Modest Proposal*, suggests that the two problems of overpopulation and insufficient food could be solved by the simple expedient of eating young children. As he expected, his readers were revolted by this proposal. What underlies this sense of revulsion is the reactive attitude, since people were being asked to treat as food, members of their own species. *No reasons* could be given for this sense of revulsion, since it is at an instinctive level. It is rather that any reasons we might give for the way people should be treated would derive their substance from such a natural response. One might say, for instance, that a certain way of treating people was appalling because it amounted to treating them as cattle. Similarly, a reason for opposing the institution of marriage, or at least traditional attitudes to marriage which are still only too prevalent, might be that it perpetuates the notion that, as a wife, a woman is still to some extent regarded as an object, as the property of her husband. The force of both, as *reasons*, derives from an implicit appeal to the natural reactive attitude to other human beings.

It may be worth emphasizing again that the reactive attitude is ultimate, in that it is not underlain by reason or hypothesis. For instance, responding sympathetically to other people is part of this attitude. Thus, that someone winces or cries out in an appropriate situation is not evidence from which I infer, from a general theory about human beings, that he subjectively, 'internally' is in pain and deserving of sympathy. There is no sense in the notion of one's having formed such a theory, or in understanding what could justify it. My attitude, expressed in my response, is *ultimate*. While, in a sense, I have a reason for responding to him as I do, it is not an *underlying* reason, which *justifies* my response. There is no sense in the notion of such underlying reason or justification. My response is not based on a theory about the kind of entity I am confronted with; it is not based on a theory at all; it is based on *nothing*. Or, to put the point another way, it is not that my attitude is based on a belief, but that the meaning of a belief that he is suffering is given by the *attitude* to him as a *human being*. Thus, my belief, in a particular case, that someone is suffering is based upon the fact that it is a *fellow human being* who is wincing and crying out, and I simply *have*, instinctively, a reactive attitude to fellow human beings. Learning how to respond to others is based upon an implicit appeal to this attitude. Roughly, it is not that the response is based on a reason, but that the reason is given its meaning by natural responses to other human beings. Similarly, a child is not given *reasons* to justify his initial responses to the arts. On the contrary, he learns to share and engage in artistic and related activities. This learning is achieved, at the early stages, not so much by explicit teaching as by being initiated into the activities and responses of the arts. This point, which is central to my thesis, may be difficult to grasp at first. It will, I hope, become clearer as the book progresses.

◊

There is a complex relation between feeling and reason, in general and in the arts. My arguing, in Chapters 1 and 3, that there is a prevalent neglect of the importance of reasoning does not in the least imply a depreciation of feeling; my arguing here that understanding the arts depends ultimately upon non-rational attitudes and responses does not imply a depreciation of the importance of reasoning. Natural responses give sense to reasons, yet reasons can open a vast and varied range of feeling which could not be experienced without them. At most, the subjectivist conception, even if it made sense (which it does not) can claim merely that the arts, like language, can *express* supposedly 'inner' experiences which one *already* has. By contrast, my thesis shows clearly that the arts, like language, actually *confer* possibilities of feeling and experience; without the arts there could be no such feelings. In this sense, the arts are enormously *creative* emotionally. This offers a far more important and comprehensive account of the educational potential of the arts than the subjectivist view.

It is important to keep alive natural responses to the arts as one develops rational understanding. This point is related to the importance of intuition, and by no means only in the arts. Some people are said to 'have a feeling for' a subject. Part of what that means is that they can make what are often fruitful conjectural leaps, ahead of the evidence or reasoning. Of course such leaps have to be substantiated, in general, by evidence or reasoning, to be regarded as reliable — in that sense intuition depends upon continued tuition. Nevertheless, without such intuitive leaps, no progress could be made — the scientist, for instance, would have no idea in which *direction* his search for evidence should proceed. In the arts, as in every other sphere, the feel for the subject should be cultivated, not weakened, as one extends enormously the scope of one's rational understanding.

I wrote above that one's responses to the arts are both natural and learned. This will sound odd, or even contradictory, to those who assume that there is a sharper distinction between the two terms than can coherently be drawn. What could be more natural than to respond emotionally to powerful music, to a superbly performed play, or to a vividly written novel or poem? A particularly clear illustration is the way in which children respond to the reading of a story. Yet learning is necessary for all such responses. An animal, for instance, could not respond in that way; neither could the people in the society with no concept of representational art respond, for example, to a drawing of a sad or agonized face.

It should be remembered, too, that I am using the term 'natural' in a broader sense than as equivalent to 'innate'. In some cases it is difficult to distinguish between what is entirely instinctive and what has been learned even, for instance, with animals in the wild. The distinction is not relevant to my principal interests, which are with the roots of reason and understanding in the arts.

Conclusion

The roots of artistic understanding are our natural responses to and engagement in the arts and related activities. Although reasoning is of crucial though often neglected importance, it should not be misunderstood as providing an underlying justification for artistic appreciation. It is rather that the natural responses to, actions involved in, and activities of, the arts give sense to the reasons. A child learns how to respond to the arts before he could possibly grasp any purported rational principle of justification of such response. Moreover, no explanation of any such principle would be comprehensible to anyone who had not already some experience of responding to the arts. Thus we shall be looking in the wrong direction if we try to discover what is fundamental to artistic experience in this sense. Indeed, as I have already hinted, the mistake of assuming that there *must* be something which provides the underlying justification for the arts is what leads to an assumption of unintelligible metaphysics. The roots of artistic, as of any form of understanding, are to be found not in an underlying rational principle but in what is much simpler, namely, in what is involved in a child's learning, in the natural ways of responding and acting which are the preconditions of learning. In this sense, it is irrational to be too rational, for artistic meanings and responses are not derived from an underlying rational principle; indeed, on the contrary, if any principle could be formulated it would be answerable to the natural ways in which people respond to the arts. This is why it is to rationalize in the wrong direction to examine the roots in order to try to find a principle. If there should be such a principle, it will be found at the top of the tree, supported and nourished by the roots of natural responses. To adapt Kerr (1986, pp. 92–93), we are so dominated by the mind/body dichotomy that it is difficult to acknowledge a whole range of characteristically human activities which are neither the result of ratiocination nor the effect of mechanical conditioning.

One might say that it is neither feeling nor reason but *action* which is the root — action which takes place within and inseparably from a *social* context, and which is an expression of cultural practices. But, of course, action itself, is, at least frequently, inseparable from feeling, cognition, rationality. *Unreflective reactions* are no less intelligent, rational and human for being natural, immediate, and automatic, than comforting an injured man or a bereaved woman, or shunning them in dread.

Chapter 3

Reasoning

My insistence in Chapter 2 that there can be no principle which underlies and justifies our responses to and engagement with the arts should not be construed as denying the possibility of justifying artistic judgments. On the contrary, it is the possibility of rational justification which shows that the arts are fully educational. That it makes no sense to suppose that there can be a rational justification for the natural responses which are the *roots* of the concept of art does not in the least imply that there cannot be rational justification of judgments made *within* the concepts of art which have grown from those roots.

There is a prevalent tendency among those concerned with the arts, and perhaps especially with the arts in education, to overlook or even to repudiate the place of reason. While the role of feeling is generally assumed to be obvious, the notion of reason in this sphere is often regarded with suspicion. Hence it is commonly said that the arts are a matter of feeling rather than reason. The subjectivist is right to insist that feeling is central to the arts, but he is seriously mistaken to assume that therefore artistic appreciation is a matter of irrational or non-rational feelings or attitudes, and thus that reasoning is irrelevant or even inhibiting. Of course, an inappropriate emphasis on reasoning *can* prevent a full understanding of the arts, but equally an inappropriate emphasis on feeling can prevent such understanding.

Reason is equally important to questions of appreciation, meaning, interpretation, judgment and evaluation, so I shall not differentiate between them. For convenience, I shall centre my argument primarily on appreciation, although it should be emphasised, because I have been misunderstood in this respect, that it applies equally to the creator and the spectator. There is a common assumption, usually revealing precisely the philosophy of mind which I aim to expose as fundamentally confused, that whereas reasons may be appropriate to appreciation, the creation of art is purely subjective, in the sense that there is no place for reason.

Since the role of reason in the arts is sometimes regarded as questionable, I shall compare it with the sciences, where the role and importance of reasoning are normally unquestioned. Although of course there are considerable differences between the two areas, there are also important similarities with respect to the nature of reasoning and objectivity.

For expository purposes I shall often consider the case of exchanges of opinion, but it should be remembered that at least equally important is the common and enriching experience of reflecting about a work of art. This involves reasoning one's own way to an opinion and feeling about it.

Education

It is worth emphasizing that the question of educational implications is not separate from or peripheral to the central philosophical questions. One does not, as it were, first do the philosophy and then consider the consequences for education. The question whether reason has a place in the arts *is* the question whether the arts necessarily involve cognition or knowledge. And, as Plato insisted, the question of whether knowledge is possible *is* the question of whether there can be learning and teaching.

Education is not, of course, limited to what goes on in schools, colleges and universities. There is a great deal to be learned from the arts during the whole of one's life. Nevertheless, unless artistic experience is answerable to reason and cognition, there can be no justification for including the arts in our educational institutions. Arts educators are often their own worst enemies, in that they tend readily to accept and proclaim the subjectivist doctrine — probably because they see no alternative. Yet that is to concede that there is no role for reason, and therefore that judgments are not justifiable. And that is to say that there is *no* place for the arts in education. Accountability, for instance, depends not only upon the quality of the work, but upon the reasons which can be offered for the inclusion of that kind of activity in the curriculum. It is only if rational justification is possible within an activity that the activity can justifiably be regarded as educational.

Subjectivism

The subjectivist correctly insists on the importance of individuality and freedom; on the wide differences of opinion there may be about the same work of art; on the centrality of feeling and creativity. He cannot see how these can be compatible with an insistence that objective reasons are equally important. Yet there is no sense in the notion of *learning* anything, if it does not involve objective criteria for progress and evaluation, including self-evaluation. Thus the dilemma for a subjectivist teacher is that as a teacher it is incumbent on him to encourage progress so that each individual student can develop his or her artistic potential, yet as a subjectivist he cannot attach any sense to that notion. For it is part of the subjectivist doctrine that artistic meaning or value depends solely upon what each individual feels about it, in which case no sense can be given to understanding or meaning.

Subjectivists usually fail to recognize this inevitably self-defeating consequence of their own position. For instance, the principal of a well-known dance academy once wrote: 'Dance is such subjective matter that there is nothing that can or should be said about it.' One wonders how he can reconcile this with accepting his salary, since it amounts to denying that he and his staff can teach anything to their students. Some years ago an American dance professor, recognizing that an implication of her professed subjectivism is that anyone's opinion is as good as anyone else's, and that any feeling in response to a work of art is equally 'appropriate', was unable to object when some of her students, as their dance performance, simply sat on the studio floor eating crisps. Despite her commendable honesty, she lost her job. Such explicit recognition of the consequences of subjectivism is rare. Usually the subjectivist is in the bizarre position of denying a platitude, for he is well aware that the arts have meaning, and that some works and performances are better than others. Despite what he may *say*, he reveals this in what he *does*, for example, in the way he responds to different works of art, and in those he wants to see or hear again.

There is a line of thought which appears to support subjectivism, and which may cloud the issues. It may be stated as follows: 'The impression I have of a work of art must come through my senses, therefore it is my impression and no one else's, and therefore it must be subjective.' But a similar argument would apply to such unquestioned cases of objectivity as mathematical propositions and statements about physical objects. It is by means of my own faculties that I see that $2 + 2 = 4$, and that the table is brown. Nevertheless, such statements are not subjective. That an impression of art is my impression, in that it depends upon my senses, does not in the least imply that artistic judgments are subjective. The fact that it is *my* judgment, based on *my* impression, obviously does not imply that it cannot be objectively correct or incorrect, as the $2 + 2 = 4$ example clearly illustrates.

A closely related argument, which also appears to support subjectivism and which will be further discussed in Chapter 4, is that an artistic judgment, like a moral and philosophical judgment, but by contrast with what might be called 'judgments of fact', requires one' s own assessment, rather than accepting what even experts say. However, this significant aspect of artistic judgments is by no means inimical to reasoning. On the contrary, the ability to reflect on artistic meaning and value, and to formulate one's own individual opinion, *requires* reasoning.

The term 'subjective' is notoriously slippery, and the subjectivity of the arts is often defended with such fervour that it may be worth stating certain theses for which I am certainly *not* arguing, and indeed to which I am strongly opposed. In opposing the subjective with objectivity, in the sense of the possibility of giving reasons, I am not denying the importance of individuality and personal involvement, nor am I suggesting that there is a single standard which every rational being must accept. On the contrary, one of the central and most rewarding aspects of engagement with the arts, and one of the most important contributions of the arts in education, is the progressive development of individuality and personal involvement, with consequent differences of feeling and opinion. There is no incompatibility between an insistence on the importance of reasoning, and those important aspects of artistic experience on which the subjectivist rightly insists. On the contrary, as I argued in Chapter 1, the feeling involved in artistic experience *is* rational in character.

Nevertheless, although the meanings of the terms will become clearer as the book progresses, it may be helpful if I offer now a brief outline of what I mean by 'subjective' and 'objective'. The two senses of 'subjective' which are the principal sources of philosophical confusion, and educational damage, are as follows:

(a)   'subjective' in the sense of the purely private, 'inner' mental experience, which, supposedly, can be known 'directly' only by the person himself.

(b) 'subjective' in the sense of mere personal preference or liking. The serious fallacy in assuming that artistic judgments are subjective in this sense finds its commonest form in the prevalent view that judgments of artistic appreciation are mere expressions of whether one likes the work or not. More generally, value judgments of all kinds are commonly assumed to be merely subjective, in this sense. For instance, one often meets the riposte, 'Oh, that's just a value judgment', as if one were expressing a mere personal liking or preference, as if that is the end of the matter. Yet, to anticipate part of Chapter 4, on the contrary, the expression of a value judgment is only the *beginning* of the matter! One should be able to support it with *reasons*.

There are other senses of 'subjective', some of which will emerge in later chapters. However, it is (a) which is my main quarry, since that is the prime sense in which the doctrine that artistic experience is subjective is so confused and harmful. Yet it is widely and unquestioningly accepted, and its character and implications normally unrecognised. That is the sense in which most arts educators assume that the arts are purely subjective, although it is usually run vaguely together with, and not distinguished from (b) and other senses.[1]

The prevalent sense of 'objective' which I am *rejecting* is that of the absolute and universal. Such a notion has very little, if any, application in *any* sphere, for instance, even in the sciences, as this chapter will make clear. In relation to the arts, in arguing that the creation and appreciation of the arts are as fully objective as the sciences, I am *not* arguing that there are single, definitive, universally 'correct' interpretations and evaluations of, and responses, to works of art. Quite the contrary. But then, there are no such absolutes in the sciences either.

The objectivity for which I am arguing is mainly in the sense of the possibility of offering valid reasons. This fully allows for the possibility of cultural differences, and differences of feeling and opinion within a culture — even irreconcilable differences. It is because the possibility of giving reasons is central to my account of objectivity that my main theme in this book is the rationality of feeling. This crucial notion of objectivity, in terms of the possibility of giving valid reasons, will become clearer later in this chapter.

But an artistic judgment, perhaps especially in education, should also be objective in the sense of being impartial, unprejudiced. In that sense, whatever the teacher's personal preferences or prejudices, he or she should obviously try to judge objectively what is artistically valuable, and what is in the best artistic and educational interest of each individual student.

Scientism and Subjectivism

A principal source of misconception on this issue is an inappropriate comparison with what is regarded as a paradigm of rationality. Thus a theme of this chapter might be 'Scientism and subjectivism: two sides of the same distorted coin'. For what often impels people to subjectivism about the arts is the common assumption that the sciences are paradigm examples of rationality, coupled with the recognition that artistic judgments are obviously not open to scientific verification. This inevitably leads to the mistaken supposition that the arts cannot be fully rational.

Part of this misconception is what I shall call 'the argument from disagreement', which consists in the plausible but erroneous assumption that artistic appreciation must be subjective because, supposedly unlike the sciences, there can be such wide and even irreconcilable differences of critical opinion about the same work of art. Such a notion reveals a widely prevalent misunderstanding of the character of scientific inquiry and understanding.

A thoroughgoing example of the common assumption that the sciences are the paradigm of rationality, and that only scientific verification can justify our claims to knowledge is contained in an article on dance. The authors (Spencer and White, 1972) write:

> Numerous claims for dance have been made, yet . . . little published research is available to give substance to the claims. The position taken in this paper is that dance is a form of behaviour, and as such, is open to scientific examination. That is, if something exists, it exists in quantity. The major method by which knowledge is developed in the behavioural sciences as well as in the physical sciences is by empirical investigation. Dance as a body of knowledge can be furthered in the same way. (p. 5)

Yet none of these branches of science can discover anything in a dancer's movements to support artistic or aesthetic judgments. So a subjectivist argument might continue: 'Since all human behaviour is scientifically examinable, yet the aesthetic quality of movements cannot be discovered scientifically, such aesthetic quality is clearly not *in* the behaviour, in which case, if any sense at all can be made of the notion of aesthetic quality, it must be a purely subjective matter. Thus it follows that aesthetic and artistic appreciation cannot be rationally substantiated.' For example, in a very similar vein, Louis Arnaud Reid (1931, pp. 62–3) writes:

> How does body, a nonmental object, come to 'embody' or 'express', for our aesthetic imagination, values which it does not literally contain? . . . How do the values get there? The only possible answer is that we put them there — in imagination.

This is a classic statement of the kind of subjectivism which is still so dangerously prevalent, and which it is a main aim of this book to expose as radically confused philosophically, and fatal to the case for the arts in education. According to this pervasive but deeply misconceived notion, aesthetic values cannot literally be *in* the behaviour, they are imposed on the object, or the physical movement, by one's subjective imagination. Exactly similar assumptions are commonly made about the other arts.

This is why I said that subjectivism about the arts is the other side of the same coin as scientism. For the subjectivist assumes that judgments of artistic appreciation are obviously not supportable by reasons on the grounds that they cannot be supported by the kind of reasoning which is employed in the *sciences*, an important characteristic of which, he also assumes, is that definitive conclusions are reached. That is, the subjectivist accepts the doctrine of scientism that the only rational verification is scientific. Small wonder that critical appreciation of the arts has been characterized as the natural home of rapturous and soporific effusion.

As I mentioned above, there is a strong temptation to assume that since no scientific analysis can locate an aesthetic or artistic element, then it cannot be actually *in* the physical movements of the dancer, and therefore it must be subjective, in the sense that it is merely projected imaginatively into the movement by the spectator. This common kind of assumption is aptly captured by Hume when he writes: 'Beauty is no quality in things themselves — it exists merely in the mind which contemplates them' (in MacIntyre, 1965, p. 278). Ducasse writes (1929): 'The feeling is apprehended as if it were a quality of the object' (p. 177); Perry (1926): 'It seems necessary at some point to admit that the qualities of feeling may be "referred" where they do not belong . . .' (p. 31); and Reid (1931): 'the value embodied in the perceived object or body is not literally situated in the body. The joy expressed in music is not literally in the succession of sounds.' (p. 60) It is clear that these last three writers make the assumption that artistic value must be subjective because it is not possible to discover it *by the methods of the physical sciences*. It is an understandable but confused assumption. Central to it is the notion which appears in the article on dance, quoted above, that if something exists it must exist in quantity. The confusion here was exposed in a cartoon depicting a couple of lovers embracing in the moonlight, with the young man exclaiming ruefully: 'I can't tell you how much I love you — I forgot my calculator.'

It is important to recognise clearly that although it is undoubtedly true that behaviour is open to scientific explanation, it does not follow, nor is it true, that all explanation or justification is of a scientific kind. The young man in the cartoon could prove how much he loved the young lady, but not by scientific methods. Similarly, Epstein, asked whether he believed that absolutely everything could be expressed scientifically, replied: 'Yes, it would be possible but it would make no sense. It would be a description without meaning — as if you described a Beethoven symphony as a variation of wave pressure.' It would have been clearer, perhaps, if he had replied: 'No.'

Objective Assessment without Measurement

There are important practical consequences of this issue, for instance, for accountability in education. Assessment tends often to be equated with quantification, and where an activity cannot be quantified it is too easily assumed that it cannot be assessed. Yet, to take an obvious case, the validity of a reasoned argument can be assessed, although it obviously cannot be measured. A philosophy student's progress in producing valid reasons to support his case can be assessed, but not by measurement. Moreover, anyone who wished to dispute my contention that assessment cannot be equated with measurement could do so only by reasoned argument. Hence even the attempt would be self-defeating — since he would have to appeal to our non-quantifiable assessment of the validity of his reasons which are intended to show that there cannot be non-quantifiable assessment. He would be pulling the rug from under his own feet even to try to dispute the case.

Only *some* kinds of assessment are quantifications. For example, one may assess a move in chess as a good one, yet clearly no sense could be made of quantifying it. Moreover, the most important assessments we make in life, such as those involved in understanding other people, are not quantifications. How, for instance, would one set about measuring facial expressions in order to assess their meaning? We can recognize that people are sad, sensitive, or troubled, and we are constantly making such assessments of the character, mood and responsiveness of other people. One can be right or wrong, one can learn to improve one's ability to judge other people, or another person, but the notion of measurement here is completely out of place.

Similarly only some kinds of progress can be quantified. A good teacher can objectively assess a child's developing maturity, sensitivity to a subject and sense of responsibility, but it would make no sense to suggest that these crucial aspects of a child's educational progress could be measured. Part of the temptation to equate assessment with quantification is that the latter is so much easier and less personally demanding than judgment. Simone Weil writes (1962, p. 18): 'For men burdened with a fatigue that makes any effort of attention painful, it is a relief to contemplate the unproblematic clarity of figures.'

However tempting it may be, it is a serious and harmful misconception. The most important areas of education require sensitive, informed judgment, and thus there can never be a substitute for high quality teachers.

Reasons for Interpretation

It is sometimes claimed that whereas there are recognized methods of resolving scientific disagreements, there are no such methods of resolving conflicts of critical opinion about a work of art, since a scientific statement, unlike a critical judgment in the arts, can be verified by empirical tests and observation. The apparent force of this objection derives from its conflating what are in fact two distinct assertions. The first amounts to a confusion of standards, since to assert that artistic judgments cannot be verified by the empirical tests and observations characteristic of the sciences amounts merely to asserting that artistic appreciation is not science. That is trivially obvious. The point at issue is not whether artistic judgments are scientifically verifiable, but whether they are verifiable.

The second assertion implicit in the objection is clearly false, for there obviously are recognized methods of resolving differences of critical opinion, as anyone who engages seriously in the arts knows very well. For example, a critical opinion of a literary work may fail on the grounds either of internal inconsistency or of having less adequate support from the text than another critical opinion. What appears to give substance to the initial contention is the elision of an assertion which is trivially true but irrelevant, namely, that artistic judgments cannot be verified scientifically, with an assertion which is substantial but false, namely, that there are no methods of resolving conflicts of critical opinion.

It has already been remarked that there tends to be too rigid and narrow a conception of the character of reasoning. There are different kinds of reasoning, such as the deductive, which is characteristic of mathematics and syllogistic logic, and the inductive, which is characteristic of the sciences. Yet there is another kind of reasoning which is, if anything, even more important than these. Although I dislike technical terminology, and thus I am reluctant to create any myself, I sometimes call this 'interpretative reasoning' in order to indicate its character. This kind of reasoning can give an interpretation, evaluation or picture of a phenomenon or situation, and it is *central* not only to the arts, but also to scientific and other forms of knowledge. As an illustration, consider one of the figures sometimes used in the psychology of perception, which at first, however hard one scrutinizes it, appears to be just a meaningless jumble of lines, but in which, when it is pointed out, one can clearly distinguish a face . The reasons offered in support of the judgment that there is a face visible would consist in drawing attention to the relevant features in the drawing. Moreover, it is significant for some of our later discussion of the possibility of coming to see, evaluate or understand a phenomenon or situation under a certain interpretation, description, or concept, that once one has seen the face it may be hard to imagine how it was not immediately apparent, and one may be unable to see the figure in any other way subsequently.

However, the situation is often more complex, in that there may be a variety of possible interpretations. Clearly, so far from undermining objectivity, or the role of reasoning, one has, in such a case, to appeal to reason to decide which is the most convincing. Sometimes this cannot be achieved, since two interpretations may be equally possible and valid. For example, consider this figure which can be seen as a duck or as a rabbit.

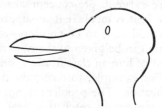

Each of two people, one contending that it is a duck, the other that it is a rabbit, could support his contention by citing, as reasons, features of the figure — for example, 'There are its ears'. However, there is obviously not an arbitrary, completely *unlimited* possibility of interpretation. Yet an inevitable consequence of subjectivism is that there are *no* limits. For a subjectivist *any* interpretation or response is as 'good' as any other. But that supposition makes no sense. The figure cannot be seen as the Eiffel Tower, for instance.

While it is true that, in one sense, reasoning cannot improve eyesight and hearing, it is crucial to recognise that it can open up possibilities of perception which would otherwise remain closed. (I shall shortly give an example of the limits of perception which may be set by the language one speaks.) One's attention may be drawn to the significance of previously unrecognized subtleties of a work of art which suffuse the whole work with a new meaning and value, yet, from a purely physical point of view, one sees nothing which one did not see before.

Although a work may be open to various interpretations, this lends no support to subjectivism, since beyond certain limits a judgment could not count as an interpretation at all, precisely *because* it could not be supported by reasons. That is, there may be in some cases an *indefinite*, but there cannot be an *unlimited*, scope for intelligible interpretation; the very sense of 'interpretation' requires limits. There has been a variety of interpretations of Shakespeare's *King Lear,* but a conception of the play as a comedy, in normal circumstances anyway, could not intelligibly be regarded as an interpretation. Within the limits, of course, there may be an indefinitely wide scope for argument about whether a particular interpretation is valid or invalid.

Although there are different traditions and concepts of art, this does not imply that each is equally available to us, in the sense that we could choose which to adopt. Neither does it imply that one is limited to understanding only the arts of one's own culture. This is an issue which will be discussed in Chapter 5. At this juncture I mention it in order to bring out an important distinction between conceptualization and interpretation.

The conceptual, which is fundamental, gives sense to reality, and it sets the limits for intelligible interpretation. To bring out what I mean I shall refer briefly to two common kinds of thesis which I shall call realism and relativism. Although, for simplicity, I shall discuss the issue in terms of language, it should be emphasized again that the contribution of the arts, and other activities, to conceptual understanding cannot be coherently distinguished from that of language. The realist supposes that there are facts about the world which are independent of, and determine, the concepts expressed in language. There are trees, rivers, clouds, births and deaths, to which we attach names and descriptions in order to communicate about them. For the realist, the structure of language mirrors, or ought to mirror, accurately the pre-existent, pre-conceptualized phenomena. However, as we have seen in Chapter 2, it is incoherent to suppose that man could invent language, since language would have to be presupposed for the invention to be possible. Moreover, no sense can be given to the notion of recognizing divisions in a 'real' world independent of human classification, since the recognition would itself *require* classification. For example, to recognize that something is a tree is already to employ a classification. The problem is not quasi-empirical; it is not that however hard we try we cannot reach this 'real' world, but that nothing could possibly *count* as reaching it. Which is to say that the notion of a reality which is independent of language makes no sense. What we are looking at in the real world would have to be *understood* to carry out the check, and understanding is given *by* concepts; thus to verify the correlation of concepts with a supposed external, concept-free 'reality' would require one's having unconceptualized concepts which, of course, is senseless.

In a perceptive radio play based on a true story of Pocohontas,[2] an American-Indian woman in Western society, Mick Mangan (1991) has Pocohontas saying: 'Your eyes are as good as mine but there are so many things you haven't yet learned to see. Perhaps they can only be seen in my language' . . . 'There are too many things that cannot be seen in your language, Benjamin.'

Later in the play, it becomes clear that the Indians cannot see death in our terms. Pocohontas finds it impossible to express her thoughts in English. 'The English say that the Virginia Indians hold it a disgrace to fear . . . (She has difficulty saying it) . . . death'.

Many of these issues concerning the impossibility of seeing the world given other cultures are powerfully brought out in Mette Newth's moving novel *The Abduction* (1989), about the capture of a young Greenland Inuit couple. The brutality and tragedy of their treatment has its source largely in a fundamental failure of understanding of a very different culture, and thus in a failure to see the Inuit as at least equal, if different, *human beings*.

The crucial point is that it is unintelligible to suggest that language could be true or false. To quote Kerr (1986, p. 97) 'There is no world for me or anyone else other than the world that language gives us. It is a world that we (i.e. people in the same culture) have in common.' Although propositions expressed *in* language can be true or false, it would make no sense to suppose that concepts can be true or false, since they are the *standards* of truth or falsity. The standard metre in Paris determines what counts as a metre, and the accuracy of metre rules could be checked against it. But it would make no sense to question the accuracy of the standard. Similarly, the concepts implicit in language and the arts determine what counts as truth and falsity, hence they also determine the *possible* constitution of reality. Consequently, if there were two different societies with different languages, it would be a senseless question to ask which was the more accurate one. Such a question would be rather like asking whether the rules of chess were more accurate than the rules of football. Analogously, an action can be legal or illegal, but it would be senseless to ask whether laws are legal, since laws determine what counts as legality.

The relativist recognizes that the concepts which determine what counts as reality are implicit in language, and since there are different languages, he contends that reality is relative. Yet, although there is something in this contention, it may be equally misleading if construed as implying that the different conceptual schemes are all equally available to us. For in that case reality would be what one chooses it to be. For the realist, reality is independent of any possible conception, while the relativist regards language as a pair of coloured spectacles which can be changed at will to see a different reality.

Both the realist and the relativist are mistaken, although each is indicating a valid and important aspect of the problem which is overlooked by the other. The realist is right to insist that reality is not what we choose it to be, but he is wrong to assume that this is because reality is *independent* of concepts. The relativist is right to insist that reality is given by concepts, which may be different with different languages, but he is wrong to assume that they are all equally available to us. The important point for my argument is that it is not a matter of choosing to see reality in certain ways, but rather of learning a language, and the natural responses and actions which give sense to it. (It is the primitive reactions common to humanity, as outlined in Chapter 2, which give the possibility in principle, although it may be very difficult in practice, of coming to understand the language, values, customs, conventions and social practices of other cultures.) The conceptual network embodied in language presents reality to us *in its terms*. Thus the relativist stands the position on its head. It is not that one sees reality according to one's interests and purposes, but that to a very large extent the concepts one has acquired in learning a language determine the interests and purposes it is possible to have. The qualification is necessary (a) because there are, of course, pre-linguistic purposes and intentions of the kind a very young child may have, and (b) because, more importantly, there is not a sharp distinction between them since, as was emphasized in Chapter 2, language is rooted in such natural interests and purposes expressed, for instance, in instinctive action and response. Moreover, as we shall see in Chapter 5, the initial limits of intelligibility given with a language can be developed and extended according to people's interests and purposes.

Similarly, the network of concepts which one acquires in learning language and the arts constitutes the *limits* of the intelligibility of reasons, values and knowledge. To repeat the point made earlier, there is no world for me or anyone else other than the world which language, the arts, cultural practices, give us. It is a world which those of us of the same culture share, in common. *Within* these limits an indefinite number of interpretations of a work of art may be possible. A distinction of two levels can be seen here, the reasons for interpretation deriving their sense from the underlying concepts. The notion of interpretation implies agreement about *what* is being interpreted. That there may be differences of interpretation of a play or novel presupposes agreement at least that it *is* a play or novel. It follows from the meaning of 'interpretation' that disagreement is possible, and disagreement makes sense only by reference, if only implicit, to a shared conception. One can disagree only if there is something to disagree *about*, and if one can recognize conflicting reasons *as* reasons. For example, the possibility of different interpretations of a play presupposes agreement, to some extent at least, about what happens in it. There are various interpretations of the character of Iago's actions in Shakespeare's *Othello,* and these are based on and given their sense by the unquestioned fact of the virulent force of his determination to destroy Othello.

Nevertheless, to anticipate the argument of Chapter 5, this is not to imply that understanding is irrevocably confined to the conceptual limits which one has acquired in growing up in a culture. Other conceptions are available to the extent that one can learn other languages, arts, attitudes and ways of acting and responding. For the purposes of the present discussion of the character and scope of reason, it should be recognized that reason can be employed at both levels, in that it may achieve comprehension not only of different interpretations, but also of different underlying concepts. Although, as we have seen, it would make no sense to suggest that the concepts given with language and the arts could be adopted at will, they can be changed or enlarged where there is some overlap with other concepts which may initially be beyond one's comprehension. For instance, different languages overlap to *some* extent, or there would be no justification for referring to each *as* a language. In this respect, the way in which relativism is often formulated gives the misleading impression that each language is entirely discrete. Yet even very different cultures have some points of contact which can offer starting points for reasons which may achieve greater mutual understanding. For instance, the arts are often and characteristically concerned with issues such as man's attempts to come to terms with death and suffering, and these may provide starting points for such reasons.

The fundamental issue of the relation between concepts and reality is of considerable significance for the arts, and education generally. Some psychologists suggest that in order to perceive what the world is really like, it is necessary for all concepts to be eliminated. Thus Witkin (1980, pp. 90–1) writes of 'direct realism' or 'direct apprehension' which, he claims, can be achieved by taking away 'everything that memory adds' in order to see what is there *in itself.* The aim of his thesis, couched in realist terms which are initially plausible, is to encourage fresh visions of reality. But, as we have seen, it is senseless to suppose that these could be achieved by *eliminating* all concepts. Fresh vision requires not the *absence* of concepts (which makes no sense anyway) but *fresh* concepts. The point can be brought out by revealing the incoherence which centres on this tempting use of 'direct'. Our perception of reality is normally direct. If I am looking at a chessboard, in normal light, what could be more direct? The sense of 'direct' used by those who argue in this way renders senseless any possibility of understanding or referring to what is supposed to be perceived 'directly'. Someone from a society with no knowledge of chess or any similar game cannot directly apprehend the reality of a game of chess, however hard he looks at it, precisely because he does not have the requisite concepts. Perhaps he can directly apprehend oddly shaped pieces of wood on a black and white squared board, and this may tempt one to think that at least he can see the reality of size, shape and colour without concepts. Yet concepts are necessary for that too, and it is worth remembering that they may be different in different languages. To bring out the point in a different way, someone who suffers a total loss of memory does not, as a consequence, understand reality directly. On the contrary, he understands nothing. For example, he could no longer directly see a tree, since he no longer knows what a tree is. Similarly, someone with no conception of a rabbit could not directly apprehend that interpretation of the figure, no matter how carefully he scrutinized it.

Reason, Concept and Interpretation

Near the island of Skomer, which is a sea-bird sanctuary in Pembrokeshire, the West Wales Naturalists' Trust has provided the 'Lockley Lodge Interpretative Centre' in order to help visitors to recognize the birds they will see and hear. This illustrates the close analogy there can be between interpretation and conceptualization as far as the role of reason is concerned. The Centre tries to help visitors to classify or conceptualize correctly what they see and hear, but the ways in which reasons can be given to achieve this are so similar to, that it is natural to refer to them as, interpretation.

Of course, there are also significant differences. Whereas answerability to reason is always appropriate in the case of interpretation, this is certainly not always true in cases of applying a concept since, as we have seen, any reason necessarily presupposes a ground in a concept which gives it sense. More obviously, when I refer to a tree, a chair, the sky, and so on, I not only do not but could not give reasons for that application of the concept, and neither (to put the same point another way) am I interpreting anything. I simply see a tree. And if I were asked why I refer to it as a tree, the only answer would be that I have learned the English language. Given that, and in straightforward cases, there is no room for the further question of why I call it a tree. If, in normal light and when I was standing in front of it, someone were to say 'I realize that you know the language, but why do you call that a tree?', his question would make no sense. By contrast, such a question about an interpretation would always make sense even if, in an obvious case, it might be surprising. Nevertheless, that there is not always a clear distinction between conceptualization and interpretation is illustrated by this example, since, in the Centre's terms, to interpret correctly what one sees and hears is to be able to recognize this as, for instance, a razorbill rather than a guillemot; it is to be able to bring what one sees under the correct description or concept.

A precisely similar situation frequently arises in the sciences in order to give sense to what is perceived. Discovery is not a matter simply of accurate sensory perception. The greatest problem for a scientist is often not to conduct experiments and make observations, but to interpret his results. As we have seen, everything we call 'observation' involves conceptualization, but interpretation of the results is often required. Bronowski (1973) with respect to the problems of understanding the electron, and the rival interpretations of two opposing factions at the University of Gottingen, writes:

The quip among professors was (because of the way university time-tables were laid out) that on Mondays, Wednesdays and Fridays the electron would behave like a particle; on Tuesdays, Thursdays and Saturdays it would behave like a wave . . . That was what the speculation and argument was about. And that requires, not calculation, but insight, imagination: if you like, metaphysics. (p. 82)

He goes on to say:

. . . new ideas in physics amount to a different view of reality. The world is not a fixed, solid array of objects, for it cannot be fully separated from our perception of it. It shifts under our gaze, it interacts with us, and the knowledge that it yields has to be interpreted by us.

Giving reasons for interpretations, whether of a work of art or of a scientific observation, is very like giving reasons for judging something to be of a certain kind, and it may be difficult to decide whether a particular case of disagreement or change would be better described as the same facts interpreted differently, or different facts because of a different conception. Kuhn (1975, p. 56), discussing the discovery of oxygen, writes: 'that a major theoretical revision was needed to see what Lavoisier saw must be the principal reason why Priestley (who had first encountered the phenomenon) was, to the end of his long life *unable* to see it'. And, with respect to X-rays, which had created an unexpected glow on a screen, he writes (p. 58): 'At least one other investigator had seen that glow and, to his subsequent chagrin, discovered *nothing at all*' (my italics).

A particularly pointed illustration of the dependence of scientific fact upon underlying theory or interpretation appears in the following remarks by the mathematician and astronomer Bondi (1972).

I regard the very use of the word 'fact' as misleading, because 'fact' is an emotive word which suggests something hard and firm. What we have in science is always a jumble of observation, understanding of the equipment with which the observation was carried out, interpretation and analysis. We can never clear one from another. Certain experiments that were interpreted in a particular way in their day we now interpret quite differently — but they might well have been claimed as 'facts' in those days . . . It's important to realise that in science it isn't a question of who is right and who is wrong; it is much more a question of who is useful, who is stimulating, who has helped things forward. (p. 226)

It is sometimes assumed that measurement or quantification provides a standard of certainty which transcends the dependence of human judgment on concepts and interpretation. Yet the aphorism 'Lies, damned lies, and statistics' reminds us that figures by themselves are meaningless. To be meaningful they have to be interpreted.

It is also sometimes assumed that reason is exclusively or peculiarly the province of mathematics and the sciences, by contrast with the imagination and creativity which are supposed to be the peculiar province of the arts. Yet both reason and imagination are necessary in all areas of knowledge and inquiry. *Reasons* may give understanding of different interpretations and evaluations in the sciences as much as in the arts and, as some of the examples cited above clearly illustrate, in both it requires *imagination* to grasp their significance. It was a recognition of this point which induced Einstein to remark that in science imagination is more important than knowledge. As I have already pointed out, it might have been clearer if he had said that scientific knowledge is inseparable from imagination.

There is, then, a parallel between the two areas in that the sense of what is perceived, and of the interpretation of what is perceived, is derived from concepts given by underlying scientific theory, or artistic tradition, respectively. The point can be illuminated by considering examples of the ways in which radical changes or differences affect the character of what is perceived in each case. Consider, for instance, the enormous effort of conceptual imagination required to grasp what Galileo said about the earth's revolving round the sun, after centuries of acceptance of the earth as the centre of the universe. This conception was deeply embedded, and was expressed in linguistic expressions which we still commonly use, such as talk of the sun's rising and setting. To change it necessitated a considerable readjustment not only of scientific, but also of religious and other interlocking patterns of thought. It required a radical and fundamental readjustment of underlying theory in order to be able to see the universe in Galilean terms. The observed facts were *determined* by those conceptions.

After we had been discussing issues of this kind at the University of Victoria in Canada, one of my students recounted the interesting anecdote that for the first time in his life, standing on the West coast of Vancouver Island, he had actually seen *not* the sun setting, but the earth revolving away from the sun. He said that, even now, with our present understanding of the universe, to see this had made great demands on his will power and imagination. Such is the power of language.

It may be said that at least we can be absolutely certain now that Galileo was right, since numerous observations, for instance by cosmonauts, have shown that it is an indisputable fact that the earth revolves round the sun. While I do not wish to be taken as denying or doubting that the earth revolves round the sun, this way of thinking misses my point. For, before Galileo and Copernicus, it was equally indisputable that the sun revolved round the earth, and any serious denial of this 'fact' was literally inconceivable. Scientists could no more consider an alternative than I can see through someone else's eyes. Similarly, we are now operating within a different set of theories and concepts which do not allow us to conceive of the possibility of a comparably immense change of view in the future. As J.B.S. Haldane once observed, 'the universe is not only queerer than we suppose, but queerer than we *can* suppose'.

The analogue in the arts is clearly exemplified by the difficulty for their contemporaries of comprehending the artistic innovators. Examples abound: Giotto, Turner, the Impressionists, Picasso; James Joyce, Samuel Beckett; serial music, the revolution in modern dance initiated by Martha Graham.

The necessity of grasping the relevant artistic tradition in order to be able to make valid or intelligible artistic judgments can be illustrated by the following two anecdotes. Ravi Shankar, the eminent Indian sitar player, during a concert in Britain was rapturously applauded. He thanked the audience and assured them that they should certainly enjoy the rest of his concert, since so far he had been merely tuning up. While in Canada some years ago I was given another illustration of the point. A party of Inuit people, attending a performance of *Othello*, were appalled to see what they took to be the killing of people on the stage. They had to be reassured by being taken backstage after the performance to see the actors still alive. The Inuit had assumed that new actors would be required for each performance.

Reasons: Lateral and Non-Verbal

To give reasons, in the sense under discussion, is to offer a picture, an evaluation, of, a certain perspective on, a work of art. The justification of a judgment consists in citing features of a work, under a description which invokes the criteria of the art form. Clearly, unless one had seen the irony in a Jane Austen novel one could not give reasons in support of the judgment that it is ironic. Such justification consists not in probing deeper for a rational principle, but in a lateral, probably implicit, appeal to the concept of art, and perhaps more widely to other aspects of life. The picture of the rational justification involved is more that of a net than that of the chain characteristic of deductive reasoning, which is too often assumed to be characteristic of *all* reasoning. For instance, reasons given in support of judgments of critical appreciation of Jane Austen's *Persuasion* might cite the development of Anne Elliott's character; whether and what she learned from her experiences; the extent to which she deceived herself early in the novel; the extent to which she overcame this later; and whether Jane Austen's irony is effective. All these aspects implicitly draw on life outside the arts. For instance, the judgment that character development is or is not convincing depends upon our understanding of people in life generally.

To come to see irony where one had not recognized it before is an obvious example of a way in which reasoning can bring a work of art under a new light. Another example is hearing a description of the composer's intentions, or the circumstances in which a piece of music was written, or even simply its title. The *Symphonie Fantastique* by Berlioz is an example, as are tone poems and impressionist music.

Reasons in the arts may not be exclusively verbal. One's interpretation and evaluation of a work may be given in various other ways, and especially through the particular artistic medium, perhaps by comparisons and contrasts. For example, a musician might help us to understand an interpretation of a piece by playing certain passages with particular emphases, or with subtleties of phrasing, which cast a different light on the piece as a whole. One has seen, in television's *Master Class,* a sensitive musician demonstrate, by playing with such emphases, his interpretation of a passage of music, and how important that interpretation was to his conception of the whole work. A painter might show how a different use of colour might bring about a significant effect on a painting. Indeed, there are numerous and various non-verbal ways in which understanding can be shown and achieved in life generally. For example, in support of a judgment expressing condemnation of war and jingoism one might simply point to the corpses on a battlefield, or to photographs or paintings of scenes of consequences of war. This would be at least the equivalent, in certain circumstances, of offering a verbal judgment and supporting it with verbal reasons, and it might well be far more powerful.

There are numerous examples of non-verbal, or not-exclusively-verbal, reasons which can contribute to, or reveal artistic understanding. A point made by Chekhov to an actor playing the part of Astrov, in *Uncle Vanya,* effectively illustrates the point (Stanislavsky, 1961):

> During the intervals Anton Pavlovich dropped in on me and spoke with admiration, but afterwards he made one observation concerning Astrov's departure.
>
> 'But he whistles, listen . . . Whistles! Uncle Vanya is weeping, but Astrov whistles!' After that I could not make him explain any further.
>
> How is that, I asked myself, sadness, despair and — jolly whistling?
>
> But Chekhov's remark came to life of itself at one of the later performances. I just began to whistle, taking him at his word, to see what would happen. And straightaway I felt it was true! Just right! Uncle Vanya is dejected and full of gloom, but Astrov whistles. Why?
>
> Well because he has lost faith in people and life to such an extent that his disbelief in them has reached the point of cynicism. People can no longer cause him pain in any way. (p. 259)

There are those who are dubious about the notion of non-verbal reasons. This is a further manifestation of deep, pervasive and long-held preconceptions about the character of reasoning, which have the consequence of imposing constricting possibilities on human experience, and especially on education, not only in the arts but in a wide variety of ways. Sometimes, for instance, non-verbal reasoning can achieve more than could be achieved by verbal reasoning. To take a clear example, consider Samuel Beckett's play *Act Without Words,* in which, as the title implies, the only character never speaks. A certain view of life is expressed in the play, and it might be said that it would be possible for the character to express, even if in a severely etiolated sense, the same judgment verbally, and support it with verbal reasons. Yet in its present form the play expresses that view of life, and offers reasons for accepting its validity, in a richer sense without words — so much so, indeed, that there would be considerable point in insisting that *this* sense could never be adequately conveyed in words. Similarly, some of Goya's and many of Francis Bacon's paintings express a conception and evaluation of life, and offer support for it. One could cite similar examples from all the arts.

The important point is that a principal characteristic of a reason, in any sphere, whether verbal or not, is to give *understanding,* or a change of understanding. Of course this is not to say that *everything* which produces understanding could count as a reason. As we have seen, there are limits to the intelligibility of the notion of a reason, and it must connect with, or appeal to, what already comes within the understanding of the person to whom the reason is given. The notion of a reason, too, involves validity or invalidity — the possibility of being right or wrong. Nevertheless, if there are those who remain uneasy about the notion of non-verbal reasons it is not important for my argument. I have given reasons for supporting it, but what is most important, as my examples above reveal, is that there are various non-verbal ways of achieving, giving and revealing understanding.

Reason and Propositions

Metaphor, analogy, allusion and many other ways of presenting or drawing attention to a certain perspective or judgment on a work of art are also examples of reasons, or giving understanding, in this sense. This indicates why I reject the widely accepted assumption that reason is tied to the notion of knowledge as necessarily propositional. This way of construing the character of knowledge and reasoning is, for example, associated with the philosopher of education, Hirst, (1974; see esp. chs 3 and 6). I shall not here consider this approach in detail, since I am more concerned to propose a thesis than to criticize others. I give a more complete account elsewhere (Best, 1991) of why I reject the notion of knowledge as necessarily propositional, and of the harmful implications of that widely held assumption for education *in general*, i.e. not only for the arts. I raise the issue now in case it is not already clear that in arguing for the importance of reason in the arts, I am certainly not supporting, indeed I am repudiating, a propositional approach. For example, the poets of the First World War, such as Owen, Sassoon and Rosenberg, both expressed a conception and evaluation of war, and supported it with reasons which consisted in offering a vivid vision of what war amounts to. In support of one's view of war one could now cite their poetry. This is clearly not propositional, but a judgment of the truth of war is expressed and rationally justified. Moreover, it should be emphasized again how important is the possibility of reasoning one's *own* way to a judgment, conception or evaluation.

According to Hirst (1974), the domain of knowledge is centrally 'the domain of true propositions or statements' (p. 85). This contention may be initially plausible for the sciences, although, as I have already indicated, further consideration reveals its inadequacy even here. But it is not even initially plausible for the arts. Ray Elliott once said that the arts are forms of love, not of knowledge. While one sympathizes with the spirit of this remark, it is misleading to say that we cannot legitimately talk of knowledge with respect to the arts, and worse to imply that knowledge precludes love. It is, unfortunately, all too often true that the methods of teaching in what are popularly regarded as the central forms of knowledge (e.g. in the so-called 'core subjects' of the curriculum) *do* preclude love — but that is an indictment of the education system. Mathematics and the sciences, as well as the arts, should be forms of knowledge *and* of love. To regard the two terms as exclusive is as mistaken here as it is with respect to love of other people. So far from its being the case that love is inimical to knowledge, it is difficult to see how one could love another person without knowing him or her quite well.

The danger is that to continue to equate knowledge and rationality with the ability to produce true propositions will help to perpetuate the damaging misconception that where the arts are concerned we cannot legitimately speak of knowledge and rationality. For recognizing (a) that what one says in appreciation of a work of art may not be *propositional*, and (b) that appreciation of a work may not be revealed exclusively in what one *says*, those involved in the arts often feel impelled *ipso facto* to accept that the arts cannot be cognitive and rational. Thus, in offering a proposed rationale for the arts, at least one philosopher of education has argued that they are 'pre-cognitive', and 'pre-epistemological'; that the notion of truth-conditions cannot be applied here because a work of art cannot be said to be true or false. There are those of us who would argue that the notion of 'truth-conditions' *in general* is highly questionable, but I cannot digress to discuss that issue (see Best, 1991). More relevantly, this is a clear illustration of the narrow conception of truth, knowledge and rationality which is still so common. For of course some works of art can and do express profound truths, and some are false. It has been said, for instance, that Barbara Cartland's novels positively *impede* a knowledge of the human condition. If this notion of truth cannot be fitted into the rigid categories of 'truth-conditions', so much the worse for those categories.

In a similar vein, Witkin (1980) writes: 'The arts stand in relation to the intelligence of feeling much as the sciences do in relation to logical reasoning' (p. 89). This is a classic example of the oversimple subjectivist assumption that feeling and reason are quite independent of each other, and even inimical, and thus that they are legitimately developed in separate aspects of the curriculum. But the preconception that rationality and cognition have no place in artistic experience involves throwing out the baby with the bath water. Knowledge, understanding and reason are *central to*, and *inseparable from*, artistic experience, and are necessary for the educational credentials of the arts. But that certainly does not entail the ability to produce true propositions. Indeed, as we have seen, this conception is inadequate even for the rationality involved in scientific and other forms of knowledge often regarded as unquestionably propositional. In short, a principal source of the misconception that the arts are a matter of feeling, not of reason and knowledge, is the unquestioning acceptance of a rigidly narrow conception of reason and knowledge.

The Limits of Reason

It is widely assumed that the question 'Why?', asking for a reason, is always appropriate, and that to decline or to be unable to offer a reason, reveals a lack of rationality. Yet there are situations in which to be able to provide reasons might be regarded as inappropriate and even repugnant. To refer again to the example used in Chapter 2, Swift, in *A Modest Proposal*, suggests that the two problems of overpopulation and shortage of food could easily be solved by the simple expedient of eating young children. One's natural reaction to this, as Swift anticipated, is repugnance. It is not just that one does not feel the need, or may be unable, to argue rationally against it, but rather that even to engage in reasoning about such a question is *already* an indication of a moral position which one cannot seriously entertain. That is, sometimes the fact that a position is not open to rational questioning is a mark of how fundamental it is to a moral position or to a culture. Any alternative is, in the literal, rather than the currently debased, sense of the term, unthinkable.

More important for my thesis, to argue for the central place of reason in the arts is not to argue that the request for a reason is always appropriate. The notion of explaining and justifying our artistic judgments is familiar enough and, as I have indicated, it takes a variety of forms. One might, for example, refer to striking progressions, or rhythmic variety, or subtlety of harmony, or sensitivity of playing, in music; one might refer to the structure of a novel, or the perceptiveness of character-portrayal; one might refer to the composition or use of colour in a painting. But what if, after being given such reasons in considerable detail, someone were to say that he could not see why that made it such a good work of art? One would have no idea what to say, and one would have to conclude that he just did not understand this art form. One's reasons cannot be understood unless one can find something which he recognizes as a reason, or unless one can find something incompatible in his position. Even then one is not necessarily helpless — although in fact there may be little point in continuing. One may need to reach to the foundations, by trying to bring him to respond to and understand the art form or approach to art *as a whole*.

Again, the difficulty is, in principle, no different from other areas. If someone simply cannot see why deductive reasoning leads to a certain conclusion in logic, or why an addition in arithmetic gives a certain answer, or why a certain conclusion is drawn from a scientific experiment, and if his request for a reason is not of the kind which could be answered by offering him further explanation from *within* the activity, then one must either give up, or attempt to *introduce* him to the activity. For no reason will count as a reason for him until he grasps and responds appropriately to it; there is no sense to the notion of an external justification.

Conclusion

A major source of the prevalent and educationally disastrous subjectivist assumptions about artistic appreciation is a fundamental misconception about the nature of objectivity, knowledge and reasoning. This is the distorted coin of which scientism and subjectivism are the opposite sides. The argument from disagreement is fallacious, and the source of the fallacy is a failure to understand the character of both the sciences and the arts. The possibility of differences of opinion, interpretation and evaluation lends no support to subjectivism, whether in the arts or the sciences. Artistic appreciation, like understanding in any sphere, allows for the indefinite but not unlimited possibility of interpretation, and of an extension of understanding which gives sense to interpretation and judgment. In short, knowledge and objectivity of any kind rests on underlying conceptual grasp and human judgment. That assessment in the arts is necessarily a matter of judgment concedes nothing to subjectivism, since such judgment derives its sense from the publicly shared arts, language, attitudes and activities of a culture. The assessment may itself always be open to possible revision, of course, but that is not to say that judgments can never be completely sound. What often underlies the feeling that judgments can never be quite reliable is a craving for an ideal which makes no sense — an ideal of knowledge and objectivity as something absolutely fixed and certain, beyond the possibility of change and revision. That 'ideal' makes no sense because it would make 'knowledge' and 'objectivity' unattainable, and unintelligible.

Notes

1   I am grateful to Ingeborg Glambek for the interesting suggestion, which would repay further reflection, that subjectivism seems to have arisen with modern art. It would, she said, never even have occurred to artists and appreciators of the arts of the preceding era that the creation and appreciation of art was a matter of purely subjective 'inner' individual feeling. It would have been unquestionable that the appreciation of the work of Leonardo da Vinci, Michelangelo, Constable, Turner (perhaps more questionably his later work) etc. would have been be in terms of

objective features of the works of art themselves. But with, for example, abstract expressionism, cubism, even much impressionism, perhaps, the tendency may have arisen to locate artistic appreciation in 'inner', subjective feelings. This, of course, paves the way for the vapid pretentiousness of some purported modern 'art', which is not, it is said, answerable to the work, but to 'inner', subjective feelings.

Let me emphasise that I am not in the least castigating all modern art. Very far from it. Neither am I saying that subjectivism is acceptable for modern art. On the contrary, subjectivism makes no sense, no matter to which kind of art it is applied. The point, presumably, is that it is an easy evasion, if people do not understand some supposed piece of art, simply to say, or more usually imply, that they lack the mysterious 'inner' subjective experience of which only the élite circle of modern-art subjectivist *cognoscenti* are capable.

2   I am grateful to David Sheasby, the producer, for kindly sending me the script of the play, and to the author for allowing me to quote from it.

Chapter 4

Questions

Succeeding chapters will consider in more detail issues which arise from Chapters 1 to 3. However, it is worth discussing immediately some of the questions which are most likely to arise, and which can be answered, at least in outline, relatively briefly.

Value

I have emphasized that artistic appreciation is a fully rational activity, in that the judgments involved are fully objective, i.e. supportable by reasons. The objection is sometimes raised that even though judgments of meaning and interpretation may be open to rational discussion, these are irrelevant to the central issue, since the *real* problem of artistic appreciation is that of value judgments.

First, it is clearly implausible to contend that interpretation is irrelevant to evaluation since it is obviously impossible to evaluate a work unless one understands it. For instance, one's evaluation may change, and even change radically, if one comes to recognize that it has ironic or other subtleties which one had previously failed to appreciate. Moreover, some evaluative judgments are obviously incompatible with certain interpretations.

More important, as I intimated in Chapter 3, evaluative judgments cannot be differentiated in this respect: they are as fully objective, as fully open to rational justification, as any other judgment. The assumption that value judgments are necessarily subjective, is one of the most prevalent and pernicious aspects of the traditional subjectivist doctrine. It is surprising how often one encounters the unquestioning conviction that value judgments must be merely subjective. If it were so *no* education at all, in *any* subject, would make sense. For, to put it crudely, to learn *any* discipline, including, for example, sciences and mathematics, *is* to learn to discriminate what counts as *good or bad* within it.

This aspect of the subjectivist doctrine is very commonly related to the Myth of two realms or domains which we discussed in Chapter 1. It will be remembered that there is supposed to be, on one hand, an 'objective', cognitive/rational realm, and on the other hand, a subjective/feeling/individual/creative/personal realm. Value judgments are supposed to be in this latter category of the hopelessly subjective. As I have already clearly shown, the whole bizarre Myth, *very* common though it remains, is based on deep and damaging philosophical confusions. One of the principal confusions is a grossly oversimple conception of objectivity, which caricatures the nature of the sciences. The sciences are emphatically *not* concerned with accumulating knowledge of absolute, universal, imagination-free, value-aseptic facts. The arts are emphatically *not* concerned with non-rational, non-cognitive, occult, subjective feelings. The sciences involve imagination and value-judgments as do the arts. The arts are as objective and rational as the sciences.

It should be noticed that the non-rational responses or attitudes which underlie reasoning *involve* evaluations. Responses of wonder, delight, excitement and disappointment, for instance, clearly *are* evaluations of their objects, and these responses and evaluations may change on reflection, or as a result of recognizing the cogency of reasons for a different point of view. Thus arts education, for instance, is inevitably concerned with the education of value judgments; with what counts as good within the particular art form. To repeat, it really is surprising that one so often encounters scepticism about the objectivity or rationality of a cultural practice or activity on the grounds that values are involved in it. For to be inducted into *any* subject, discipline, or area of knowledge is to learn to grasp its criteria of value. One has, for instance, to learn what counts as good, better, or worse reasoning or evidence, and clearly to judge evidence as good and reasoning as weak *is* to evaluate. Thus one could not be said to have even the slightest understanding of a subject unless one had to some extent learned to evaluate by its criteria. Moreover, as Holland (1980) puts it:

> Those for example who profess enthusiasm for everything in music from Bach to boogie must actually be indifferent to music or interested in it solely as a diversion, otherwise it would matter to them what kind of music they heard . . . How much a person cares about a pursuit, whether it means much or little to him is attested by the liveliness of his appreciation of the distinction between the superior and the inferior in that *genre*, between the genuine and the faked, the impeccable and the slipshod. (p. 24)

Discussing the long history of philosophers, especially of the empiricist tradition, who have persistently misconstrued value judgments as mere subjective feelings or intuitions, in sharp contrast to those areas of knowledge which supposedly deal in value-aseptic logic and facts, Bambrough (1979) writes:

> Value, far from being contrasted with fact and logic as swamp with firm ground, or little sister with big twin brothers, is more fundamental than either . . . Neither logic nor history nor physics nor philosophy nor any other sphere in which this is *preferred* to that, where one view may and must be compared in *soundness* with another, where reasons may be adjudged good or bad, strong or weak, can be a point of vantage from which a philosopher may look down on the concept of value, unless we talk of looking down to mark the necessary but rare recognition that here if anywhere is the bedrock in search of which so many philosophers have scanned the sky. (p. 106)

It is of the utmost importance, not only for the arts, but for morality and education generally, to root out ruthlessly the remarkably prevalent, and harmful assumption that evaluation is purely subjective. For instance, as mentioned earlier people sometimes say: 'Oh, that's just a value judgment', as if that is the end of the matter, and nothing more can be said, since, it is assumed, value judgments are the expression of mere subjective preferences to which the notion of objective reasoning is wholly inappropriate. In fact, so far from being the *end* of the matter, the expression of a value judgment is only the *beginning*, since, of course, one can and characteristically does offer reasons in support of one's value-judgments, and not only in the arts. One may be mistaken, there may be disagreements, but such possibilities *presuppose rationality*.

This assumption is part of the prevalent notion that artistic appreciation is, or is primarily, an expression of personal likes and dislikes. One is reminded of the deeply confused 'Boo-Hurrah' theory of ethics, that is, the notion that moral judgments amount merely to non-rational subjective boos or hurrahs of approval or disapproval. Yet although even cursory reflection reveals how obviously false it is, such a subjectivist assumption, about ethical, artistic and even religious questions is still quite common.

Despite the prevalence of this assumption, it is difficult to give any sense to the notion that evaluative judgments are, or can be reduced to, mere personal preferences, or subjective likes and dislikes. Much of the argument of this book is devoted to exposing that fallacy and related ones, but there are immediately obvious objections which can be raised against it. For example, a consequence would be that it would be impossible to distinguish between, on one hand, evaluative judgments, and on the other hand, likes and dislikes, whereas this is a distinction which obviously can be made. Taking on such a view, the sentence 'He is a superb operatic tenor, but I dislike operatic tenors' would be self-contradictory, or it would have to be denied that 'superb' is an evaluative term, which is nonsense. Similarly, we can and often do distinguish between liking, and artistically evaluating, films and television programmes. Someone might like *Dallas*, while recognizing that it has no artistic value whatsoever. Conversely, someone may recognize that Shakespeare's plays are great art, while not particularly liking them.

A largely contributory factor to this misconception is the assumption that where reasoning is appropriate it is always possible to reach definitive conclusions. Yet, as we saw in Chapter 3, that assumption is equally mistaken in other disciplines, such as the sciences. That reasons can be adduced in support of evaluative judgments does not imply that where there are disagreements it is necessarily the case that they can be resolved by rational argument.

It should be emphasized again that there could be no place at all in education for the arts if artistic judgments, by teachers and students, amounted merely to expressions of subjective, non-rational personal preferences. This point should not be misunderstood. It clearly is an important aim of arts education to encourage a genuine love of the arts, a desire to engage in them, and a recognition of how much is to be gained from involvement with them. It is an aim of education to encourage students' likes and dislikes to coincide as far as possible with their evaluative judgments.

Beauty

There is a common assumption, which has a long history in traditional philosophy, that artistic appreciation is centrally or even exclusively concerned with questions of beauty. Thus it is sometimes objected that although reasons are important for interpretation, it is not clear how they can apply to such explicitly evaluative judgments as 'This is a beautiful painting'.

The common misconception about value judgments has been considered above. There are two further issues here. First, it is equally strange to claim that reasons cannot be given for one's judgment that something is beautiful. Even in the case of natural phenomena such as sunsets and landscapes, one could give reasons to support one's judgment. That someone may not accept them, or may fail to recognize their point, tells as little against the possibility of rational support here as it does, for instance, in the sciences. As we saw in Chapter 3, reasons may be given which may allow someone to see a situation or an object under a different aspect, so that he sees beauty where he did not see it previously.

Secondly, a major source of this assumption is the common, but seriously confused conflation of the aesthetic and the artistic which will be considered in Chapter 12. Moreover, although it is true that judgments of beauty have traditionally been assumed to be central to artistic appreciation, and thus have been central to philosophical debate, even on cursory reflections this assumption can be seen to be obviously mistaken, and it is surprising that it continues to be so prevalent. Terms such as 'beauty' appear very little in informed discussion of the arts, for instance, by knowledgeable critics. If someone were to express his opinion of music, concerts, plays, paintings, dance performances, and literary works such as poems and, for instance, the novels of Dostoievsky and George Eliot in terms of 'They are (or are not) beautiful', or some similar comment, and if these were the only kinds of comment he were to make, that would be a good ground for *denying*, or at least entertaining grave scepticism about, his *capacity* for artistic appreciation. That is, if that were all he could say, or even if that were the predominant tenor of his conversation, it would clearly reveal that he had little or no understanding of the arts.

It is very doubtful whether there are any terms which are typical or characteristic of artistic appreciation, and I shall offer a reason for this in Chapter 12. However, terms such as 'sensitive', 'imaginative', 'carefully observed', 'lively' and 'perceptive insights' are used far more often than 'beauty' and its cognates.

Art and Science

To repeat, since the issue is important and has been misunderstood, I am certainly not arguing that scientific methods are parallel to, or can be used in, the support given to artistic judgments. My argument is that judgments in both sciences and the arts are open to rational justification. The difficulty of grasping the point may stem from the common assumption that the scientific is the paradigm, the standard, by which other claims to rationality are assessed. Yet what this amounts to is a confusion of standards. As an illustration, consider the contention, from the recent history of philosophy, that not even scientific propositions for which there is the soundest possible empirical evidence can be regarded as certain, since they do not have the infallibility of the deductive knowledge of, say, mathematics. Thus, for instance, according to this view, although the sun may have risen every morning of recorded history, this cannot justify my claim to know that it will rise tomorrow, since it is *logically* possible that it will not. But questions of logical possibility are irrelevant. My claim is justified by the fact that there is sound *empirical* evidence for it — that is what justification amounts to in this context. It would be a similar confusion to deny that I can know that a window will break if I hit it hard with a hammer, on the grounds that there is no logical contradiction involved in asserting that it will not break. I know for certain that it will break because windows always do break in such circumstances, and logical possibilities are irrelevant.

It is a confusion of standards to regard the deductive as *the* paradigm to which any scientific claim must attain if it is to be regarded as genuine knowledge. It is equally a confusion of standards to regard the scientific as the paradigm to which moral, religious and artistic judgments must attain if they are to be genuinely objective and rational.

To say that scientific judgments cannot be certain because they do not have the deductive certainty of mathematics and the syllogism is merely to say that induction is not deduction, or that science is not mathematics. Similarly to say that artistic judgments are not rationally supportable because they are not scientifically supportable is merely to say that the arts are not science. That is an obvious, uninformative truism. What is important is to recognize that there are kinds of rational justification *other* than the scientific.

Nevertheless, since I do argue that judgments in both spheres are rationally justifiable, it is incumbent upon me to show the relevant similarities between them. Doubts are sometimes expressed about whether there is such a parallel. For example, if we compare the possibility of proof in the two areas, it may seem that there is a significant difference. Consider the following:

(a) Philip believes that Rembrandt's portraits have no artistic merit.
(b) Philip believes that water freezes at 100°C.

There may seem to be a contrast between the two cases in that whereas in (b) a proof of the mistaken belief can be achieved by a simple empirical test or observation, there is no parallel in the case of (a). Yet (b) is not the straightforward case of an empirically verifiable proposition which it initially appears to be, for it would make no sense to say that Philip *understands* the Centigrade system and still needs empirical evidence to convince him that water does not freeze at 100°C. The very *sense* of the Centigrade scale is given by 0° freezing and 100° boiling. Philip's mistake is *conceptual*, not empirical — rather as it would be if he wanted to measure a foot to confirm that it was twelve inches long. He does not understand the Centigrade system.

Similarly, it would make no sense to say that Philip understands Western art and yet can seriously assert that Rembrandt's portraits have no artistic merit. Whether or not he dislikes them, if he is unable to recognize in them *any* artistic merit, even of technique, for instance, that would reveal unquestionably, analogously, that he simply has no understanding of what *constitutes* good painting in that tradition. The cases are parallel, in that in both Philip's failure is one of conceptual grasp, and the proof in each case will consist in helping him to grasp the concept.

It has also been objected that whereas no one could deny that $2 + 2 = 4$, this contrasts with the differences of opinion which so often arise about the meaning and value of a work of art. This marks a significant distinction between the two cases, the objection continues, with respect to the possibility of giving reasons in justification. But the example fails to provide a parity of cases, since a simple case from one area is being compared with a complex case from the other. A legitimate comparison with '2 + 2 = 4' might be '*King Lear* is a tragedy'. It would make no sense to say that someone could understand the play, and the concepts of tragedy and comedy, and still believe that *King Lear* might be a comedy, any more than it would be intelligible to say that he could understand numbers and believe that 2 + 2 = 5. Parity of cases reveals parity of answerability to rational justification.

The cases cited above are those in which disagreement immediately reveals a failure of understanding. Most cases in science and art are not like this. In science the more usual cases are those in which someone understands the relevant concepts and can be offered empirical proof. Similarly, in the arts, someone with the relevant background of understanding could, for example, be shown, where he had previously failed to recognize it, that certain passages in Chaucer or Jane Austen are ironic; or he could be given reasons for recognizing the underlying melancholy in a Shakespearian comedy such as *Twelfth Night*.

Another serious misconception, with important consequences for learning from the arts, is expressed in the objection that a significant difference between them is that the sciences are concerned with the truth, whereas the arts are much more a matter of imagination. It may already be clear from what has been said about interpretation that the objection implies a naïve and ultimately incoherent, or at least irrelevant, notion of truth (see Best, 1991), since scientific truth is given by theoretical interpretation, an understanding of which requires imagination. Scientific discovery, the search for truth, as we have seen, is not simply a matter of accurate sensory perception but also necessarily requires imagination. It is a fallacy to assume that truth and imagination are distinct and perhaps incompatible notions since it frequently *requires* imagination, in any sphere, to reach the truth. Truth, one might say, is an imaginative concept.

There are two principal points to be made with respect to the arts. (a) Even if the value of the arts were to lie not in the truths they express but rather in presenting imaginary situations, there are objective criteria for the effectiveness with which they succeed in achieving this, and these criteria can be adduced as reasons in support of judgments. (b) More important, it is often a mark of the greatness of a work of art precisely that it *does* reveal profound truths about the human condition. To take a clear case, an allegorical work such as St-Exupéry's *Le Petit Prince* reveals truths about humanity through wholly imaginary situations.

Reading Meanings In

Another persistent misconception is that, unlike the sciences, any values and meanings attributed to the arts are merely read in. This is simply another version of the misconception inherent in the notion that beauty is in the eye of the beholder, that is, that the characteristics cited as reasons for artistic judgments are mere subjective projections of the spectator. Again, a consequence of such an assumption would be that the notions of valid interpretation, and thus of artistic meaning, would make no sense. Yet, on the contrary, it is precisely the mark of a valid interpretation that it is *not* read in, but is *objectively* supported by *features of the work*. To the extent that it is read in it is invalid. To be valid, a judgment has, for instance, to be supported by the text, by the painting, by the performance. Thus there is an exact parallel with the sciences where a valid conclusion has to be supported by the evidence.

Of course, such reading in occurs, in both disciplines, perhaps as a consequence of trying to launder recalcitrant evidence to fit a theory in the sciences, or of approaching a work of art with certain predispositions. Yet this is equally distorting in, and contrary to the character of, both disciplines, and in both it is important to learn to avoid any such tendency. Education in artistic appreciation largely consists in learning to recognize and eradicate readings in, and in developing the ability to discern increasingly perceptive, objective interpretations and evaluations of the works of art themselves.

The same misapprehension often arises over the notion of feeling in the arts. For example, Reid (1931) writes of the feelings expressed in art that they '. . . belong, analytically and abstractly regarded, to the side of the subject and not the object'. (p. 79) It may immediately strike some as undeniable that, at least with respect to feelings, subjectivity has to be conceded, since a painting, for instance, cannot feel sad. I shall consider this issue in later chapters, but such a reaction ignores a central problem of philosophy of the arts which is parallel to some of the issues discussed above. There is an important distinction here which tends to be overlooked. The feelings expressed in Picasso's *Guernica*, in the poetry of Gerard Manley Hopkins, in Beethoven's Ninth Symphony, and numerous other works, are *qualities of the works themselves*. These qualities may not coincide with how one may happen to feel in response to them. One may recognize that a work expresses sadness while having a quite different response to it. It is important to distinguish between what one may just happen to feel in response to a work of art, and the feelings which are expressed in it. While it is, of course, true that only animate beings can *have* feelings, it is equally true that a work of art can *be* sad, or can express sadness, and the quality of sadness is as much a quality of the work as it is a quality of a person when he is sad.

A further very important factor here is the frequent conflation of two senses in which feelings can be said to be subjective. As a consequence, a point about feelings which is trivially true is conflated with a point about feelings which is radically mistaken, and thus the *latter* is assumed to be obviously true. (a) In the first sense, to say that a feeling is subjective is to say that it is felt by someone, and it is, of course, trivially true that only people (and animals) can have feelings. (b) In the second sense, to say that something is subjective is to deny that there can be any limits, and thus to say that feelings are subjective is to deny that there can be any sense in the notion of *appropriateness* of feelings. While (a) is obviously true, (b) is radically mistaken, for there are as obviously appropriate feelings in response to a work of art as there are to situations in life. For example, in normal circumstances, we should be at a loss what to make of someone who, when offered an ordinary toasted crumpet, responded with extreme fear. Such a response would be so inappropriate as to raise questions about his mental state. However, the important point I want to bring out is the danger of sliding between, or conflating, (a) and (b), so that a platitude is confused with a serious falsehood. This conflation of two senses of 'subjective' partly explains how one of the most fundamentally damaging misconceptions about artistic judgments, can appear to be obviously true. The serious misconception is to assume that because artistic judgments may be partly expressions of feeling, there is no place for appropriateness and answerability to reason. To repeat, the danger is a failure to recognise the distinction between (a) 'subjective', in the sense of 'felt by someone', and (b) 'subjective' in the sense of 'unlimited' (which is a denial of any sense in the notion of appropriateness of a feeling to its object). If the distinction is not recognised then a very damaging falsehood (that artistic feelings are not answerable to reason), is conflated with a trivially obvious truism (that artistic feelings are felt by someone).

Artistic judgments are often at least partly an expression of one's feeling about a work, but they are nevertheless fully *objective*, in that one can give reasons for the feeling by reference to features of the work.

Judgment

An exactly similar confusion can arise from taking human judgments to be necessarily subjective. A prominent figure in educational drama, when addressing a conference, stated that all judgments by drama teachers were subjective. After his address he was pressed by a member of the audience to clarify whether he really *meant* that all drama teachers' judgments were subjective. He expressed considerable surprise and replied: 'Of course they are subjective, what other kind of judgments could there be?' To which the obvious reply is: 'Objective judgments.'

Of course, like the parallel case of 'feeling' discussed above, he may have been using 'subjective' to be *entailed* by 'judgment'. That is, he may have assumed without question that since a judgment is made by an individual human being, on the basis of his own background of knowledge and experience, then it *must* be subjective. But that obscures an important distinction between those judgments which are unduly influenced, for instance, by prejudice or predisposition, and those which are based on the evidence, or on qualities of the object or situation. An example will illustrate the confusion which can arise. I once heard a young teacher, in support of his contention that all human judgment is subjective, cite the assessment of trainees on teaching practice in school, which, he said, is always 'disgracefully subjective'. The use of the pejorative, of course, reveals the confusion since it clearly implies that such judgments should, and therefore could, be *objective*.

That we do not always know which kind of judgment we are making lends no support to subjectivism. One might, for instance, make what one fully believed to be an objective appraisal of music, drama, or dance, only to realize later that one had been unduly influenced by a mood, prejudice, or other misleading predisposition. Such a possibility does not in the least, as we have seen before, invalidate the distinction. Indeed, we need to be keenly and increasingly aware of it if we wish to extend our capacity for artistic appreciation. The reasons given in support of judgments should be based on the *qualities of the work*, not our subjective prejudices.

Sometimes what underlies the tendency to insist that all judgments must be subjective is the notion that judgments are made by human beings, and thus they depend upon our constitution and cannot be guaranteed 'objective', in the sense of 'infallible'. Enough has been said about this notion in Chapter 3. It merely reveals a very common craving for an unintelligible ideal of objectivity and knowledge as totally *beyond* human conception. The absurdity of such a conception becomes very clear when we recognise that an inevitable consequence of it would be that scientific and mathematical judgments would be equally subjective.

There are, of course, important differences between mathematical or scientific judgments, and artistic judgments. One important difference is that personal involvement is implied in the arts, whereas in the sciences it is more normal to accept conclusions reached by others. In relation to cars and electrical appliances, for instance, we just use conclusions without knowing how they were reached. In the arts, by contrast, it is doubtful whether one can be said even to *understand* a judgment which one has not reasoned through for oneself. Also by contrast, an artistic judgment commits one much more personally, in that the making of it implies one's own first-hand experience of the work. If I were to say 'George Eliot's *Middlemarch* is a fine novel, but I have never read it', there is an oddity about my remark which is not present if I were to say 'A Rolls Royce is a fine motor car, but I have never driven one'. One could, with propriety, say 'I am told that it is a fine novel', but that is not the same thing, and concedes my point. This characteristic, that artistic judgments cannot be made at second-hand, misleads some into assuming that they are subjective in the sense that *all* that is expressed in them is a personal commitment or attitude. It is true that an artistic judgment may partly or largely express the feeling or attitude of the speaker. But the subjectivist exaggerates this to the point of *equating* an artistic judgment with an attitude or feeling, which is usually construed as a mere subjective personal preference. But this is to ignore the equally important content of that judgment, namely, the question of its truth or falsity, or whether it can be objectively, rationally supported. That is, while an artistic judgment expresses a personal attitude to a personal experience, *there are objective reasons for it*. The subjectivist does not so much put the cart before the horse as ignore the horse altogether. For he ignores *that on which the personal attitude or commitment is based*.

That artistic judgments may be partly or largely expressions of feeling, involving personal commitment, does not, then, imply that artistic appreciation is a matter of mere subjective personal preference, prejudice, or predilection. The judgment expressing the feeling and commitment is answerable to reason, in the sense that one could give reasons for it, and it could in principle be changed by more cogent reasons or reflection. In spheres such as morality and the arts, where feeling and personal involvement are so central, it is if anything even more important than in other spheres, though possibly more difficult, to make judgments which are supportable by objective reasons. Moreover, it is of the first importance that education in the arts and morality should extend students' capacity for making and recognizing the validity of such judgments. Only in that way can one escape the restrictions of predispositions, and enlarge one's horizons. In my view, the most important contribution of education, in all areas of the curriculum, is progressively to offer our children and students an opening of conceptual horizons, by which I mean continuously *expanding* possibilities of feeling and understanding. This involves progressive escape from the confines of the socially determined ways of thinking and feeling — too often television-induced clichés — which so frequently constitute their tragically restricted possibilities of *being*.

Associations

A related, and equally common, misconception is that the only way to explain the personal response characteristic of involvement with the arts is by reference to personal association. It is true that in particular cases associations may be partly relevant to one's understanding of a work of art. For example, the meaning of a particular painting may depend to some extent on associations with the mushroom-shaped cloud characteristic of a nuclear explosion. But clearly not *any* association can be constitutive of artistic appreciation. That I may have feelings of sadness when I hear a joyful Mozart rondo, because of its associations with my dead mother, is completely irrelevant to its meaning. In such a case it could not intelligibly be said that my response was one of artistic appreciation, since it would not be logically related to objective features of the music. Indeed, if the supposition is that meaning, whether linguistic or artistic, is entirely constituted by purely individual associations, as is often believed, then that supposition is transparently subjectivist and senseless. For in that case there could be no meaning at all. If the supposed 'meaning' of every word and work of art were totally constituted by each person's individual associations, that would amount to saying that the word or work had no meaning *in itself.*

The very notion of associations *presupposes* that artistic and linguistic meaning is *objective*. That is, there has to be an objective *meaning* of a word or work of art about which one may have associations. The word 'dentist' may have painful associations for one, but 'dentist' does not mean 'painful'. And it is *only* because 'dentist' has objective meaning that it makes sense to say that one can attribute associations to it.

In the great majority of cases, personal associations are neither necessary nor sufficient for artistic understanding and personal response. In particular cases one may need a prior understanding of and associations with the relevant life-situations, as in cartoons generally, and, for instance, a lampoon of Mrs Thatcher, but such cases are very much in the minority. One does not need previously to have experienced, and to have associations with, anything similar to the situations depicted in most works of art in order to understand them, and to be fully engaged in them emotionally. I have just been reading again Jane Austen's *Persuasion*, and I was completely absorbed in it. I have no experiences or personal associations of relevantly similar kinds, but this certainly did not prevent my artistic appreciation of the novel, in a fully involved way. In the novel, Captain Wentworth learns that it was his pride which prevented him and Anne Elliott from recognising their love for each other, and thus being together, eight years earlier. Through a personal involvement with the novel, one may learn similar lessons, in advance of any possible experience of situations which may give appropriate personal associations.

There is a huge range of emotion-concepts, and therefore possibilities of experiencing emotional feelings, which are actually *acquired* through the arts. Most obviously, children learn to understand and respond to people and numerous life-situations through literature, stories and play-acting well before they have met the relevant situations in life. And it is equally true of adults that we learn to respond to situations in art when we have never experienced anything similar in life. Indeed, to insist that it is necessary, in general, to have personal associations in order to appreciate and respond fully to the arts is actually to *belittle* the power, and especially the educational power, of the arts. Part of the reason why there is so much to be learned from the arts is precisely that associations are *not necessary* for personal involvement and appreciation.

Moreover, personal associations are certainly not sufficient for artistic appreciation. Even where associations are in an obvious sense highly relevant, they may detract from or even prevent artistic appreciation and response. For example, a friend suffered so much from a possessive and unjustly jealous husband that she now finds it impossible to appreciate and respond adequately to performances of Shakespeare's *Othello*. Ironically, and understandably, the more powerful and convincing the performance, the less can she appreciate it. There are many such examples — for instance, the difficulty of appreciating painters of the Renaissance because of religious associations; the difficulty of appreciating Athol Fugard's plays, and J M Coetzee's novels, because of strong personal associations with the sufferings of black people under apartheid; the difficulty expressed by some people of appreciating Wagner because of associations with the Nazis. Even in less extreme cases, a personal association, even when very similar to a situation depicted in art, may actually *detract* from the close attention to and involvement with the objective features of the work of art which is central to *artistic* understanding and response. For the association may divert one's attention from an objective involvement with the work of art itself. Associations are then, in general, neither necessary nor sufficient for the personal involvement characteristic of artistic appreciation.

It is true, and important, that a general experience of life is necessary for adequate appreciation of very many works of art, which is why a very young child is incapable of appreciating Shakespeare or George Eliot. Furthermore, there may be no *sharp* division between relevant associations and what we could call a general experience of life. Nevertheless, in general, personal associations are neither necessary nor sufficient for personal responses to art.

It is central to the argument of this book that artistic appreciation, and the learning involved in artistic experience, is essentially personal, but that is not to say that it depends upon personal associations. The assumption that personal involvement necessarily entails individual associations is another guise of subjectivism. In this case, it amounts to the assumption that personal emotional response is a subjective experience, *separate from* the objectivity of artistic *understanding*. It is this division of the two realms, expressed, for instance, in the Myth discussed in Chapter 1, which is central to subjectivism. But it *is* deeply and widely held. Most people are so completely in its grip that they cannot even question it, and thus cannot even seriously *consider* the radically different conception of artistic experience for which I am arguing.

It is a profoundly misconceived dichotomy — a dichotomy *created* by subjectivism — to regard artistic values as *either* objectively in the work of art, *or* subjectively in people. The personal involvement and response characteristic of artistic appreciation IS the appreciation of the *objective* qualities of the work of art.

Reason and Individuality

A related tendency is to assume that the individuality which is such an important characteristic of involvement with the arts commits one to subjectivism, and is thus incompatible with the answerability to reason of artistic judgments. Yet so far from there being any incompatibility between the two notions, the possibility of artistic individuality necessarily *presupposes* the culturally shared criteria of an art form which allows for the adducing of reasons. This issue will be discussed in later chapters, but it is worth mentioning now because it is so often assumed that individuality implies subjectivism.

In relation to moral judgments Bambrough (1979) makes the position very clear:

To suggest that there is a *right* answer to a moral problem is at once to be accused of or credited with a belief in moral absolutes. But it is no more necessary to believe in moral absolutes in order to believe in moral objectivity than it is to believe in the existence of absolute space or absolute time in order to believe in the objectivity of temporal and spatial relations and of judgments about them. . . The fact that a tailor needs to make a different suit for each of us, and that no non-trivial specification of what a suit has to be like in order to fit its wearer will be without exceptions, does not mean that there are no rights and wrongs about the question whether your suit or mine is a good fit. On the contrary: it is precisely because he seeks to provide for each of us a suit that will have the *right* fit that the tailor must take account of our individualities of build. In pursuit of the objectively correct solution of his practical problem he must be decisively influenced by the relativity of the fit of clothes to wearer.

Similar examples may be indefinitely multiplied. Children of different ages require different amounts and kinds of food; different patients in different conditions need different drugs and operations; the farmer does not treat all his cows or all his fields alike. Circumstances objectively alter cases. (pp. 32–3)

The same consideration applies to the arts. For example, the good teacher, at any level, will be concerned with what is right for *each* student, and with the development of each student's *individual* abilities. Yet, so far from there being any incompatibility between them, the possibility of individual expression and interpretation requires a grasp of the criteria of an art form which gives sense to the notion of reasons given within it. Again, in principle, the situation is the same in other disciplines. Scientific progress, for instance, requires individual freedom for innovation, but that is possible and makes sense only by reference to the canons of what counts as sound and unsound evidence.

Indeed, if anything, because of the greater complexity, scope, and requirement for very sensitive individual judgment, the necessity for rigorous objectivity is even greater, and poses greater difficulty, in the arts. To help each student to develop her or his *individual* potential makes great demands on the teacher's ability to be rigorously objective. For the teacher has to learn, as far as possible, and increasingly, to detach herself or himself from preferences, prejudices etc. in order to try as far as possible to do what is in the best interest of that individual student. It is all too easy for the arts teacher to relax into the self-indulgence of imposing her or his own kinds of approach to art. But it may be imposing serious limitation on one's student to do so. To repeat, although sensitive objective judgment is crucial in all aspects of education, if anything, the demands on objectivity may be even greater and more complex in the arts than in other areas.

The anxiety sometimes arises that the notion of answerability to objective reason in the arts implies artistic authoritarianism. For example, doubts of this kind are sometimes expressed in questions such as: 'If the creation and appreciation of the arts are answerable to reason, that implies that there is a correct interpretation or evaluation of, and a correct way to create, a work of art, in which case who decides what is correct?' There are two important misconceptions in the first part of the question. Enough has been said to dispel the fallacy that rationality implies a single correct interpretation or evaluation. Answerability to reason does not in the least imply definitive answers of that kind. Changes of conception have occurred even in the most soundly established scientific theories. Moreover, secondly, the notion of differences of opinion, so far from supporting subjectivism, makes no sense at all on a subjectivist basis. If you and I disagree, there is a position which one of us asserts and the other denies, and an implicit agreement between us about what objectively counts as a reason of the kind which would settle the issue, or at least offer support to one or the other. Without such a background of agreed, culturally shared grounds of rationality no *sense* could be made of the notion of disagreement. On a subjectivist basis a 'disagreement' would amount merely to personal likes and dislikes passing each other by. And *that* kind of passing-by could not count as a *disagreement* at all. Disagreements are characteristic of the sciences not *despite* but *because of* their being objective, rational disciplines. The objective criteria of the subject give sense to what counts as support for the contending positions, and therefore to the notion of disagreement.

The second part of the question, 'Who decides what is correct?', reveals a common yet really rather silly misconception, which can be exposed by asking the parallel question 'Who decides that $2 + 2 = 4$?'. In this case the incoherence of the question is obvious. We do not accept the latter because of some authoritarian edict, and no one *compels* scientists to accept a particular conclusion for which there is overwhelming evidence. To decline to accept such a conclusion, at least provisionally and in the absence of sound countervailing reasons or evidence, is a manifestation not of unbridled individuality, but of a failure to have understood the scientific discipline. Similarly, to decline to accept an interpretation of a novel or play for which the textual evidence is overwhelming, and in the absence of sound countervailing reasons, is a manifestation not of unfettered individuality but of a failure to understand the work and the relevant concept of art. The question of obeying or disobeying an authority does not remotely come into it.

In fact, on the contrary, so far from conducing to authoritarianism, a genuine commitment to objectivity or rationality *precludes* it, precisely *because* a judgment has to be answerable not to edict but to *reasons*. Moreover, to be objective, one's judgment may have to be modified or rejected in the light of sound reasons for a better interpretation or evaluation. Thus a commitment to rationality implies the *repudiation* of dogmatism, and any attempt to impose interpretation or evaluation by the exercise of authority. The danger of authoritarianism is far greater from the subjectivist, since there is no way in which he can be shown to be wrong.

It may now be apparent that, in this sense, as in many others, subjectivism is self-defeating. It arises largely as a result of a commendable and correct emphasis on, but a radical confusion about, individuality expressed in the possibility of differences of opinion. Differences of opinion are possible only if there can be an exchange of reasons for one's judgments, if there is agreement about what counts as a valid reason, and if there is agreement about the issue which is in dispute.

Artistic appreciation is certainly an individual matter, in that fully to appreciate a work of art one must have experienced and thought about it for oneself. But so far from implying subjectivism, that amounts to a *repudiation* of subjectivism. For what can thought here amount to if it is not thought *about the work*? The response is not simply a subjective experience; it does not depend solely upon the constitution or attitude of the spectator. The point becomes particularly clear, perhaps, when one considers not discussion with others, but working out one's own interpretations and evaluations of art. To focus on the formulation of one's own opinion underlines the fact that the work is *independent of the spectator*: his response is given by his understanding of the *work of art*. Although there can and should be individual responses, and the possibility of differences of interpretation, such differences and individuality are possibilities which have and arise from limits. Beyond certain limits, as we have seen in previous chapters, one's response would not be an expression of individuality, but of lack of understanding. *Not anything* can count as a response to a work of art, just as not anything can count as a reason for artistic appreciation.

Chapter 5

Differences

... nothing changed in Mr. Knott's establishment, because nothing remained, and nothing came or went, because all was a coming and a going. (Samuel Beckett, *Watt*, 1963, p. 130)

It was argued in Chapter 2 that reasoning derives from learned natural actions and responses. Since the latter are assimilated from the ways of life of a particular society, this raises the questions of (a) how, if at all, one can come to understand the arts of other cultures, or differences of concept within a culture, and (b) how conceptual change is possible. It is, perhaps, largely because conceptual change and differences (i.e. fundamental differences in what *counts* as art) are so obvious and significant a characteristic of the arts that many are impelled to subjectivism, since it is difficult to see how it is possible to justify one's judgments with reasons. If understanding is rooted in natural actions and responses assimilated from a culture this seems to imply either that there can be no place for objective reasoning, or that reasoning is relative. The notion of an objective reason may at first sight seem to imply universal validity, although I hope that enough has been said by now to demolish that oversimple caricature of an objective reason. Nevertheless, to some it may still be difficult to see how the notion of objective reasoning can be reconciled with the wide differences in concepts which are characteristic of the arts. For how can judgments made from within very different concepts be justified or supported by genuinely objective reasoning? On the other hand, if it be said that the justifying reasons are relative, this seems to be denying a central characteristic of the notion of a reason.

I shall approach the issue via relativism, since it may appear to be an inevitable consequence of my general thesis, and since it is commonly assumed that schools of thought within a culture, and especially the art forms of different cultures, are entirely discrete, in that the judgments within each can be justified only by its own internal canons of validity. The question I shall consider is, then, whether the reasons to which artistic judgments are answerable are relative. As so often in philosophy, much depends on what is meant by the term. There is unquestionably a sense in which artistic appreciation is relative to socio-historical context, in that certain concepts may not be or may not have been available as possible factors in judgments at other places or periods. To take an obvious example, Freudian interpretations of the arts would not have been possible in pre-Freudian times. Moreover, different schools of thought, or approaches to art, incorporate different criteria.

It is worth a brief digression to explain what I mean by the term 'criterion'. I shall use it to mean 'necessarily a reason for'. Its meaning can be brought out by contrasting it with evidence. If, through my window, I see people walking past with raincoats on and umbrellas up, this is evidence that it is raining. If I put my hand out of the window and feel cold, wet drops, this is a criterion of its raining. Thus a criterion is directly related to meaning. It would be quite possible to know what 'It is raining' means without knowing that people put up umbrellas when it rains, but if in normal circumstances someone who feels the cold, wet drops does not know that this is a ground for saying that it is raining, then he does not understand what it means to say that it is raining. It should be noticed that a criterion is not equivalent to a sufficient condition. One could easily imagine cases where there were cold, wet drops even though it was not raining. There is much more which could be said about the notion of the criterion, but it is not necessary for the purposes of my argument.

In relation specifically to the arts, a criterion is necessarily a reason both for what counts as art, and by which good art can be distinguished from poor art. Similarly, for instance, if a criterion of something's being a knife is that it is an instrument used for cutting, then a criterion for a good knife is that it should be an instrument which cuts well. In the case of the arts, the change from purely representational art to impressionism or abstract expressionism involved changes of criteria. Where formerly a criterion for what counted as art, and as good art, was accuracy of representation, the change of concept necessarily involved changes of criteria. Clearly there is a close relation between criteria and concepts, in that a criterion is an expression of a concept; where concept or meaning changes, so will the criteria.

To return, then, to the issue of the criteria of different concepts of art, the problem we are considering can be seen clearly in cases of conceptual innovation. Thus the question might arise whether *Finnegans Wake* is a novel. Consider the slighting remarks by critics when Martha Graham's Dance Company first came to Britain; how the terms 'impressionism' and 'fauvism' were first used dismissively by critics of the respective styles of painting. There are numerous other examples, such as serialization in music, Henry Moore and Barbara Hepworth, Ingmar Bergman and Samuel Beckett. Each introduced a conceptual innovation requiring such a readjustment in the grounds of artistic judgment that many people were unable to make it. Such readjustments would not necessarily be easier for the knowledgeable and perceptive since they might be more prone to a hardening of the conceptual arteries. Many, inevitably, continued, at least implicitly, to refer to the old concepts of art as *grounds* to judge the new works. But these new works were *changing* the grounds of art, i.e. they were changing in the practice of artists the concepts of what *counted* as art. Hence a work did not qualify even for the pejorative extreme on the scale of critical judgment, since it could not be understood as *art* at all — it was not even a painting, but merely an impression; the perpetrators were as crazy as wild beasts (fauvism).

The problem of understanding conceptual differences can be most sharply brought out by considering the arts of very different cultures. There is a great temptation to say, and obviously some point in saying, that judgments, and the reasons given for them, must be relative to the cultures within which they arise.

Nevertheless, they cannot be *entirely* relative, if by that is meant that they involve criteria which bear no relation whatsoever to any other. For to be able to recognize something as even very different art, dance, drama, music, and so on, in another culture, necessarily presupposes *some* overlap with our concepts. If someone were to claim that an activity of another culture, which bore no relation whatsoever to art in ours, should be regarded as their art, we should be at a loss to know why he wanted to use the term 'art' for it at all. Wittgenstein writes (1969): 'To say: in the end we can only adduce such grounds as *we* hold to be grounds, is to say nothing at all' (§599). That is, we can operate only with the concepts we have, and which give meaning to the terms we use. If it were asserted that the concept of art in another society was literally *nothing at all* like ours, then the assertion would be meaningless. For example, imagine that someone were to say that it is possible that there could be a different concept of mathematics such that $2 + 2 = 5$, where this was not merely a terminological difference, that is, where the supposition is not that '5' in their language is equivalent to '4' in ours. The supposition is meaningless. To make the point with an apparent truism, an activity can be understood as mathematics only if it can be understood as mathematics. The same applies to art.

It is sometimes assumed or argued that, because of its peculiarly innovative character and its being subject to frequent and radical change, the concept of art has no boundaries, and thus that *anything* can be understood as art. Yet those who argue in this way contradict and defeat themselves, since they inevitably have implicitly to presuppose what they are explicitly denying, since, ironically, only if 'art' has meaning can such a claim be made. And to say that the concept has no boundaries *is* to say that 'art' has no meaning. For example, attempts are sometimes made to argue that sport is art on the grounds that *any* activity or artefact is art if the creator intends it to be art, and that such an intention is a matter solely for the individual. My refutation of this confused notion appears elsewhere (Best, 1988). But, to put the point briefly, it makes no sense to suggest that an intention can be logically independent of concepts, practices and context. Intending is not a sort of context-independent subjective wishing or willing. What I am writing on this page cannot become mathematics by my 'intending' it to be so. Or rather, to put the point more clearly, it would make no sense to suggest that I can intend this to be mathematics.

There are, of course, cases where we are uncertain whether to call something art. But it certainly does not follow from the fact that a concept has vague, uncertain boundaries that it has *no* boundaries. Still less does it follow that in that case *anything* could be art. On the contrary, if there were no boundaries to the concept, *nothing* could be art.

The overlap which justifies our use of the term 'art' to describe an activity of another culture offers the possibility of coming to understand and appreciate the arts of different cultures, at least to some extent. Examples include listening for the first time to Japanese music played on the shakuhachi, and to Indian classical music, and watching Oriental dance. One needs to be cautious, though, for whereas an activity may have some relevant overlap, which allows us to call it 'art', it may also have, for instance, a mystical or religious significance in another society which it does not have in ours. It may be only in some respects like art in our culture. Thus one will need to understand the place of the activity in the whole culture.

The problem of relevance should be mentioned here. *Some* similarity can be found between *any* two objects or activities, so the overlap has to be in *relevant* respects. Given the complexity of the concept of art, it is, of course, impossible to state precisely and in general what would count as a relevant overlap, since that would amount to saying that 'art' can be defined, in terms of necessary and sufficient conditions. The fact that 'art' has, and necessarily has, vague, indefinite boundaries renders it commensurately difficult to state what counts as relevant. Nevertheless, it is possible to indicate in a general way some of the kinds of consideration which would count. For example, I argue in later chapters that an art form must allow for the possibility of the expression of issues from life, and that the object of one's attention and feeling may be fictional. Moreover, there is an important sense in which the concept of art is ultimately non-purposive, by which I mean that any supposed purpose of a work of art cannot be identified apart from the artistic means of achieving it, which is the same as saying that, in the arts, there is no distinction between means and end. (I consider this issue more fully elsewhere; see Best, 1978, ch. 7.) Of course, art *can* be regarded as purposive, as, for instance, when a painting is regarded as an investment. In such a case it would be evaluated according to the *extrinsic* criterion of its potential increase in financial value. But the concept of *art qua art* is not purposive; artistic values are *intrinsic*.

(This raises an interesting set of related questions, in the current educational and industrial context, in many countries, of the relationship between fine art and design. For example, should fine art be regarded primarily or partly as a *means* to producing creative, e.g. graphic, design? Important though such questions undoubtedly are, they are outside the scope of this book. I hope to deal with them in another.)

In practice it may be rare for someone of another culture to be able to develop the complete grasp of artistic meaning and value which is possible for a native. This is, of course, equally true of language. In relation to prayer, Simone Weil (1951) writes: 'Except in special cases the soul is not able to abandon itself utterly when it has to make the slight effort of seeking for the words in a foreign language, even when this language is well known' (p. 117). The difficulty is largely created by the fact that both art and language are not independent, but are inextricably interwoven into the whole way of life of a society. This is a consequence of the issue discussed in Chapter 2, that both are grounded in natural ways of acting and responding, and it also relates to the question of the relation of art to life, which will be examined in Chapter 13.

In this respect, to anticipate an issue which I shall discuss further shortly, it is important to distinguish between what is possible in principle, and what is possible in practice. That a remarkably complete grasp of a foreign language is possible is shown by cases such as Conrad, whose sensitive grasp of the subtleties of the English language is far superior to that of most, even educated, native-speakers. But such cases are very rare.

It will be clear from what has been said earlier that the possibility of coming to understand the arts of a different culture depends upon the possibility of sharing responses to them. In Chapter 2, I gave the artificial example of a foreigner with no grasp of the conventions of drama or any related activity. As I pointed out, it is difficult if not impossible to imagine a society in which there were *no* such related activities as children's make-believe stories, and so on, to which they had learned to respond and which would give some overlap with drama in our society.

As we have seen, the attitude which one assimilates as the substratum of artistic understanding is not subjective, in the sense that it can be adopted at will, or in the sense that any such attitude would be equally 'appropriate'. Coming to understand *is* coming to respond in a certain way, and the notion of choice does not come into it. Thus there are two related issues here: (a) there are limits to what can count as art and as a response to art, that is, there is no question of choice; (b) someone who understands art cannot choose what counts as a response to it. If someone were persistently to respond in a way, or to reveal an attitude, which was completely at variance with the norms, that would constitute good grounds for saying that he did not understand the art form at all. To have learned to be involved in artistic appreciation *is* to have acquired such an attitude, revealed in the way one engages in and responds to the arts. There is nothing which justifies one's having such an attitude, since it is that attitude which constitutes the *grounds* of justification and appropriateness.

To repeat the point because of its importance, despite the almost universal unquestioned adherence of arts education theorists to the deep and self-defeating subjectivist/metaphysical doctrine, which is the influential legacy of Kant, Cassirer, Langer, and Louis Arnaud Reid, there is no sense in the notion that artistic understanding depends on supposedly private 'inner' mental processes, or on the private, subjective 'intuition' of metaphysical forms of feeling. On the contrary, understanding the arts, like the ability to use language, is rooted in unhesitating responses to the relevant situations. In the case of the arts this will include, for instance, responding immediately and with emotional involvement to fictional objects. This is why it reveals a radical misconception to ask whether, or, suppose that, responding emotionally to what one knows to be a fictional situation or character in a novel, play, or film is irrational. The unhesitating, immediate response is fundamental, and not only in the arts, but in language, mathematics and the sciences; that response is the ground which gives sense to the rational. It is not an unquestioning assumption, and it is not intuitive knowledge, since both assumptions and intuitions are grounded ultimately in the possibility of justification and falsification, and thus depend upon grounds which underlie them. This is not to suggest that one cannot speak of what is expressed in a work of art, or a verbal utterance, as true or false to reality. The point is that natural responses and ways of behaving are the *roots* of the meaning of truth and falsity, and therefore of what count as sound and unsound reasons. At this level, there can be no room for questions or doubt, since such responses and actions are what gives sense to questions and doubts. Thus it is not intelligible to ask what justifies one's having such an attitude to the arts; such a question is not open, since it is that attitude which constitutes the grounds of justification and appropriateness. The natural responses and actions which are an expression of the artistic attitude are not a *consequence* of the recognition of artistic qualities, they are fundamentally involved in the very *formulation* of concepts of artistic qualities.

This, again, shows that the reasons given for artistic judgments, which are founded upon such an attitude, must be relative in some sense. In order to bring out my own position, I shall briefly consider an interesting symposium on Objectivity and Aesthetics by Sibley and Tanner (1968). Both symposiasts assume that a genuinely objective judgment requires the possibility of at least a fairly wide measure of agreement, at least in the perceptive 'elite', even though, as Sibley puts it, this may be more like a concentrated scatter than convergence on a point.

Sibley contends that although there may be disagreement *in fact*, objectivity consists in the possibility of achieving widespread agreement. One of Tanner's strongest criticisms of Sibley's case for objective judgments in this sphere is that it depends upon 'a pretty impressive amount of agreement' (p. 63) which, he argues, is in fact lacking.

Since he contends that Sibley overlooks the ways in which, for instance, socio-historical factors can affect artistic judgments, Tanner argues that it is necessary to introduce, in addition to the subjective-objective dichotomy, a third category. He illustrates his point by imagining a case where mankind is divided into two equal groups, and there is a class of objects which is seen by one group as blue, and by the other as yellow. Of this he says:

> the fact that there are two groups shouldn't in the least incline us to say that their judgments are subjective. Equally, we may feel rightly uneasy about saying, simply, that members of each are making objective judgments. It looks indeed as if we need . . . the term 'relativism' and its cognates. (pp. 60–1)

The first point to be made about this example refers back to the translation issue, that is, the appropriateness or otherwise of applying a term from one language to an activity in a different society. The two groups are supposed to agree generally in colour-judgments but to differ over one class of objects. Thus someone in group A could find a B member concurring, for instance, that the sky is blue yet saying that a dress, which A judges to be the same colour, is yellow. B is shown the cloth from which the dress was made, and he agrees that it is blue. He is shown a rag doll being made from part of the dress, and at some stage he agrees that it is blue. Yet he still insists that the dress is 'yellow'. There is clearly a serious difficulty about this hypothesis. There are grounds for saying that he is making colour-judgments, in that in most cases there is a general agreement. Yet, on the other hand, since what he is doing in this case is so completely at variance with what can be understood as making colour-judgments, we also have grounds for doubting whether he is making them. Much depends on how the example is filled out. If this should be a single aberration, we might conclude, for instance, that in some odd way this class of objects affects group B's vision. However, if this kind of incident were to occur more generally we might have to conclude that we did not understand what kind of judgments these were, and the use of 'yellow' would be of no help.

More important, Tanner's formulation of the issue suggests that since there may be differences *between* cultures, this precludes the attribution of objectivity to colour judgments *within* a culture. It is true, and may be part of Tanner's point, that such differences in judgments by people of different cultures cannot be described as differences about objective matters of fact since, because of their different concepts of colour, what *counts* as a fact will be different. The point here is that there is no way to discover what their concepts are *apart from* considering the judgments which they make. There is no standard *external* to those judgments by which they can be judged. If the judgments of the two cultures were radically enough different, this would mean that they had different concepts. Nevertheless, this does not imply that there cannot be objectivity of normal colour-judgments. That there is no disagreement between two groups who have different colour-judgments does not imply that there cannot be objective colour-judgments *within* each group. Both symposiasts accept that objectivity requires the possibility of wide agreement, at least in the 'elite'. Sibley argues that, with qualifications, such agreement is possible, whereas it is because he believes such agreement is unattainable, that Tanner doubts the possibility of objectivity, and introduces the category of relativism.

It seems to me that the issue can be more clearly discussed in terms of giving reasons in support of judgments. The issue is the same, in that in each case the possibility of reaching agreement will depend upon an initial overlap of conception and natural response or attitude, which will make sense even of the minimal notion that what is under discussion is art rather than something else. It is no help to say that it is proper to speak of an objective judgment only where it agrees with the facts or reality, since what one *means* by the facts or reality is given by the underlying conception. The notion of the truth or falsity of a proposition presupposes grounds by reference to which it is possible to decide for or against its truth. It is not that we have an *independent* grasp of the truth which we can apply to a proposition, but that what counts as a proposition is that which carries with it canons of truth and falsity within a particular context or activity. That is, it would make no sense to suppose that the facts or reality give us our picture of the world; it is rather that the picture determines what can count as a fact, and as reality. The same applies to objectivity, and to what can count as a valid reason. Thus, partly because of the misleading connotations of 'objectivity', as being concept-independent, and partly because it is more germane to my general thesis, I shall continue the discussion primarily in terms of reason.

Two matters should be mentioned before continuing to discuss this issue. First, neither the view that artistic judgments are relative, nor the view that they are not capable of universal agreement, lends any support to subjectivism. A reason for an artistic judgment cannot be whatever I decide will count as a reason, even if it remains an open question whether the grounds of reason and objectivity are relative or universal. What counts as a reason is still grounded in the normal responses and attitudes of a *society or culture*.

Secondly, as we saw in Chapter 3, one can make legitimately objective judgments, or judgments for which one has sound reasons, which may nevertheless be fallible, and which may not be universally true. 'Objective' or 'rationally justifiable' should not be equated with 'infallible' or 'absolute'. There is a tendency to assume an idealized notion of objectivity such that 'objective' can be legitimately predicated of a judgment only if it is absolutely true and infallible. These two notions are often conflated. To say that a judgment is absolutely true is to say that anyone, in any culture, if he reasons correctly, must arrive at that conclusion. To say that a judgment is infallibly true is to say that it is not even in principle open to question. Neither is implied by saying that a judgment is objective. I shall consider the notion of the absolute shortly. In relation to the assumption that 'objective' implies 'infallible', almost the opposite is the case, for that a judgment is objectively true implies, at least frequently, that there must be, in principle, the possibility of showing that it is false.

As we have seen, there are different grounds, and grounds can change. Consequently what counts as rational, or objective, may also be different and may change. This is not an insuperable problem for, but reveals an important yet often misunderstood characteristic of, rationality, which is not universal and timelessly set. Tanner's feeling impelled to propose the *additional* category of relativism seems to reveal this misconception. For rationality and objectivity in any sphere are relative to the grounds of natural action and response which give them sense, and these grounds may be different at different times in the same culture, and in different cultures. Thus the imagined case where mankind is in two equal groups with different colour-judgments, shows not the necessity for a third category of relativism, but that the grounds of objectivity and rationality may be different. They may also change.

The duck-rabbit figure is a useful illustration. If there were a society with knowledge of ducks but not of rabbits, the question of whether the figure could be interpreted as a rabbit could not even arise. Yet if rabbits, or illustrations of rabbits, were introduced, this would allow for that interpretation. Different grounds give the possibility of different judgments and reasons to support them. This is a simple analogue of the way in which a concept of art may change, sometimes as a result of contact with a different culture, sometimes as a result of a change in the life of society.

Of course, conceptual differences cannot always be resolved, and changes understood, as simply as this. It is a matter of degree. To the extent that there is *some* overlap, there is a meaningful possibility of disagreement, and with it the possibility in principle of reaching understanding. For example, there are societies where the notion of a moral principle relates solely to its application to other members of that society, and where, consequently, robbing, cheating and even killing foreigners is not against the moral code. The overlap of a moral sense which applies within the society gives the possibility of reaching an understanding of a concept of morality which applies universally.

However, sometimes differences cannot be resolved or understood as simply as this. Sometimes they cannot be resolved or understood at all. If differences are sufficiently great, they cannot intelligibly be regarded as conflicts or disagreements at all, but are rather positions which simply pass each other by. But again, in relation to the arts, the question arises whether, in such a case, there would be any justification in referring to the difference as one of *artistic* understanding or appreciation. The possibility of coming to understand a very different concept, and thus extending one's own notion of what counts as intelligibility, depends upon connections with those concepts which already constitute the grounds of one's present understanding. The more tenuous the connections, or the further the innovation has moved from the grounds from which its meaning was derived, the more the innovator is likely to be regarded either as a fool and a heretic (Wittgenstein, 1969, §611), or as a creative genius. This is true, of course, in *any* sphere, not only in the arts.

An interesting problem arises at the limits, for one might feel that there is a sphere of rich artistic experience which is beyond one because one cannot grasp, or at least has not grasped, the relevant grounds of judgment. How can one account for this? Tenuous connections may allow some inchoate sense to this possibility, or one's feeling may be based on respect for the judgments of those whose views one has learned to trust within concepts of art one does understand.

It is the lack of such connecting reasons which justifies one's conviction of the vapid pretentiousness of purported works in which, for example, one is invited to regard as serious art an artist walking about with a plank on his head, splashing about in mud, or contemplating his navel. Certainly those artistic innovations whose value and significance were not recognized in their own time are salutary reminders of the need for care and open-mindedness. Nevertheless, the onus is on the innovators or their apologists to provide the connections. Moreover, in contrast to the cases cited above, in the case of a genuine but different concept of art one may at least be able to recognize technical competence.

Change, and the recognition of different concepts which offer new grounds for rational judgments, are made intelligible only by implicit reference to some of the previous criteria. The notion of a logically free judgment is unintelligible. One cannot simply *choose* either to regard something as art, or one's criteria of evaluation. Where there are fundamental differences, to reach an understanding of another concept of art may well involve not so much a single work of art as a different approach to art, just as, in other contexts, it may involve progressively coming to understand not just a single proposition but a whole system of propositions. Moreover, given the inextricable relation between art and life which will be discussed in Chapter 13, different grounds of approach to art may often amount to a different *Weltanschauung,* a different conception of life.

Consequently, convincing someone of the validity and value of conceptual innovation, in any sphere, requires not proof but rather persuasion. This raises the problem of how to convince the sceptic who assumes that, in default of a proof to the contrary, what purports to be the rational discourse of artistic appreciation amounts merely to a thinly disguised, pretentious attempt to justify what are in fact no more than expressions of mere subjective preferences. The sceptic's demand reveals a fundamental misconception, for the notion of an *external* proof makes no sense. The only way to convince him is by progressively bringing him to understand the arts. No doubt he would be sceptical, and accuse us of what Tanner calls 'semi-circularity'. Yet the same 'semi-circularity' applies to the sceptic's paradigms of reasoning, since in these too the grounds which confer validity on the proof have themselves simply to be *accepted.* For example, this is true even in the case of the simplest deductive syllogism. In 'All men are mortal, Socrates is a man, therefore Socrates is mortal', the conclusion follows *only* if one accepts, not only without proof, but *without any reason whatsoever,* that such a conclusion does follow from such premises.

Given, then, that artistic appreciation is relative to the grounds of natural response and behaviour, to what extent is it possible to reach agreement or understanding between diverging positions? There is a far greater possibility of reaching understanding than is often believed. To repeat, it is important to recognize the distinction between a disagreement or divergence which is of its nature incapable of resolution, and one which will actually, in fact, not be resolved. Even within the same culture and concept of art there are obviously intractable differences of opinion. Moreover, there are cases where each person in the dispute may fully understand the other's interpretation or evaluation of a work even though he does not share it.

A similar situation arises in moral disagreements, although again, if one can recognize a position *as* a moral position, that gives good grounds for the possibility in principle of reaching agreement. Nevertheless, one may come fully to understand a differing opinion without sharing it. For example, one might fully understand and respect opposition to abortion because of a consideration of the sanctity of life, yet still incline to the view that, at least in some circumstances, abortion is justified. In the sciences, too, there may be situations where disagreement may persist although both parties have the same facts. There is still a geoplanarian or flat-earth society, whose members construe differently the "same" observations as those who are convinced that the earth is spherical. That is what may superficially appear to be the *same* observations or data are construed so differently that it may make little or no sense to call them the same. Kuhn (1975) gives other examples. In some such cases, it may cease to have much meaning to continue to insist that a conflict of opinion is resolvable in principle. Each case has to be considered on its merits. Nevertheless, the distinction between what is possible in principle and what is possible in practice is a useful one, and the acceptance of the general principle that it is possible to resolve conflict will encourage the search for the common ground or shared response which will provide the basis for a fruitful debate, and with it the possibility of achieving agreement, or at least understanding. It may or may not require a prolonged exploration of each other's positions to find such a shared response and understanding, which may be in an example or analogy to which appeal can be made as to what counts as a valid reason for both sides in the disagreement. Without such a shared response it will not be possible to conduct rational debate, for a genuine disagreement is founded upon a background of shared agreement or response at a more fundamental level. That is, a disagreement is about *something,* and is thus founded upon an agreement about the position in dispute, and about what counts as supporting or detracting from the conflicting views. It may be difficult to locate those shared foundations of disagreement, and it may require an extensive exploration of a network of related issues. The same considerations apply to reaching an understanding of a different approach to art, or a different interpretation, for *oneself,* as a result of reflection.

Of course, it is often true that, in practice, one has to recognize the futility of attempting to continue rational debate, or the search for understanding, and this is as true of philosophy and the sciences as it is of morality and the arts. There is, for example, a distinction between having a valid reason, and having a valid reason which the other person can understand. In philosophy generally, as much as in the arts and morality, there are those with whom one does, and those with whom one does not, share a common language. That is, with some, one shares assumptions and ways of approaching issues which one cannot take for granted with others. Debate may be so exhaustingly fundamental that one may regard it as not a fruitful enterprise, or even if one does undertake it, one may not succeed in locating the common ground. But that does not necessarily imply that further fruitful debate is in *principle* impossible. The possibility of further progress may be impeded by a failure of understanding, perhaps on both sides, which further discussion may remove.

Indeed, universal agreement in practice is neither desirable nor even, at least in some cases, coherent. Both a conviction that it is possible in *principle* to resolve problems and conflicts, and yet the intractable persistence *in practice* of problems and conflicts, are essential for the continued progress and even existence of any area of inquiry. Kuhn (1975) points out, for instance, that contrary to what is often assumed, it is a mark of the fruitfulness of a scientific theory not that it *solves* all problems and conflicts, but rather that it continues to *generate* problems and conflicts. Understanding is extended *within* areas of disagreement and difference.

What is of particular importance for my argument is that, because of the character of the arts and morality, to wish, even if it were conceivable, that there should be a considerable degree of agreement would amount to wishing that people were all the same. Leibniz expressed a profound insight, which would repay much more discussion, when he contended that to come genuinely to understand another person is to see life in his terms, and is thus to grasp another *Weltanschauung,* another perspective on the world. Differences of opinion, and, perhaps even more important, debating with *oneself* about the interpretation and evaluation of what is expressed in a work, are central to the character of artistic appreciation. Exchanges of opinion about, or reflecting upon, those possibilities of different interpretation, may give an extended and enriched understanding not only of the arts but of other people and life generally, since considerations other than exclusively artistic ones are often relevant to fruitful debate and reflection about the arts. This partly anticipates Chapter 13, where it will be argued that it is a misconception to regard art as entirely autonomous. For example, reflections on moral insights, character traits and personal relationships may be relevant in important ways to considering artistic interpretation and validity. The arts are constituents of an inextricably interwoven network of related activities which together provide concepts of truth, reality and value.

I have argued, then, that this inevitable and desirable range of individual variation in response, interpretation and evaluation is certainly not incompatible with objectivity, rationality and the possibility of reaching understanding and perhaps agreement. I have tried to show that it is to mistake the character of rationality, or objectivity, to suppose that a separate category of relativism is necessary, since objectivity and rationality are, in an important sense, relative to their grounds of learned natural action or response.

Moreover, one may be convinced that the most important aim of education should be to stimulate critical, independent thinking, but that is certainly not to imply that it should encourage subjectivity. On the contrary, independent thinking in the arts, as much as in science, mathematics and philosophy, is not only compatible with but *presupposes* objectivity and rationality. What is required is not conformity but that independent thought should be answerable to valid reasons. In that sense, rationality is a precondition of the individual differences in the creation and appreciation of the arts which are such significant expressions of the rich diversity in human personality. It is a fundamental misconception about this issue which is a major source of subjectivism. For example, in arguing the case for objectivity, or answerability to reason, one has sometimes encountered the, usually hostile, objection: 'Who are you to tell me how to interpret or respond to a work of art?' But who am I to tell the subjectivist that 12 x 12 = 144? As we have seen in Chapter 4, one can appreciate the hostility if objectivity, or answerability to reason, is taken to imply authoritarianism and a denial of the importance of individual response. My argument carries no such implication but, on the contrary, strongly *supports* and offers an intelligible account of originality and individuality. As Wittgenstein puts it (1969): 'There is no subjective sureness that I know something' (§245), and, 'a ground is not anything *I* decide' (§271) Bambrough, with typical perceptive acuity, (1984) writes: 'In every sphere of enquiry the learner may come to question what he has been taught, but when he does so he is appealing *to* what he has been taught as well as *against* what he has been taught' (p. 48).

Some years ago a group of art students in Madrid were so determined to give art a completely fresh, original start that they wanted to destroy all existing works of art in order to prevent what they believed to be the suffocation of potential 'real' artistic originality by the supposedly limiting influence of tradition. What if they had succeeded, and after the holocaust someone had created a work in the conventional style of one of those destroyed? By what criteria could they reject it as too prosaic or conventional? To achieve their aim, all memories of art would have had to be destroyed too and if they could have achieved that, how could anyone in the future create *any*, still less an *original*, work of art? For in that circumstance nothing could even count as a work of art. Innovation makes sense as such only in a context of a tradition or convention. So if they were able to destroy altogether the conventional, and even memories of it, they would *ipso facto* be destroying the possibility of originality.

Could the whole of space be six inches to the left? Could everything be twice the size it actually is?

The subjectivist 'ideal' of artistic individualism, in this sense, is self-defeating. Since it connects with nothing there is nothing against which change, reaction and individuality can make sense.

Mozart's oboe quartet has passages of striking originality, which have similarities to Stravinsky, and some of Turner's later paintings are remarkably like precursors of modern abstract expressionism. In each case what gives sense to the attribution of originality is an implicit reference to a background of contemporary artistic conventions.

Ironically, if subjectivism were intelligible it would be condemned to eternal conservatism, the permanently static, since there would be no ground on which to move. It is only a relatively stable background which can make meaningful the notion of movement and change. Hence the passage with which I introduced this chapter:

> . . . nothing changed in Mr. Knott's establishment, because nothing remained and nothing came or went, because all was a coming and a going.
> (Samuel Beckett, *Watt* 1963, p. 130)

Chapter 6

Free Expression

The light dove, cleaving the air in her free flight, and feeling its resistance, might imagine that her flight would be still easier in empty space.
(Kant, 1929, p. 47)

An important issue which is closely related to some of the preceding chapters and which has been central to discussion of general educational policy for some years, is the conflict between those who emphasize freedom of expression to allow unrestricted individual development, and those who emphasize learning the discipline of an activity or subject. Learning the discipline, in this sense, means progressively mastering the techniques and criteria so that, for instance, the valid can be distinguished from the invalid, the more competent from the competent, and the more from the less perceptive. The issue applies equally to the artist and audience, or creator and spectator, and although it is particularly significant in the arts, it raises a question of general educational concern.

This chapter considers one of the most widespread and damaging consequences, in practical educational terms, of the confused subjectivist assumptions which are still so prevalent. Subjectivism continues to wreak severe damage on the credibility of the arts in education, and in society generally. It is a common misconception that philosophy is a remote, abstract enterprise, of little or no practical relevance. This chapter attempts to refute that dangerous distortion of the character of philosophy. For it is *only* by a careful philosophical examination of the assumptions which lie behind them that we can understand what has led to the disastrous *practical* effects, in the classroom, of subjectivist doctrines (often dogmas) which have infected educational *practice* on a remarkably wide scale for many years.

Psychology and Philosophy

There has been for many years a reaction against the 'bad old days' of an educational policy whose overriding emphasis was on the formal imparting of knowledge and drill in techniques. But in many ways the reaction has swung to an equally damaging opposite extreme of permissiveness, sometimes amounting to absurdity and incoherence. In Chapter 3, I gave the example of a professor who refuses to teach the discipline of dance, and to assess her students' work, on the grounds that this would illegitimately restrict their individual freedom of expression. She insists that there should be no such 'external imposition' of criteria and techniques, but that each student should be free to develop in his or her own way, and to decide what is and what is not of artistic value. Hence she was unable to object to the eating of crisps as a purported dance performance. It has sometimes been objected that this is an extreme example, but in fact the dance professor was at least commendably consistent in recognizing the inevitable consequences of her subjectivist convictions, unlike those who explicitly propound or accept subjectivism yet who implicitly contradict their theory in practice. The subjectivist teacher is always and necessarily in a self-contradictory position, since to help students to learn necessarily requires the employment of the objective criteria of the particular activity. There is no other way of knowing that a student is progressively developing her or his individual potential. Thus, despite the continued prevalence of the doctrine that the arts cater for the subjective area of humanity, there is obviously no sense at all in the notion of arts *education* on a subjectivist basis. For instance, as a consequence of her students' actions, the dance professor lost her job, although she had merely carried consistently to its logical conclusion a policy towards her subject which was well known to and therefore presumably implicitly approved by those who employed her. It was *they* who were inconsistent, since they also felt that it was incumbent on them as responsible educationists to require their teachers to help students to attain higher standards. In this they were right, since clearly no one can teach without some form of assessment. A teacher needs to know whether, and to what extent, his students are understanding and learning, and to achieve such knowledge is assessment. To fail to assess is to fail to teach. What *form* that assessment should take is, of course, another matter.

This point can hardly be over-emphasised, with respect to all aspects of education. Objective judgment, the teacher's increasingly objective judgment, is of central educational significance. The most important aspects of education will always require sensitive, informed, objective judgment. The skills of good judgment, assessment skills, *are* the skills of teaching well. Which is why there will never be a substitute for high quality teachers, who not only make such judgments, but who continuously refine their sensitive ability to do so.

There are similar, and equally disastrous, confusions, about intervention. For example, I once heard a Senior Primary Adviser, talking to a large group of teachers, emphasise that, in art, a teacher must *never* intervene in a child's work. This is a classic example of the extreme 'free expression' doctrinaire subjectivism which is so harmful. For how on earth can the notion of *education* in art be justified at all if the teacher must never intervene? On this view, there is no justification whatsoever for employing arts teachers. Yet, almost unbelievably, arts educators themselves proclaim the subjectivist doctrine.

It is, of course, true that inappropriate or excessive intervention may restrict or distort a child's individual development. But it certainly does not follow from that that therefore *all* intervention is harmful. Far from it, for it is *equally* true that to *fail* to intervene appropriately may severely restrict a child's individual artistic development. This is why we need high quality teachers who can make the difficult objective judgments required to assess when and how to intervene.

To refuse to intervene is to refuse to educate.

The misconception in the subjectivist, 'free expression' policy can be clearly exposed by considering the parallel with language-learning. As we saw in Chapter 2, a language is an expression of a conception of reality, so that in learning the discipline of correct linguistic usage a child is learning to see and understand the world in terms of that language. But it would be palpably absurd to suggest that this understanding is restrictive, and that for *real* freedom of individual development each child should grow up alone on a desert island, where he could form his own concepts and understanding of the world, free from supposed conformist influences. Clearly, so far from conferring greater freedom of thought, this would severely *limit* the child's possible freedom of thought and individual development. A person with an inadequate grasp of reading, spelling, grammar and vocabulary incurs a limitation of the possibility of free expression and individual development. The subjectivist fails to recognise the distinction between limits and limitations. Thus the subjectivist regards all learning of techniques as imposing *limitations*, instead of recognising that it is the grasp of those techniques which alone enables students progressively to *free* themselves from limitations.

Nevertheless, even though it is sometimes exaggerated to the point of absurdity, there is an important truth underlying this 'free expression' approach. It arose as a reaction against an educational policy which undoubtedly was restrictive in, for example, elevating the ability to write grammatically to the status of an end in itself, rather than regarding it as a means to the end of making possible greater freedom of expression. Thus imagination was stifled in an over-emphasis on stringent standards in modes of expression at the expense of a concern for what was expressed.

Some individuality managed to survive the conformist pressures, yet it underlines the point I am making that even a D.H. Lawrence was free to castigate the system *only* because he had mastered the disciplines conferred by that system. For instance, he condemned too much reasoning as morally and emotionally crippling, in that, in his view, it leads to a calculating and insufficiently spontaneous nature. Yet, although, in one sense, he was undoubtedly indicating something importantly true, it is significant for the point I am now making that inevitably he had to support this contention with persuasive reasoning.

This is also a further illustration of one of the central aspects of Chapter 3, namely that there is a much wider possibility in the notion of reasoning than is usually assumed. For example, in an exquisitely perceptive passage, Lawrence (1962) writes, about Bertrand Russell:

> What ails Russell is, in matters of life and emotion, the inexperience of youth. He is, vitally, emotionally, much too inexperienced in personal contact and conflict, for a man of his age and calibre. It isn't that life has been too much for him, but too little. (vol. 1, p. 351)

Putting it this way *is* giving a reason. In effect, Lawrence is pointing out that an inappropriate and predominant emphasis on reasoning imposes severe limitations on personality. This is a powerfully effective way of formulating his reason.

The example also illustrates the main theme of this chapter, that it is understanding of and competence in the medium which allows for freedom from limitations. In this case Russell's limitations emotionally, vitally, are his relative isolation in the 'safe' ivory tower of academia, and thus his lack of understanding and experience of the medium of life in general, and of personal contact and conflict in particular.

The philosophical misconception which seems still to underlie some subjectivist-infected educational thought is that to have the opportunity for *really* free individual development is to have been exposed to *no* influence, to have acquired *no* discipline, to have received *no* teaching. The conceptual error encapsulated in that kind of assumption is aptly exposed in the quotation from Kant at the beginning of this chapter. For just as the dove would have no freedom to fly without the resistant air, so there can be no freedom for artistic individuality of expression without a grasp of the artistic medium. In both cases, there can be no progress in a vacuum.

There are two factors which contribute to this pernicious subjectivist doctrine. The first is a failure to distinguish between the psychological and philosophical issues involved. The valid insight of the 'free expression' school of thought is a psychological one, namely, that there are attitudes to and methods of teaching which can stifle individuality, imagination and self-confidence. This is quite distinct from the philosophical point to which I am drawing attention, namely, that if certain disciplines are not acquired, whether of language, the arts, or any other subject, students are not allowed but *deprived of* certain possibilities for freedom of expression and individuality.

Perhaps the confusion arises in this way. It is correctly recognized that *some* methods of teaching disciplines lead to restrictions on freedom, and from this it is erroneously assumed, at least implicitly, that to remove *all* teaching of disciplines is to remove *all* restrictions on freedom. Thus a valid psychological insight is taken to the invalid extreme of a philosophical confusion, with seriously damaging educational consequences.

A contributory factor, then, to this misconception is a conflation of the psychological and the philosophical issues, as a consequence of which 'free expression' is assumed to be incompatible with assessment, technical competence, and the learning of objective criteria. In fact there is no incompatibility here at all. It is quite consistent to maintain, and it may well be true, that a 'free' approach is the most effective method of attaining competence in the discipline without restricting individuality. It is important to recognise that 'free' does *not* mean the same as 'random' or 'arbitrary'. Someone who seriously insists that 3 x 7 equals whatever he feels he wants it to equal is exhibiting not freedom and individuality, but a failure of understanding. This is not an expression of freedom, but of limitation.

Individual and Social

The second contributory factor to this subjectivist confusion is more complex and brings up an issue which is central to the argument of this book. It arises from a common misapprehension about the individuality of a person, and is underlain by a failure to recognize that it makes no sense to suppose that the identity of an individual person — the character of his thoughts and feelings — can be regarded as independent of the character of society. It is obvious that a society is necessarily composed of individual people, but less obvious is the converse relation which is of far greater significance, namely, the way in which individual personality is logically inseparable from the language and practices of a society. This question is of great significance with respect to understanding other cultures, and therefore to multicultural education.

The subjectivist tendency is to conceive of the individual personality as a totally autonomous entity logically distinct from its social context. That is, the subjectivist thinks of the real person, what he really is, his essential individuality, as that which underlies and is independent of 'extraneous' factors such as the social practices in which he engages. It is what Kerr (1986) calls the mentalist-individualist picture of the self. This misleading tendency is sometimes manifested in psychological theories of 'self-actualization' and 'self-realization', which imply that the real character of the individual can be fully revealed only by seeing through such distorting and irrelevant 'accretions'. This kind of assumption is particularly tempting where someone exhibits disparate and perhaps conflicting dispositions and attitudes. Yet an individual's personality cannot coherently be regarded as distinct from what he does and says. It is possible to make sense of the notion of an individual's personality apart from *some*, but certainly not from *all*, his actions. Clearly what he *says* depends upon the social practice of language. Less obvious, perhaps, is that what he *does* also, to an overwhelmingly large extent, cannot intelligibly be regarded as distinct from the social practices which he learns as he grows up in a community. For example, his paying for something depends upon the social institution of money and financial exchange.

One can appreciate why the subjectivist regards linguistic and artistic disciplines as inhibiting, for according to the subjectivist doctrine they appear to be extraneous influences, obscuring a person's essential character and hindering its free and natural development. Yet this kind of conception is fundamentally mistaken, and not only with respect to the arts. Discussing the question of how we can understand other people, Phillips (1970) writes:

> The problem is not one of discovering how to bridge an unbridgeable gulf between a number of logically private selves, contingently thrown together. On the contrary, unless there were a common life which people share, which they were taught and came to learn, there could be no notion of a person . . . Our common ways of doing things are not generalizations from individual performances, but the preconditions of individuality. The public is the precondition of the private, not a construct of it. This being so, what it means to be a person cannot be divorced or abstracted from these common features of human life. (p. 6)

This is not to deny that there are thoughts, feelings and experiences which are not expressed (although it is important to note that the ability to keep them to oneself is limited, and is a secondary, acquired, sophisticated matter). What I do deny is that at anything above a primitive level any sense can be made of the notion that the thoughts and feelings of an individual person can be regarded as logically distinct from the public media or cultural practices of a society, which necessarily incorporate certain objective criteria and values. Yet the enormous significance of this point is frequently overlooked. For example, Argyle (1975) writes:

It looks as if what is being expressed in music is an elaborate sequence of inner experiences including various emotions. It is because music can represent these experiences so well that it has been called 'the language of the emotions' (p. 386).

This is a classic expression of the subjectivist assumption which I am exposing. It clearly implies that the 'elaborate sequence of inner experiences' exists in the mind prior to and independently of the public medium of music, and that, as a matter of contingent fact, it can be expressed in that medium (i.e. it just happens to be the case that it can be expressed in music). The notion is that such experiences are, as it were, awaiting the availability of the most appropriate form of expression so that they can be most effectively articulated. According to this conception, the 'inner' experience could exist even though the art form of music did not exist. But that is to assume that the experience would be possible in the absence of a medium in which it could be formulated, and which alone gives sense to the notion of such an experience. To take a clear example, no experience could possibly count as that of making a checkmate move in isolation from the discipline or practice of playing chess. Apart from that public medium and discipline, whatever physical movements were performed, it would make no sense to say that they could give the same experience. Thus the existence of the public medium of chess and of music is a *precondition* of the possibility of the individual's having the respective experiences. Moreover, the individual must have learned the discipline of the public practice in order to have the possibility of such an experience.

It is important to recognize the full force of this point, since it involves the common subjectivist view exemplified by Argyle, who, significantly, writes of music that it can represent the experiences *so well*. This shows that Argyle regards the problem as *empirical*, that is, as if there were no problem about the independent existence of the experiences, but only the practical problem of discovering the best way of expressing them. Yet, as we have seen, the problem is not practical or empirical, but conceptual; it is a question of whether it *makes sense* to postulate the existence of such experiences which are independent of the art form of music. Argyle implies the intelligibility of comparison, in that, in his view, it is possible to express the *same* experiences in other media, but when they are all tried music is found to be the most effective. Yet no sense can be made of the suggestion that the same experience could be expressed in some other way even if not so well. For what could count as the *same* experience? Taking on this view point, it would be intelligible to suppose that, in principle, a poem or a painting might be found which could express the 'inner' experience even better. Thus, on a cold night, one could say: 'Don't bother to go to the concert. Stay at home and read this poem which expresses the same experience as well as or even better than the symphony.'

Again, the example of chess is a clear illustration, for it is obvious that the suggestion that the game of chess allows *very well* for the representation of checkmate experiences is nonsensical. Or, to bring out the point in another way, one could ask the subjectivist who argues in this way to which experience he is referring. The only way in which that question could be answered would be by reference to the *objective* notion of checkmate in chess. Similarly, it is not simply a practical difficulty which prevents what is expressed in a symphony from being expressed and experienced in a different artistic medium. On the contrary, this common subjectivist supposition — or consequence of subjectivism — simply makes no sense. The experience is necessarily related to, *uniquely* identified by, the existence of that piece of music. The public medium is not merely the convenient but extraneous means of expression. If there were no such medium there could be no such experience. Thus it is only by learning the discipline of the medium that an individual can *have* such an experience.

It may be remembered that a similar point was made in Chapter 2 about the subjectivist supposition that men *invented* language. As we saw, this makes no sense, since the ideas given uniquely with language, and even the very *idea* of the shared medium of language, would have to be presupposed in order to invent it.

Educational Consequences

The consequences of my argument are of great importance for education since it should be remembered that the case of music, which was considered above, is merely a particular example of a subjectivist conception which is held as a general principle applied, for instance, to all the arts and language. The position we have reached in this book by contrast to the subjectivist position, makes sense, and also amounts to a far stronger argument for the immensely significant contribution of education. It is the argument of this subjectivist doctrine, if it were intelligible (which it certainly is not), that the relevant experiences could not be, or could not be adequately, *expressed* without the appropriate medium of expression. It is assumed that the supposedly private, 'inner' experiences exist independently, and that learning the art form provides the possibility for expressing them overtly. But the rejection of the subjectivist conception as nonsensical reveals a position of enormously greater significance for education with respect to responsibility for the development of individual potential. For it is a direct consequence of my argument, by contrast with subjectivism, that if, for instance, there were no art form of music, the respective experiences would not be merely inexpressible, but, more important, *they could not intelligibly be said even to exist.* Moreover, the *individual* could not have such experiences unless he had acquired some grasp of the public discipline and objective criteria of the art form of music. Thus the existence of the art form, and the learning of its techniques and criteria, are necessary preconditions of the possibility of individual experience and development.

This clearly exposes the pernicious subjectivist fallacy that freedom for unrestricted personal development depends upon the *avoidance* of the disciplines, since, on the contrary, the freedom of the individual to experience the relevant feelings necessarily *depends upon* his having learned those disciplines.

The examples we have considered are manifestations of a general misconception to the effect that ideas, thoughts, experiences and feelings are only contingently (i.e. they just happen to be) connected with their overt forms of expression in social practices. One of the most seriously misleading manifestations of this general doctrine is expressed in the common assumption that language and the arts are symbolic forms. For, in the way that assumption is most naturally construed, this expresses or lends support to the prevalent misapprehension that language, like the arts, is merely a system of signs or symbols to convey messages, or purely private 'inner' experiences, which are formulated prior to and independently of language. (I have considered symbolism more fully elsewhere; see Best, 1978, ch. 8.) Thus it is often proposed as an intelligible supposition that it is possible to *think* without any medium of expression, even if one requires language to communicate the thoughts. Yet it is a consequence of this assumption that one could intelligibly suppose an owl to be capable of profound philosophical ideas, even though it so happens that he has not managed to learn the language in which to express them. Clearly, however wise owls may be in fable, such a supposition makes no sense, since, without the requisite ability to express oneself in language, nothing could *count* as having the ability to formulate profound philosophical ideas. One may be able to ascribe some thoughts to owls, but certainly not the kind of thought involved in philosophy. For example, to recognize even a simple self-contradiction obviously requires a grasp of language, and it would make no sense to attribute any such thought to a creature without such a grasp. Thus the learning of the discipline of language is a precondition of the possibility in an *individual* for philosophical thinking and ideas. It is in this sense that the discipline, so far from inhibiting or distorting freedom of thought and individual development, is the only way of making it possible.

This common assumption that linguistic and artistic meaning are symbolic, or that they express symbolic forms, indicates why I sometimes refer to the 'subjectivist/metaphysical' preconceptions of most arts educators, i.e. why the subjective often collapses into the metaphysical. For if, with respect to a *general* theory of symbolic meaning, we were to ask 'symbolic of what?' the answer is frequently either a postulated general metaphysical Form, or a postulated individual, subjective occult 'inner' experience. But since, in terms of the theory itself, these latter cannot be known to anyone else (since they are purely private) there is an inevitable resort to mysterious metaphysics to 'substantiate' the claim for their existence.

How, according to this subjectivist/symbolic theory is meaning and communication possible *at all*? Taking this view, the only way in which I could know that a word or work of art symbolises even approximately the same for you as for me is by 'metaphysically' entering your mind to find out. And that, in terms of the theory itself, is nonsensical. Similar problems arise for the closely related and widely assumed reliance on intuition, which Suzanne Langer calls 'the basic intellectual act', since, in that sense, no one could possibly know whether his own 'intuition' is even approximately correct, or coincides with anyone else's. This is certainly not to deny the importance of intuition, in almost every sphere of human life. But it *is* to deny that it makes sense to regard intuition as 'the *basic*' intellectual act, i.e. it cannot be the *ultimate* arbiter. On the contrary, intuition is valuable and meaningful only to the extent that, at least normally, it can be *verified*, i.e. by something *other* than intuition. As Ben Shahn has aptly put it: 'Intuition in art is actually the result of prolonged tuition'. And that applies not only to the arts but to *all* intuition. In that, non-subjectivist, non-metaphysical, sense, intuition is crucial to almost every human activity, and in every sphere of intellectual enquiry. Neither am I denying the *possibility, sometimes,* of symbolic meaning in art. What I do deny, because it makes no sense, is that artistic and linguistic meanings are always and necessarily symbolic.

For instance, I was once given the example of a play in which an empty chair stood on the stage throughout, symbolising the continuing dominant influence of a member of a family who had died long ago. There is nothing metaphysical about that. It makes perfectly good sense, and, indeed, it was a powerful part of the play. By contrast, the supposition that *all* art is symbolic, e.g. every piece of music, almost inevitably runs us into unintelligible metaphysics.

It is, then, a seminal fallacy to regard language or an art form as a mere convenience, a message-carrier, supervenient to the thoughts, ideas, activities and experiences of individual people. On the contrary, language, and the other social practices of a culture, such as, centrally, the arts, provide the standards of truth and falsity; they give the structure of possible reality, as the expression of the form of life of a society. As Rush Rhees (1969) has aptly put it: 'What do we learn when we learn a language? A list of verbal expressions would be no answer.' It would be no answer because a language gives a *whole way of life*, a vast and varied range of thoughts and feelings which would be impossible *without* language. This is why I wrote in Chapter 2 that, in an important sense, it is language, and the other cultural practices, which *create* human beings, and *not* the converse. That is, the kind of people we are, our thoughts and feelings, are to a very large extent, and at anything beyond a very primitive level, *determined* by language. Our dependence upon language and cultural practices is so *total* that we become oblivious of it. As we saw in Chapter 3, the American Indian Pocohontas, after living among the English settlers for some time, became puzzled by the apparent lack of visual acuity among the English, and at one point exclaimed: 'It seems that I can see things in my language which you cannot see in yours.' This echoes a point which resonates through the whole thesis of this book, that language, like the arts, cannot be coherently regarded as independent of a whole way of life, and the natural actions and responses set in a cultural context.

With respect to the grounds of the reasons which are adduced in scientific proofs, Wittgenstein remarks (1969, §298): '"We are quite sure of it" does not mean just that every single person is certain of it, but that we belong to a community which is bound together by science and education.'

The notion of a logically independent individual personality is, then, misconceived. Kerr (1986) aptly calls it the 'mentalist-individualist' conception. This formulation captures the absurdity of the subjectivist notion we are considering, which entails that each of us is born with all the thoughts and feelings expressible in language and the arts. They are all supposed to be there from birth (and even before?). The problem for each of us is supposed to be to find means of expressing them so as to communicate with other mentalist-individuals.

The subjectivist notion presents a radically misguided but widely assumed picture of the autonomous self as, in Kerr's words (1986) the 'self-conscious and self-reliant, self-transparent and all-responsible individual which Descartes and Kant between them imposed upon modern philosophy' (p. 5). It may easily be identified, in various guises, in the work of most arts educators.

Yet, on the contrary, one's possible ways of thinking and experiencing, and therefore one's very *being*, are inextricably bound up with the language and practices of society. For example, the thought that it is five o'clock obviously depends on the existence of a society which has practices involving clocks and watches. This carries implications, which I can only briefly adumbrate here, of another misconception implicit in essentialist notions of the individual, often implied in the use of terms such as 'self-actualization', and 'self-realization'. For the notion of 'the *real* character' of a person seems to convey a picture of a self waiting to be released from the bonds and obscurities of what has been learned; a self which is permanent below the superficial changes on the surface. Yet there is an important sense in which it is more appropriate and intelligible to regard a person as being in a constant state of creation. It is an important insight of existentialism to conceive of each person as faced with an indefinite range of choices which will progressively determine the character of his own individuality. This conception has the added psychological benefit of emphasizing the active possibility, indeed inevitability, of responsibility for what one is, and it is more constructive in that it allows for change where one is dissatisfied with one's self. However, in one important respect the existentialist view is seriously misleading, for clearly there are limits to the possibility of change. It would make no sense to suppose that one's choice is logically unlimited. To take an obvious case, and one which is most relevant to my thesis, one cannot choose to change in ways of which one simply has no conception. Someone in a society with no conception of chess cannot choose to become a chess player; someone in a society with no concept of art cannot choose to become an artist. The possibilities of changing oneself depend not only on inherent abilities, but also on the language and social practices which one has learned. This emphasises again my conviction that the most important contribution of education, in all areas of the curriculum, is opening horizons of understanding. Such extensions of understanding necessarily depend upon learning the techniques and criteria of the disciplines. It is in this sense that sensitive and enlightened education can be essentially liberating.

There are very significant consequences for educational responsibility, since, by contrast with the permissive subjectivist doctrine, it transpires that the educationist carries an unavoidable responsibility for the individual development of students. It is undoubtedly enormously difficult to oppose the conformist pressures, for instance, of television advertising and the so-called 'pop culture', towards a bland, superficial uniformity of cliché phraseology. But a person with only trite forms of expression is a person who is capable of only trite experiences. Although I would wish to dissociate myself from his scornful way of expressing the issue, this underlies the following passage from Oscar Wilde (Hart-Davies, 1962):

> The intellectual and emotional life of ordinary people is a very contemptible affair. Just as they borrow their ideas from a sort of circulating library of thought . . . and send them back soiled at the end of each week, so they always try to get their emotions on credit, and refuse to pay the bill when it comes in (p. 501).

The crucial educational point here is that if people succumb to popular pressures, and are thus limited to the circulating library of cliché forms of expression, then their capacity for *their own* individual thought and emotional experience is commensurately limited. The worst soiling is that language, and with it the scope for thought and feeling, is further debased by each member of the library, thus reducing even further the genuine possibility for others to think and feel. Thus popular, shallow, sentimental, cliché-ridden romantic novels, art, and television programmes not only impede an understanding of the human condition, they also contribute to the creation and perpetuation of shallow, sentimental, cliché-ridden feelings. They impede the possible development of genuinely individual feelings: they restrict personal possibilities.

We shall return to this crucial question of the creation of feelings, and with it the creation of freedom for individual personality development, in later chapters. Here, let us note the appalling limitation on human potential which is imposed by the shallow sentimentality of language and arts which is so widely purveyed. Its dishonesty, insincerity is aptly expressed by Dilman (1987):

> Where a person's responses to others are predominantly sentimental . . . his awareness of them as separate beings is pretty limited. For sentimentality is a taming of them, a filtering out of much in them, which one is unable to embrace affectively, an investing of them with a shallow unreal goodness. (p. 113)

This is the sense in which sentimentality is dishonest, and restrictive. It is a further indication of why subjectivism is not only senseless but severely limiting. For the only hope of avoiding, or escaping from, false feelings which not only restrict and distort the observer, but prevent a truly adequate recognition of the qualities of other people, is by *objective* perception. The scope and responsibility of arts educators is clear, and immense.

To appreciate the point I am trying to make here, imagine that one were trying to understand the ways of thinking of an individual from a very different society. At anything above a very primitive level, such as understanding that he was hungry, this would be impossible without to some extent coming to understand the concepts and practices of his society. As we have seen, it is unintelligible to suppose that thoughts could be regarded as subjectively isolated, discoverable *only* by introspection, independent of the social media in which they could be expressed. For without those social media they could not exist. In this respect it is significant that such thoughts are attributed only to human beings, that is, to creatures with language and arts. And a language like an art form, is impossible for an isolated individual; it requires a society. Peter Winch (1972) writes:

> Unlike beasts, men do not merely live but also have a conception of life. This is not something that is simply added to their life, rather it changes the very sense which the word 'life' has when applied to man. It is no longer equivalent to 'animate existence'. When we are speaking of the life of man, we can ask questions about what is the right way to live, what things are most important in life, whether life has any significance, and if so what. (p. 44)

The conception of life of an individual has to be formulated in linguistic and artistic media, and in that sense it is dependent on the cultural practices which constitute the possibilities of formulation.

Conclusion

In the arts, language and many other aspects of human life, the possibility of *individual* development in thought and experience, so far from being restricted by, actually *depends* upon, the learning of the disciplines of objective, publicly shared cultural practices. It is seriously misleading to crave for and aim towards an unintelligible 'ideal' according to which individual potential can be fully realized only by avoiding or eradicating all such formative influences. Let me extend the quotation from Kant with which I introduced this chapter, which also indicates why I am so critical of resort to the metaphysical (I shall ignore the question of whether Kant's comments about Plato are justified):

> The light dove, cleaving the air in her free flight, and feeling its resistance, might imagine that her flight would be still easier in empty space. It was thus that Plato left the world of the senses as setting too narrow limits to the understanding and ventured out beyond it on the wings of ideas, in the empty space of the pure understanding. He did not observe that with all his efforts he made no advance — meeting no resistance that might, as it were, serve as a support upon which he could take a stand, to which he could apply his powers, and so set his understanding in motion. (Kant, 1929, p. 147)

There are, of course, no clear, definitive, general criteria which will determine when an individual is ready for extending his grasp of the medium (e.g. language, art form), and when, in the interests of his particular development, it is better for him to express himself freely within the limits of the medium he has already grasped. The general philosophical principle that the possibility of free expression is extended only by an extended grasp of the medium may be a valuable guideline, but to assess the particular needs of particular individuals will always require sensitive, informed judgment. This is why there can be no substitute for high quality teachers who are able to judge the time and methods appropriate for intervention, and the teaching of disciplines, so that individual potential in students is fulfilled, not inhibited.

It should be emphasised, because I have been misunderstood in this respect, that the point I am making has no bearing on the possibility of *spontaneous* feelings and responses. The point I am making is that it necessarily *requires* an understanding of the medium — artistic or linguistic — in order to be able to respond and to feel appropriately, whether spontaneously or not.

The development of individuality, in the arts as in other areas of human life, logically depends upon the learning of an objective, disciplined structure of thought and action, in that only such a structure can provide the ground on which to stand, and which can make sense of the notion of progress. It makes no sense to suggest that one can stand on, and move forward from, *nothing*.

In short, the commonly assumed polarity between freedom to express oneself and the learning of disciplines is completely misconceived, and potentially disastrous educationally. Kant's light dove would, both literally and metaphorically, be brought down to earth with a bump if it could attain its imagined ideal of escaping the resistant air in order to achieve *complete* freedom for flight. It cannot be free to fly in a vacuum: similarly, freedom for the progressive development of artistic individuality makes no sense in a subjectivist vacuum.

Chapter 7

Creativity

This chapter and the preceding one are closely related, in that the genesis of the notion of ideally 'free' expression is almost if not quite identical with that of a certain conception of what it is to be really creative. Nevertheless, there are important additional points to be brought out in relation specifically to creativity.

The source of the confusion is a pernicious aspect of the subjectivist doctrine, which is widely pervasive in arts education. This is one of the most important and plausible of the many guises of the doctrine. It is commensurately important to identify it and expose the educational damage it does, mainly to the arts, but across the whole curriculum, and even more widely into some of the most important aspects of life in general. Although our principal concern is with the arts, it should be emphasized, because of surprisingly prevalent misapprehensions on the issue, that one can be as creative in the sciences, mathematics and philosophy, and indeed in any other subject, as in poetry, drama, music or painting. In education, for instance, there is often supposed to be a *creative* area of the curriculum, which is usually assumed to be the exclusive province of the arts. This is an expression of the subjectivist Myth which was exposed in Chapter 1. The Myth is not only a distortion of the arts, it reflects a serious distortion of the character of education generally, since creativity is equally important in all subjects.

Creativity presents a challenge to my thesis in that it is unquestionably of central importance to the arts, as it should be to all aspects of education, yet at first sight it appears to be incompatible with the objective criteria which I have argued to be necessary for the rational support of artistic judgments, and *a fortiori* for any activity which has a legitimate place in education. To put the point another way, it is not immediately obvious how the creative attitudes which are so important to the arts can be educated. If an activity cannot be rationally assessed then it cannot be educated, and it is difficult to see by what criteria creativity can be assessed. No doubt it is some such thought which, understandably, underlies the thesis of an article in a British newspaper, whose title stated starkly 'Creativity cannot be taught' — a view which, one suspects, is shared by the majority of people, including many teachers.

The crucial question, then, which covers every part of the curriculum, and, indeed, which applies to many aspects of life generally, is: 'Can creativity be taught?' In some ways it may be less misleading to ask the question in terms of whether creativity can be *educated*, since the notion of teaching may carry different connotations. I shall return to this point later. However, the issues can be brought more sharply into focus if the former question is asked, and it will allow me to bring out some aspects of the concept of teaching.

The term 'creative' and its cognates are often used very loosely, so that anything one does is sometimes regarded as creative. To put it roughly, I shall be concerned with the concept of creativity as it is related to originality and imagination. Moreover, my argument applies equally to the creator and the spectator, for it requires imagination to understand a work of imagination.

The Inexplicability of Creativity

Any account of creativity has to recognize that, in a sense, there is something necessarily inexplicable about it, so that even those who are most creative are at a loss to explain it, or to say where their ideas come from. Thus the composer Elgar speaks of plucking his musical ideas from the air; Mozart writes of his ideas: 'Whence and how they come I know not; nor can I force them'. Gauss, of an arithmetical problem whose solution had eluded him for years, writes: 'Finally, two days ago, I succeeded, not on account of my painful efforts, but by the grace of God. Like a sudden flash of lightning, the riddle happened to be solved.' And when Picasso was asked 'What is creativity?', he replied: 'I don't know, and if I did, I wouldn't tell you.'

This characteristic makes the quest for an explanation of creative acts distinctly odd. For there is a sense in which an achievement could not be correctly called 'creative' if it *could* be explained. If it were possible to provide a theory which comprehensively explained how one had arrived at it, this would be sufficient to show that an achievement was *not* genuinely creative. For it is central to the meaning of the term that to be creative is, precisely, to do something *original*, which necessarily could not be achieved solely by following rules or conforming to the norms. It is only if what is achieved transcends or even changes the rules or norms that it could be creative. Hence the surprise often experienced by those who are most creative. The touching story is told of Haydn who, on hearing his *Creation* performed for the first time, burst into tears and exclaimed '*I* have not written this'.

It is important to recognize the character of the inexplicability of creativity. It has been objected against my thesis that the process of creativity is not now as inexplicable as it was. I do not deny that causal, perhaps psychological, conditions may be or may have been found to be conducive to creativity in certain kinds of activity, and even that it is conceivable, if highly unlikely, that a regularity should be found which would justify our confidence that creative acts would inevitably ensue when certain conditions were present. What I do deny is that such a regularity could be an answer to the question 'How did he produce that creative act?' Similarly, as I have stated above, I deny that rules, or a series of steps of learning, could be formulated which would constitute an explanation of how someone was able to be creative. The inexplicability is not empirical, and solvable in principle, but is internal to the concept of creativity. Any act which could be explained comprehensively could not, in virtue of the *meaning* of the term, count as creative. Thus, it is necessarily the case that there is and always will be something inexplicable about creativity.

It is, of course, precisely this problem which has led to the common assumption that there cannot be criteria for creativity; that creativity is a mysterious, purely subjective, 'inner' process which therefore cannot be taught. Once again, we are into the realm of unintelligible subjectivism. Its intrinsic self-contradictions become rapidly apparent, even on cursory reflection. For how is one supposed to understand supposedly occult 'inner' subjective mental processes, which the doctrine *itself* insists are totally impenetrable and incomprehensible to anyone else? So why have not arts educators, education theorists, psychologists, and many more, recognised these obvious flaws? The answer is to be found in a point which I have already emphasised, yet which can hardly be over-emphasised, namely that the subjectivist doctrine is so deeply ingrained that it can hardly be regarded as an *assumption* at all. All of us have been brought up on it, so that it takes a great effort of will and imagination to escape from it in order objectively to consider whether or not it makes sense. We are so thoroughly impregnated with it that we are oblivious of it. So completely are we in its grip that it is the *foundation* of, the starting point for, our thinking about the arts and creativity generally. Moreover, it is constantly reinforced by influential theorists. Yet, as I have said, there is no hope of providing a sound justification for the arts in education until this stale and fatally damaging subjectivist doctrine is decisively rejected, and replaced by fresh, rigorous thinking.

The difficulty, then, is to look at the situation without the doctrinal coloured spectacles which distort the vision of most arts educators. The fresh conception is intrinsically much easier to understand than the subjectivist doctrine. However, the deep difficulty is to recognise that the intelligible answers to the problems of understanding creativity *lie on the surface*. Linguistic and artistic meaning are not symbolic, and given by reference to deeper occult 'inner' experiences, or metaphysical Forms. The depth of the meaning lies on the surface, in the way in which language is used, and the art work is created, within a certain cultural context. Similarly, it makes no sense to locate creativity ultimately in occult mental experiences. Creativity occurs, and is recognisable, on the surface, in what people *do* and *say*.

The subjectivist doctrine involves some obvious and bizarre inconsistencies. For example, after even cursory reflection, it is obvious that those who assume creativity to be a matter of a purely subjective 'inner' process, for which there can be no objective criteria, inevitably contradict themselves. They insist that there can be no criteria for assessment of creativity, yet they usually have the highest esteem for those who are creative. But on what is this esteem based? Certainly not by unintelligible reference to incomprehensible 'inner' processes. Only, of course, on the basis of *objective* criteria can one assess Mozart as more creative than Salieri.

To recognize something as creative *is* to employ objective criteria. It is not, of course, a matter of employing a technique. It is a point of considerable significance that one can recognize something as creative even though one may not be able to *state* the criteria for creativity. Indeed, as we saw in Chapter 2, a practice such as language, which necessarily incorporates objective criteria for correct and incorrect use, must already be a going concern before it is possible to try to discern and state explicitly what those criteria are. And it is certainly possible to use language correctly, in general, without being able to state what are the rules of correct usage. Indeed, *most* people do so. We could not understand each other at all if it were not true that, in general, we all use language more or less correctly.

And the ability to use it so that we do understand each other, *exhibits* criteria for correct use. The same is true of inductive and deductive reasoning, in that the ability to state or codify their criteria of validity is possible only as a description of criteria which are already in use. The distinction is important for several reasons, of which one is that there is sometimes a tendency to deny that there are objective criteria because of the difficulty of stating explicitly what they are.

The Limits of Creativity

It may already be clear from the argument of this chapter and the previous one that the creative *process* cannot intelligibly be regarded as logically distinct from the creative *product*. That is, the process can be identified only by the product; the process can be described only by reference to the product. So to assess and consider creativity we have to concentrate on the *product*, i.e. what lies on the surface.

The implications for learning and teaching the arts are of considerable importance, for creativity can indeed be educated but only by assessing the product as creative. To be creative requires a grasp of the criteria of validity and value of the activity in question. As we saw in Chapter 5, originality is given its sense only against a background of the traditional. To count as creative an achievement must go beyond simply following rules or conventional practices, yet it cannot be merely subjective: it is not sufficient simply to be divergent or different in any way whatsoever. It has to diverge from the norms in a way which is appropriate, and this implies that there are objective constraints. The quotation at the beginning of Chapter 6 illustrates the point, for just as the dove could not be free to fly without the resistant air, so there could be no sense to creativity in the absence of constraints. To adapt a phrase from Chapter 3, creativity has indefinite but not unlimited scope, for it is the objective limits which give sense to the notion of the creative or imaginative. Similarly, there may be indefinitely many ways of scoring a goal in soccer or hockey, but clearly there are limits on what can count as scoring a goal. To put the point in a paradoxical way, not *anything* can count as a goal, and not *anything* can count as creative. Yet, on a subjectivist view, where there are no objective constraints whatsoever, *anything could* be creative. Which is the same as saying that *nothing* could count as creative.

To see the figure in Chapter 3 as a duck or as a rabbit would not count as creative or imaginative, since it would be too obvious or conventional. Yet neither could it be creative to suggest that it could be seen as the Eiffel Tower. Certainly that interpretation is not obvious or conventional, but it cannot count as creative since it goes beyond the limits of intelligibility. An ingenious member of one of my audiences once denied even this, and suggested that the rabbit is looking up, over-awed, at an Eiffel Tower which is so extraordinary and beyond his comprehension that it could not itself be represented. Whether or not that could count as an interpretation of the drawing, it significantly underlines the point I am making that in order to make that interpretation intelligible ingenious reasons have to be given which derive their sense from the features of the drawing. The same is true of the suggestion of any other unusually imaginative interpretation. In Chapter 3, I said that the figure could be seen as a duck or as a rabbit, but not as a clock. Yet it can. It is a quarter to nine, or a quarter past three for someone standing on his head. To see it in either of these ways requires imagination, but it is certainly not purely subjective. Imagination is given its *sense* by the objective constraints. I would defy anyone, for instance, to see it as half past eight.

A philosopher in a meeting of a Canadian philosophical society once raised the supposed objection that the figure reminded him neither of a duck nor of a rabbit, but of a lake he knew in northern Ontario — with an island where the eye of the duck is. But, of course, so far from constituting an objection, this supports my case, since it reminded him of the lake *only* because of its similar shape. This again makes a point which I want strongly to emphasise, since it is the key to understanding not only the problem of creativity, but also much of the positive thesis of this book, which is that imagination is *imagination* only in so far as it operates within limits. Perhaps one can see the figure as a Scottish bagpipe, and no doubt with some ingenuity one could think of many other possibilities, but what I wish to emphasize is that there is no sense in the notion of using one's imagination if *anything whatsoever* could count as a valid interpretation. The objective limits are the preconditions of and set the scope for creativity, and it is in this sense that the scope is indefinite but not unlimited.

The Grounds of Creativity

The sense of creativity is given by the criteria which are already in use, although the creative person may modify and extend those criteria to some extent. An evaluation of Picasso's work said that he had altered the horizons of art. That is, the creative genius is involved in conceptual change, in that he is to some extent changing the criteria for what counts as art, and good art. As we saw in Chapter 5, the aspiration to change *everything*, to make *all* things new, is incoherent. It is possible to move somewhere else only if one is already somewhere, and where one can move next depends on where one is now.

The point can be illustrated by analogy with the sailor who wants to restructure his ship in mid-ocean. Obviously he cannot abandon the ship to rebuild it from the beginning, since he needs the support of the main structure while he makes the changes. What changes he can make, and how quickly he can make them, depend on the character of the original. Nevertheless, progressively, he may be able to make considerable, even radical, alterations to the structure of the ship, while depending upon its support.

There is also an important disanalogy here. The problem of rebuilding the ship is a contingent one, whereas the point I am making concerns the possibility of changing or extending concepts. Since it is the concept which gives sense to art and to what counts as innovation in art, one cannot simply abandon the concept one has in order to adopt a completely new one. Any innovation, to be understood as an artistic innovation, necessarily employs many of the criteria of the concept it is changing.

This issue is related to Chapter 6 in that a competent grasp of the discipline, techniques and criteria of an activity is necessary for the possibility of being creative in it. Yet it is often believed that to be really original or creative it is necessary to avoid such supposedly conformist influences. Thus, for instance, Witkin (1980, p. 92) insists that creative vision is *inhibited* by learned technique. In fact, on the contrary, it is only if one has learned the techniques of philosophical thinking, for instance, that one can have creative vision, or be original, in philosophy. As we saw in Chapter 6, the methodological point that certain ways of teaching the disciplines of an activity can inhibit creativity should not be confused with the philosophical point that without a grasp of those disciplines it would be impossible to be creative at all. Moreover, the greater the mastery of the discipline, the greater is one's possibility of creativity, as will be clear from the example of language.

Another parallel with Chapter 6 is that artistic creativity cannot be purely private, autonomous or subjective in the sense of being distinct from the public medium of the art form. In this sense individual creativity depends upon the public practice. However, this raises another issue which I have so far ignored. I have argued that there must be criteria for creativity; that there are limits to what can count as creative. But is it the case that these criteria must be publicly expressible, or could there be private criteria? It may be objected that, although I have run these two points together, both here and in Chapter 6, it is not obvious that they are the same, or that the latter follows from the former. However, on reflection it can be seen that they are the same, since the notion of a purely private criterion makes no sense. Consider, for instance, the crucial notion of correctness. There could be no sense in the supposition of purely private correctness, since there could be no independent check, in which case there could be no distinction between seeming to be correct, and being correct. It is only in relation to an independent, publicly shared objective standard that anything can count as even approximately correct. This is not, of course, to deny the possibility of thinking silently to oneself. That is, I am certainly not arguing that a use of language, for instance, can be correct only if overtly expressed. The crucial point I am making is that it must be *potentially* expressible, since it is necessarily formulated, in a *public* medium. Similarly, the limits which set the criteria for creative acts must be public and in that sense independent. If the criteria for what counts as creative are necessarily shared, then that necessarily entails that they must be potentially expressible, even if they are not in fact expressed.

This point will arise again shortly, but it is worth pointing out that to insist on the existence of a public practice or medium as a precondition of individual creativity is certainly not to espouse behaviourism, structuralism, or formalism (i.e. roughly the notion that only the physical properties of a work of art can intelligibly be regarded as relevant to meaning and appreciation). There is a tendency to suffer from what might be called the disease of the dichotomous mind, that is, in this case, to assume that if one criticizes subjectivism one must be committed to behaviourism. Contrary to what is often assumed, these two kinds of theory do not exhaust the possibilities of accounting for mental phenomena. It is sufficient here to emphasize that my insistence that individual creativity depends upon the existence and grasp of a social practice is not a denial that there are mental experiences which are not publicly expressed. It is a denial that the relevant mental experiences could intelligibly be regarded as logically independent of overt, cultural practices or media, such as language and art forms.

The Creative Process

The preceding discussion indicates why one has suspicions about the intelligibility of a common use of the term 'the creative process', and of construing the distinction between process and product in ways which suggest that creativity is a purely private process going on in the inaccessible recesses of the mind. That, of course, would make creativity purely subjective, and impossible to assess and educate. The point can be illustrated by reference to the notion of inspiration. It is sometimes thought that inspiration consists in a sudden flash of purely private, 'inner' experience. Yet it is not the supposed mysterious mental experience which is the criterion of inspiration, but what is *produced*, and in order to be able to produce it one needs to have learned the requisite discipline of the medium of expression. A claim to be creative could not be justified by reference to a supposed inner mental experience of a creative process, in the absence of a creative product. Conversely, it would count as creative if one were regularly to produce work of striking originality even though one never had the supposed mental experience of a creative process. The product, not some 'inner' process, is the criterion of creativity.

Before continuing, I should like to mention that, although I have taken notable examples in order to make the point clearly, I do not wish to be misunderstood as implying that creativity is possible only for the genius. A child may legitimately be regarded as having manifested creative ability if he has produced something which transcends the rules even if, in comparison with others, it is not original. Similarly, an undergraduate can show creative ability by thinking his own way to a position even though it may be a conclusion reached by Plato. It would not, of course, count as creative if he had merely regurgitated the Platonic argument, or, if that were possible, he had simply followed certain logical rules which had led to that conclusion.

One reason for my raising this issue is that it is sometimes formulated in a misleading way. For instance, it has been said that the process of creating may result in a product which is not strikingly original, yet what matters is the distinctive *feeling* of being creative, since this experience is one of the great contributions which education can offer to almost all pupils. Although I entirely endorse the encouragement of creativity in all students and in all subjects, this way of putting the matter is seriously mistaken for three reasons.

(a) Although I neither deny nor accept that there may be characteristic feelings which accompany creative acts, it seems to me, in view of the huge variety of activities in which it is possible to be creative, that the occurrence of a distinctive creative feeling or experience is highly unlikely. The postulation of such a feeling may be a manifestation of the essentialist fallacy which will be discussed in Chapter 8.

(b) More important, even if there should be such a feeling or experience, it is irrelevant, since it is not the *feeling* of being creative but *being* creative which is of such importance in education. As I pointed out above, it is not the feeling, or 'inner' subjective mental process, which is the criterion of creativity, but what is produced. To put the matter another way, if it were possible to give a drug which would produce a feeling of creativity this would not in the least imply that what was achieved as a consequence was creative, nor would it have any relevance to the education of creativity.

(c) If, on the other hand, it is objected that the feeling concerned is not merely a concomitant one, that is, one which is regularly correlated with creative acts, but is rather a feeling which is uniquely identified by creative acts, then it would be parasitic upon what is produced as a creative product. That is, the notion of such a feeling is given its sense and necessarily identified by reference to behaviour or products which are recognized as creative. For example, one could make no sense of the suggestion that someone could have such a creative feeling as a result of picking up a spade, in normal circumstances, whereas it might make sense where someone was writing a poem.

This unintelligible subjectivist notion of a private 'inner' creative mental process has also been used in support of the expedient idea that the arts constitute a generic area of the curriculum. I have considered this confused, and potentially distorting, idea more fully elsewhere (Best, 1990; 1992). The claim is that all the arts involve the same, or similar, creative processes. (See, for instance, K. Robinson, in *The Future of the Arts in Schools*, 1989. But he, like many other art educators uses this notion extensively, without ever questioning whether it makes sense, and its potentially damaging educational consequences.) When one considers what is actually *done*, for instance, in the *activities* of playing the trumpet, composing poetry, creating a painting, dancing, and doing drama, there is, of course, obviously no such similarity. The proponents of the generic thesis would probably agree, for to support their claim they resort to construing the supposed 'creative processes' as purely subjective, 'inner' mental ones. Again, we are in the realm of unintelligible metaphysics. Yet it is surprising how commonly and unquestioningly this absurd claim is glibly made about the supposedly similar 'inner' creative processes involved in the various art forms.

One underlying reason for this is that when a term such as 'the creative process' is used, there is a prevalent assumption that it must *name* something. Since the varied character of creative artistic activities cannot plausibly be regarded as what is named by the term 'creative process', it is assumed that what is named must be something inaccessibly subjective. I have outlined the confusions of the common misconception that the meaning of a word is given by its naming something, elsewhere (Best, 1974, pp. 15–21). There is far more to be said than I can include here about what is known in philosophy as the denotational theory of meaning. It is a major source of fundamental confusion, in the arts and generally.

Let me offer another example of the problems engendered both by the naming view and by the subjectivist/metaphysical confusion to which it often leads. I attended a meeting to consider the critical situation for the arts in education. One of the speakers stated categorically: 'The arts *must* have common ground, if the term 'arts' means anything'. This is a classic example of the misconception that the meaning of a word, in this case 'art', necessarily entails that it *names* something. Closely related to this assumption is the essentialist fallacy, a further example of which we shall see in Chapter 8. In this case, the fallacy is the assumption that since the term 'art' is used to refer to the various art forms, it must name some *essential* characteristic which is common to them all.

So, at the meeting, I questioned the categorical statement of the common fallacy. The original speaker was supported by the Chairman, who stated as if it were general and unquestionable knowledge: 'The creative process is the same in any art form — so the psychologists tell us'. But it does not matter who tells us, the assumption is thoroughly confused. When I drew attention to the educational danger that on this assumption only one art form would be needed in the curriculum in order to develop this so-called 'same' creative process, he countered as follows. 'Some people,' he said, 'develop it better in one medium rather than another'. Clearly, this is still dangerous, because it could reasonably be contended by our educational masters that, in view of the economic constraints, *one* art form would give *everyone* the opportunity to develop this general artistic creative process at least to *some* extent.

The more fundamental and fatal objection, and the point which I mainly want to illustrate, can be expressed by asking what are the *criteria* for the creative process, i.e. what *counts* as a creative process? (I am reluctant to use this term because of its common, dubious implications.) Clearly the *only* criteria for artistic creativity are to be found in the ways in which art-works *are actually created*. And that is to say that the criteria are particular to *particular* works and forms of art — there is creative choreography, drama, poetry etc. What sense can be made of this supposed *general* creative process, i.e. independent of any particular art form and hidden in the private recesses of minds?

A remarkable example of this tendency towards the vacuity or unintelligibility of such supposed general inner mental states occurred during the strike, in the UK, of ambulance drivers and attendants. Because of the emergency in the service, troops were brought in to man ambulances. Some were army bandsmen. A radio interviewer asked a commanding officer whether bandsmen could cope with the pressures of working in the public gaze when dealing with an emergency, such as a serious road accident. Yes, he replied, he was quite confident since, as performing musicians, they were accustomed to coping with the pressures of working in the public gaze.

When I give this example at conferences etc, my audiences laugh at the obvious absurdity of believing that there is some general mental state, 'coping with the pressures of working in the public gaze', which can be applied to, and developed by, any and all of the huge variety of possible cases. In particular, it is patently absurd to believe that coping with the pressure of playing one's tuba in public has any relation to, or is any help in, coping with a serious road accident with bystanders watching. Such a notion is obviously silly (although the anecdote is a true one). Yet many people fail to recognise that the reference to 'the same, or similar, creative processes', in this sense of general, occult, subjective processes, is equally silly.

A clear example of the disastrous practical educational damage created by this kind of conception can be seen in the recent (as I write) Proposal of the Secretary of State for Education and Science (August 1991) that in the National Curriculum in England and Wales, Art and Music will not be compulsory at Key Stage 4 (the age of fourteen, approximately), but after that 'it is our view that all schools should offer some form of aesthetic experience in the curriculum for all 14–16 year olds'. The generality here is even worse than that of a supposed 'arts' general experience, and involves the common, and dangerously misleading, conflation of the aesthetic and the artistic which has already been mentioned, and which will be more carefully considered in Chapter 12. To put the point briefly, this latest diktat seems to imply that *any* aesthetic experience will do, since it will be part of and contribute to the general 'aesthetic'. In which case gazing at sunsets, or autumn colours would be adequate, and the arts would become otiose.

It is a metaphysical nonsense, which is having damaging practical educational consequences, to assume that there is a general aesthetic experience, and/or that there are general, 'inner' subjective, creative processes, which are common to all the arts (and to creativity in science, mathematics, geography, history?). Artistic experience, and artistic creativity, are *particular* to each art form. To deny children and students experience of drama and dance is to deny them experiences which it makes *no* sense to say that they can gain from other art forms. The philosophical senselessness, and the serious educational damage, of the notion of a general, 'inner' creative process, is stark.

In short, it is a serious confusion to be trying to look inwards for the criteria of creativity, as 'inner' subjective feelings or processes; we should be looking rather at the creative character of activities and of what is created. Creativity is not to be found by an unintelligible delving into occult 'inner' processes, whether one's own or someone else's. It is to be found in the character of the work of art, the use of language, the way someone behaves. To repeat, the depth of the problem lies on the surface.

It is important to recognise that there is another meaning of the term 'creative process', which does not necessarily carry implications of a subjective experience or event. To argue for the importance of the process rather than the product, in education, may be to emphasize the importance of learning to understand the character of a subject, rather than concentrating on the details of a carefully finished result; it may indicate the importance of knowing *how* to achieve a result, and of experimenting freely with various methods; it may amount to urging that students should immerse themselves in various ways in the medium, in order to come to a personally meaningful understanding of it. Nevertheless, the term 'creative process' is often taken to designate a kind of 'inner', private psychological mechanism, inaccessible to any observer, and therefore incapable of assessment or being educated. It is reported that one of his former students wrote to Wittgenstein to say that he had had the wonderful experience of being converted to Roman Catholicism. Wittgenstein replied: 'When I hear that someone has bought mountaineering equipment I want to see how he uses it.'

Much of the confused argument on this question is created by running together these two senses of the term 'creative process'. Thus in arguing that the *subjective* sense of the 'creative process' is philosophically confused and educationally disastrous, one is sometimes thought to be arguing *against* the educational importance of the 'creative process' in the experimentation sense. In fact, I strongly support the importance of stimulating the creative process, in the latter sense, as I have argued elsewhere, (Best, 1991). But, to repeat, the two meanings tend to be so frequently conflated that I have become very reluctant to use the term 'the creative process', or to offer support for it.

To emphasise the point again: the 'creative process' in the subjective sense makes no sense philosophically, and has led to disastrous educational consequences. The 'creative process' in the experimentation sense is of crucial educational value, which needs to be emphasised, especially at this time when distortingly rigid and narrow conceptions of education are being imposed.

Although this aspect of subjectivism remains prevalent in theory, in practice teachers normally contradict it by teaching the disciplines of painting, drama, music, language, and so on, and by assessing progress. They are aware of the greater scope for creativity which they give to students as a consequence. It is important to recognize that one's scope for creative possibilities will be limited unless one has a good grasp of the relevant discipline. To take an obvious example, if one has no technique at all one cannot be creative in skiing; if one has limited technique one has some scope for creative skiing; and if one has mastered the sophisticated techniques of skiing one's scope for creative skiing is considerably greater. To repeat, this is not inimical to spontaneous creativity. Martha Graham once said that it takes at least five years of training in the discipline to be spontaneous in dance, which brings out how misconceived is the notion that creativity is inhibited by learned technique. On the contrary, although of course technical competence does not necessarily give creative flair, it is a necessary precondition for such flair, in any subject, discipline, or activity.

Personal Relationships

This section is oblique to my main thesis, but it is so important that I could not resist inserting a mention of it, although I can merely hint at the outline of an argument, and how it relates to the principal questions raised in this book.

Nowhere is creativity, and objectivity, more important than in personal relationships. It is sadly significant that it so often causes surprise when I draw attention to this. Thomas Hardy, in *The Mayor of Casterbridge*, illustrates what at first sight may seem a relatively innocuous, but what is in fact a prevalent and perniciously destructive, manifestation of a lack of creativity. Referring to a couple who could be seen in the distance, he writes that their attitude of stale familiarity denoted man and wife. It is a depressing truth that one can often recognise a couple as a married couple because of this attitude of stale familiarity.

Simone Weil (1968, p. 161) points out how tragically often we *invent* what other people are thinking and feeling. That is, we *impose* our subjective feelings upon them because we have not developed the imaginative, objective capacity to move *outside* our own preconceived limitations in order to appreciate what *they* — the *other* people — think and feel.

Thus, for instance, most people are incapable of really *listening* to others, especially in this age of the blunting of sensibilities by background television and pop music, and the trite unheeded twitterings of disc jockeys and chat-show presenters. Conversation becomes a dialogue between deaf people. Consequently *real human beings* pass by as vague, undifferentiated blurs on the television screen which *comprises* life for far too many people.

Simone Weil (1952) writes that *every* human being cries out silently to be read *differently*. Yet too often we impose, as our vision of them, bland clichés; we impose the sacrilege of a wash of generalised feelings, because we have not developed the objective ability to recognise, respect and value, what is in *them*. The *objective particulars* of a unique, individual human being should be of *paramount* importance. And we should encourage a similar *particular* respect for each work of art. As Martha Nussbaum (1985) puts it: 'Our highest and hardest task is to make ourselves creatures on whom *nothing is lost*.' (p. 516)

Tolstoy makes a memorable point in his story *The Kreutzer Sonata*. The main character lives the conventional life of a Russian aristocrat, whoring, socialising, etc., and has the conventional attitude to his wife, as the mother of his children, housekeeper etc. It is only on her *death bed* that, suddenly, for the first time, he sees her, not merely as his wife, as a *human being*. As Simone Weil (1952) puts it: 'Belief in the existence of *other* human beings *as such*, is love'.

Imagination and the Truth

In a lecture, the playwright Edward Bond pointed out a common misconception about imagination in art. It is commonly assumed that because imagination is central to the arts this implies that they are concerned not with truth or reality but with fantasy, illusion, escapism. In fact, it often requires imagination to peel away illusions in order to see the truth, and it can involve a creative struggle to achieve the precise formulation of a medium necessary for expressing and recognizing true insights. The point struck me forcibly when I first studied the preliminary sketches, and then the finished work, in which Picasso expressed his reaction to the news of the bombing of Guernica. One could clearly see in these sketches the progressive creative effort to achieve a vision of the truth.

The late Francis Bacon has said about his own work that it is not imagination, it is reality. This is making the point that the imagination of a serious artist is emphatically *not* fantasy or escapism. There may be nothing of that kind in his work. Nevertheless, in a more important sense, no one who has seen Francis Bacon's work could fail to be impressed by the imaginative power of it. Imagination, in this sense, is *necessary* for the artist to express, and for us to understand, the *reality* of his vision. In this sense, it is imagination which gives the reality; imagination is inseparable from reality.

The creative vision or imagination of the artist is required to penetrate romantic illusions which preclude a truthful, objective conception of reality. An example will illustrate three of the points I have been trying to bring out, which are (a) imagination may be required to see the truth; (b) a high degree of understanding and competence in a medium is required in order to be free to express the truth; (c) creative or imaginative vision is possible only as a development out of already existent conventions. My example is that of the English poets of the First World War.

At the beginning of the war the prevailing spirit in society was that of stirring romantic nationalism, and the language of poetry was that of the Romantics such as Keats. Within this mode Rupert Brooke wrote of the glory of dying for one's country, and the spirit of national pride was evident in his writing of there being, when a soldier was killed and buried, 'some corner of a foreign field that is forever England'. Harsh and brutal experience gave a very different conception of the reality of war. Thus, as a consequence of his bitterly disillusioning experience, Rudyard Kipling wrote: 'If they ask you why we died, tell them "because our fathers lied".'

The later poets, as a consequence of their personal experience, came to see war not as a matter of romantic, flag-waving heroism, but of mud, blood, and countless, utterly pointless, agonies, and senseless maiming and slaughter. It was out of the depths of this kind of experience that Wilfrid Owen wrote of the old lie '*Dulce et decorum est pro patria mori*' — the old *lie* that it is sweet and glorious to die for one's country.

For the purposes of my example, it is important to recognize that although one can appreciate Kipling's and Owen's bitter expression, there is an important sense in which this was not a *lie*. Before and in the early stages of the war this was effectively the *only* language for, conception of, and therefore vision of, war. The early poets could use only the medium they had, and this language and conception was so dominant that it was almost impossible for them to have any other kind of thought about war. The ways of seeing and thinking were necessarily tied to the language available to them. They did not have the language, the concepts, to see what they later came to recognize as the truth. Owen and the others had to *create* a language in terms of which this conception of the reality of war could be understood and expressed. The *words* did not have to be created, since they were already available. What had to be created was a very different use of those words to give very different conceptions of the realities of war. Even though the same *words* were used, they had to be used to express different concepts.

For example, at certain periods in history, it would quite literally have amounted to a self-contradiction to say that a man who refused to fight in a war was exhibiting courage. That is, the concept of courage was such that it entailed a willingness to fight. Shakespeare's *Coriolanus* brings out very well how concepts such as courage, honour and loyalty can be logically tied to notions of military valour, and how difficult it can be to think in different ways, and espouse different conceptions of virtue. This kind of creation is far more difficult to achieve than is often realized, since it amounts to changing patterns of thought which have been deeply set — so deeply that they are the very *foundation* of thought. One needs only to consider some of the films about and propaganda of war to appreciate that hundreds of thousands of men have sacrificed their lives, at least partly because of an inability to think and feel *outside* 'the old lie'. Films such as *All Quiet on the Western Front*, and *Gallipoli*, to name only two, bring out clearly the enormous power of 'the old lie', which can induce men, in wave after wave, to climb out of trenches and charge pointlessly at murderous machine-gun fire, knowing very well that there is no hope at all even of survival, let alone success.

The enormous power of the prevailing uses of language, which set the ways of thought of a society, and the difficulty of detaching oneself from them, can hardly be over-emphasized. It is commensurately difficult to change the uses of language. It needed poets, and it could not be achieved immediately. Thus, if one examines Owen's poetry carefully it is possible, I submit, to see clear evidence of his creative struggle from his roots in the linguistic and poetic conceptions in which he grew up, and which constituted the foundations which made his originality possible. Inevitably, he often slips back to those neo-Keatsian Romantic roots, for he was involved in a creative struggle to construct a language in which his conception of the truth about war could be expressed. He was like the mariner restructuring his ship in mid-ocean. He could not start afresh, but had to depend on the given conceptions in order to alter them. Yet the changes made by Owen and his contemporaries were quite remarkable. By the end of the war they had no romantic conception of it; these poets were seeing clearly, and expressing vividly, what they could now see as the stark truth of pointless death and suffering. Nationalistic fervour, previously central to the poetic vision of war, became to-tally, inhumanly, irrelevant, and their compassion was for *all* soldiers, friend and foe, caught up in the mindless savagery of destruction.

The ability to see and express what was now recognized as the truth about war required the imagination to expose romantic illusions; it required the creation of a different poetic and perceptive medium of language; yet it necessarily had to grow out of conceptions which were already there.

Creativity and Education

In teaching the disciplines and criteria of a subject, the teacher is progressively extending the students' possibility of creativity. On a subjectivist view where, for instance, the 'creative process' is taken to be necessarily private, autonomous, and independent of potential expression in a public medium, no sense can be made of assessing what, if any, creative ideas a student may have. *Any* work produced could be the expression of *any* creative idea or none. Thus there could be no place for learning, and the progressive enlarging of understanding and scope for creativity. Moreover, for a student to recognize the progress *he himself* is making it is necessary that he should be learning the difficult task of self-evaluation — that is, of applying objective criteria to his own work.

Yet does not the most important question remain unanswered? An art educator once objected: 'I agree that you can teach and assess the techniques, but surely not the creativity *itself*, and that is the crucial problem.' There is, of course, a distinction between competence in expressive techniques, and having something to express. A work of art or an essay can be technically perfect, yet have nothing to say. It is significant, for instance, that to call a performing artist a good technician is in effect to criticize him as lacking the vital spark. But what does it amount to to say that creativity cannot be taught? One implication is that the *potential* to produce creative, imaginative original work cannot be taught. Yet it is impossible to teach *anything* to someone who has no aptitude. No amount of coaching in technical skills will make a tennis player out of a person who simply lacks an eye for a ball.

However, there may be more to this objection, and this raises the distinction between 'teach' and 'educate' to which I referred earlier. The term 'teaching' carries the implication, for many people, of something like giving a set of rules which, if followed, will produce the required results. In this sense, multiplication tables, the rules of chess, and many other activities, can be taught, whereas creativity cannot. Because of this implication, it may be preferable to ask the question whether creativity can be educated, rather than taught, although the use of the latter term does not necessarily carry the implications indicated. I shall use the two terms interchangeably, in order to bring out important aspects of both, and since my use of the term 'teaching' does not carry the implication of simply offering a set of rules.

There is a further objection which may arise. Someone may say: 'It is possible to show a person how to develop his own creativity, but it is impossible to *teach* him creativity.' But what kind of distinction does someone have in mind who says this? Often underlying it is the notion that teaching or education somehow *imposes limitations*, whereas learning is a matter of one's own free discovery. I do not wish to deny that there is something of importance in that distinction, but if we are not careful we shall be on the slippery slope to the incoherent contention which we have already discussed, namely that *real* creativity requires a complete absence of the supposed limitations of the disciplines of a medium. Yet even the most extreme disciple of free expression, who insists that the teacher must never impose on his students, will inevitably have to contradict his own view to some extent. For even setting up the conditions in which students can most effectively learn is imposing a situation on them in some sense. For example, if he were to deny this and say: 'I don't impose any limitations whatsoever. I simply give out the paint brushes, paints and paper and leave them to it', this would still impose certain expectations on them. Wouldn't it be less of an imposition to give them, for instance, sticks, horsehair and glue? But even *that* is an imposition — so what about simply showing them an oak tree and a horse?

This should be enough to demonstrate the unintelligibility of supposing that learning can be achieved without the imposition of any expectations and therefore limitations at all. What is a serious question, of course, is how much and what kinds of imposition are the most fruitful for learning. (The term 'imposition' is an unfortunate one anyway. I have used it solely to make the point clearly.) The important point is that we should try to ensure that the conditions which are set should progressively open doors for students, not close them. Nevertheless, we should be clear that setting conditions is unavoidable.

Can Creativity Be Educated?

Kant's light dove craves an unintelligible ideal. The resistant air is not a handicap to but a precondition of free flight. The notion of being creative in a vacuum is not just impossible, it makes no sense. The very sense of creativity is given by the medium, discipline and criteria of the relevant subject or activity.

In a radio interview, the extraordinarily original jazz trumpeter Dizzie Gillespie was asked whether it was his *lack* of any tuition which had allowed him to develop his highly creative, individual style. He replied, most emphatically: 'No, I should say not. A teacher is a short cut.' The interviewer pressed the point and asked: 'But wouldn't a teacher, at least to *some* extent, have limited the development of your own particular style?' To which Dizzie Gillespie replied: 'Not a good teacher.'

This indicates that a definition of good teaching or education might be that it consists in the creation of those conditions which are most conducive to the students' learning. It can now be appreciated how the original question can be answered, for in that sense creativity can certainly be educated.

Chapter 8

Feeling

As we have seen, the kinds of feeling which play a central role in the creation and appreciation of the arts necessarily involve understanding or cognition. Thus, although an animal may respond to a work of art, it is not capable of an *artistic* response, since that requires understanding. This underlines the emphasis in Chapters 6 and 7 on the medium, of language and the forms of art, without which such understanding and therefore such *feelings* could not exist. In this respect the notion of the object of an emotion, that is, the object towards which the emotion is directed, is of central importance, since it determines the character of the feeling.

An underlying misconception about mental attributes is the source of confusion in many arts educators, such as Louis Arnaud Reid, and Elliott Eisner. A central issue is the common subjectivist misconception that the arts, like language, were created in order to express and communicate discrete, 'inner' ideas and feelings. Yet it makes no sense to suppose that these ideas and feelings could exist prior to and independently of the arts and language. This has important implications for education, in that in learning to grasp the media of the arts, students are acquiring the possibility of *experiencing feelings*.

Emotions

Some arts educators, and some psychologists, are tempted to locate emotional feelings in, and even to equate them with, sensations. This temptation is reinforced by the fact that intense emotions, on which it is natural to focus to find the essence of emotional feelings, are characterized by sensations and physical changes, such as an increase in pulse rate, paling, perspiring and flushing.

However, it is seriously mistaken to assume that, even in such extreme cases, the physical changes or sensations are what the emotion essentially consists in. For instance, it would be possible in principle to produce the same sensations and physical changes by means of drugs, or electrical apparatus, but clearly the subject would not necessarily, as a consequence, be feeling the appropriate emotion. Incidentally, this reveals the confusion in the prevalent assumption that emotions can be measured, for instance, by measuring the intensity of physical changes by psychogalvanic reflex. Measuring the physical changes is not measuring the emotion. Emotions cannot be measured, not because it is too difficult but because the very notion of measuring emotions makes no sense.

The criterion of a man's being angry is not, for instance, his high blood pressure, but what he says and does. If it should be objected that nevertheless there is a correlation between anger and high blood pressure, then the point is implicitly conceded, since the behaviour has to be recognized as anger-behaviour prior to, and in order to investigate, the possible correlation. A scientist can conduct such an investigation only if he *already* knows what it is for someone to be angry. And that is to concede that it is the anger-*behaviour*, including verbal behaviour, which is the criterion of anger. Moreover, emotions which involve sensations and physical changes are by no means typical. There are no sensations, changes of pulse rate, perspirings or palings in very many cases which one describes by the use of emotion terms. For instance, I may be annoyed, disappointed, delighted or afraid without experiencing any sensations or physical changes.

The mistake is largely a consequence of the assumption that there must be some essential distinguishing feature of emotions, and the most natural place to look for this is in the extreme cases, that is, intense emotions, where sensations and physical changes do characteristically occur. To repeat, it is the underlying assumption which is the source of the confusion, namely that there *is* an essence to be found. Sometimes this essentialist fallacy, as it is commonly called, is implied in the misleading question: 'What do emotions *consist in*?'

Consider the analogous question: 'What does expecting consist in?' There is a wide variety of cases, and it is misleading to assume that there must be an essence, most easily recognizable in extreme cases such as expecting an explosion. In such a case there may be physical sensations and behavioural characteristics, for example if one were tense, covering one's ears, and with all one's attention directed on to the forthcoming event. Yet contrast that case with my expecting someone to visit me on a specific date in a few months. The appointment may be written in my diary, and I have not forgotten it. If I were asked I should reply that I am expecting the visit, but there is nothing going on in me which constitutes the expecting. It could even be truly said of me, when I am asleep, that I am expecting the visit. In such a case it would be very odd to ask what my expecting consists in. In the case of expecting the explosion, there are plausible candidates for what the expecting consists in, that is, in my behaviour, sensations and thoughts. If one assumes that there must be an essence of all cases of expecting — an essence, which is most clearly manifest in such extreme cases — this will lead to confusion in others. The temptation, again, is to postulate some indiscernible 'inner', subjective mental event as what the expecting consists in. But what shows that I am expecting the visit is not my experiencing such a mental event, (even if that were to make sense), but my saying that I remember the appointment, my not arranging to be out on that day and so on. The expecting does not *consist in* anything *going on in me now*. On the contrary, in order to appreciate that this is a case of expecting one has to take account of ways in which I speak and behave at *other* times.

Similarly, to ask what an emotion consists in tempts one to identify it with something which is going on at the time, and sensations are obvious candidates if one considers extreme cases. But, to repeat, many emotions involve no sensations, and even where sensations are characteristically involved, the emotions cannot be said to consist in them. This point underlies the humorous remark of someone who had the sensation of a lump in his throat. He said that he was uncertain whether it indicated that he had tonsillitis, or was in love. The important issue here is that contextual considerations are not merely extrinsic. On the contrary, it is not any sensation, but such wider factors as what a person does and says *at other times*, which are criteria of his being in love.

Much of what I have been trying to say here is captured in Wittgenstein's statement (1967, §504): 'Love is put to the test, pain not.' The strength and depth of a man's love, in an important sense of that term, are revealed not by the intensity of his sensations but by, for instance, his sincerity, reliability, thoughtfulness, and so on. The notion of a similar 'test' of a sensation makes no sense. The criterion of love is not the occurrence of a sensation, but rather a complex of actions and attitudes. This partly underlies Simone Weil's writing (1952, p. 2): ' "His love is violent but base": a possible sentence. "His love is deep but base": an impossible one.'

On my rejecting the notion that emotions can be equated with sensations, one art educator objected that this was merely because I did not have such intense feeling-responses to the arts, as she did. But, as I hope is very clear, this completely misses the point. As it happens, I frequently have intense reactions to the arts. But that is totally *irrelevant* to the philosophical point that it makes *no sense* to equate emotional feelings with sensations, however intense they may be.

Emotion and Object

The most important characteristic which distinguishes emotional feelings from sensations is that in the great majority of cases emotional feelings are directed on to objects. One is sad or angry *about* something, afraid *of* or irritated *by* something. The object, in this sense, is not necessarily a physical object. Thus one may be afraid of continued economic recession, anxious about a debt, saddened by a friend's disloyalty or insincerity. It is important to notice that the object of the emotional feeling can be identified only in terms of one's understanding of or belief about the phenomenon or situation. Thus a person's emotional feeling may be in relation to a mistaken belief. For instance, I shall not be afraid when I hear the sound of a burglar's footstep if I believe it to be that of my father. Conversely, I shall be afraid if I believe the footstep to be that of a burglar, although it is in fact that of my father. Similarly, my emotional response if I believe that the object lying under the table is a rope is likely to be very different from my response if I believe it to be a snake.

As we have seen, it is the failure to distinguish sensation-feelings from emotional feelings which is one of the many symptoms, or sources, of the confusions of subjectivism. To repeat, because of its importance, a central point of Chapter 1, it is precisely the crucial role of cognition or understanding which *distinguishes* emotional feelings from sensations. To reiterate the example, if I were to be poked with what I believe to be a soft, pointed rubber stick, which is in fact a sharp nail, I shall have the sensation-feeling of pain, *despite* my belief or understanding of the object. By contrast, if I believe or understand an object to be a snake which is in fact a rope, I shall have an emotional feeling of fear (of snakes). This, I hope, makes it very clear (a) that emotional feelings cannot intelligibly be equated with sensation-feelings, and (b) that in the case of emotional feelings, by contrast with sensation-feelings, *understanding is all-important*. For it is that understanding, or belief, which determines the kind of emotional feeling it is.

Of course this is not to deny that sensation-feelings are characteristic of some extreme emotions, such as intense fear, anger, jealousy etc. But the emotions cannot intelligibly be *equated* with such sensations. To underline the point again because of its central importance to the whole argument of this book, *an emotional feeling necessarily involves a certain understanding of the object of that feeling.*

The identification of an emotional feeling is not achieved by the unintelligible process of a supposed introspective peering into the occult recesses of one's private mind. On the contrary, it is achieved by taking account of the characterisation of the object, i.e. how the *object* of the feeling is *understood.*

There are complexities in the notion of the object of emotional feeling in the case of the arts which do not necessarily apply elsewhere. For instance, although sometimes the object of the feeling is quite straightforwardly the work of art, sometimes it may be at least partly the issue or situation which is portrayed in, or to which attention is drawn by, the work, as in the case of works which are concerned with social or moral issues. One's response to a poem by John Donne or Gerard Manley Hopkins may be fear of death; it is clearly not fear of the poem. Sometimes one's response may be partly to the structure of a novel or play, and partly to a character in it. Or one's feeling may be for a character, or, if one identifies with him, *as if* one were in his or her position. There are various other possibilities. Thus the normal characterization of the object of the emotion, as in the case of fear of dogs, does not carry over exactly to the case of works of art, and it is not possible to give a precise *general* account of the nature of the object of emotion in relation to the arts. (The craving for generality is a prevalent source of confusion. It is frequently the task of the philosopher to show that the attempt to impose a general theory leads to distortion. The antidote is to consider particular cases.)

As we have seen, the object of the emotion cannot be characterized independently of the individual's understanding of the phenomenon to which he is responding. The object, in this sense, is a central criterion of the feeling and it is identified by one's understanding. For instance, I could not be afraid of ghosts if I had no concept of a ghost. In the cases with which we are concerned, the object and therefore the emotion depend upon an understanding of language and the arts. Thus in the relevant cases the object is given by the concept of art concerned. For instance, if one is moved by a dramatic performance, the object of one's emotion is not normally the actor but the character in the play. Unless one had at least some understanding of the art form of drama, one would be unable to respond appropriately to a fictional character in a play. This does not imply that my argument is exclusively concerned with the spectator. It is sometimes assumed that while the art object may be of central importance to an understanding of the emotional response of the *spectator*, it is '*the emotion itself*' which is important for the artist. This kind of attitude is one of the commonest expressions of subjectivism. One often encounters it when talking to performing artists. Yet the character of the emotion expressed in the work, i.e. by the *artist*, is *identified* by the character of the art object, i.e. by the work of art it is. As we have seen, it makes no sense to suppose that it could be identified by a purely private 'inner' ostensive definition, which had no logical relation to the work. In Chapter 7, I made the point that meaning cannot be purely private, but requires public criteria. There is no sense to the notion of correct use of a term such as 'joyful', and therefore of its having meaning, on a purely private subjectivist basis. Similarly, on such a basis any 'work of art' could be the expression of any feeling or none, and thus there could be no sense in the notion of expression of feeling in a work, even for the creator of it. There are complexities here which will be considered in Chapter 9, but at this point I simply wish to make it clear that, for the characterization of the emotion, that is, for what counts as 'the emotion itself', the *art object is equally important for the artist and the spectator of art.*

Philosophy of Mind

At this stage it is important to outline the general approach to philosophy of mind on which the argument of this book is founded. This is not only important *per se*, but it further vindicates my assertion that philosophy of the arts is inseparable from philosophy of mind.

My insistence that the artist's feeling cannot be characterized independently of the work certainly does *not* imply that my thesis is a form of behaviourism or formalism or structuralism; it does not imply that the feeling can be reduced to the physical constitution of the object, or the physical behaviour which created it. Behaviourism can give no coherent account either of emotions which are not expressed, or of characteristic emotion-behaviour which is not an expression of emotion, as for instance, in the case of pretence. Indeed, more seriously, the behaviourist is not entitled to the notion of 'characteristic emotion-behaviour', since that is precisely what requires explanation. Thus the behaviourist has to characterize emotions solely in terms of the mechanical and physical movements of which, for example, a sophisticated robot would be capable. Since this makes no sense, the behaviourist has to help himself illegitimately (because of his own theory) to what he is implicitly denying, namely that emotional behaviour is possible only for living beings who have feelings which cannot be characterized in exclusively physical or behavioural terms, in the sense in which he conceives them. This does not in the least imply that the feeling is independent of and inferred from the physical behaviour. It makes no sense to suppose that meaning can be given by private observation of one's own occult, 'inner' mental processes, since, as we have seen, with no objective, publicly available criteria for what counts as correct use, there could be no sense at all in the notion of learning the meanings of emotion-terms. Any kinds of behaviour or works of art could be the expression of any emotion or none, which is to say that no sense could be made of the meaning of emotion-terms even by the person himself.

Both the subjectivist, who regards the feeling as an independent mental event, and the behaviourist, share the presupposition that mental experience can be accounted for by reference to physical behaviour, construed as a mechanistic process of bones, muscles, flesh, and so on. For the behaviourist the mental can be reduced to such mechanism; for the subjectivist the mental is a separate, subjective, non-physical, mental phenomenon which can be inferred from the purely physical mechanism. Yet no coherent account of mental experience can be given if physical behaviour, in this sense, is regarded as the only element, or as one of the basic elements. What is required is a different basic element, namely, that of *the human being*, the identity and character of whose experiences are determined, to an enormous extent, by social practices, including language and the arts.

Once again, let me draw attention to the paradox that this point is both obvious and difficult to grasp. It is obvious that it is a *human being* who thinks, feels, acts — not, on one hand, a conjunct of two independent elements, a physical mechanism, and a non-physical mysterious entity, nor, on the other hand, just the physical mechanism. Yet so deeply ingrained is the dualist/subjectivist doctrine that it can be very difficult to recognise what is obvious.

It may be worth adding now a point which we shall consider more fully shortly: that it is no good trying to overcome the intractable problems of dualism/subjectivism by simply *postulating* a correlation between the 'inner' mental experience, and the 'outer' physical behaviour, as is commonly done, by some psychologists, and, for instance, by Louis Arnaud Reid.

The deep difficulty, then, is to recognise that the answer to the problem lies on the surface. What makes this recognition so hard to achieve is the pervasive hold of subjectivism or dualism, and behaviourism, together with the assumption that they exhaust the possibilities. It should be emphasized, too, that my position is not a mid-position, or modified behaviourism, but rather a completely different approach to the concept of mind.

The fatal objection against dualism (body and mind as two distinct entities) or subjectivism is that, whatever the results of my supposed introspective observations, I have obviously failed to understand the concept of anger, if when I say sincerely that I am angry my utterance does not normally go with anger-behaviour directed on to an appropriate object. The fatal objection against behaviourism is that, equally obviously, I have failed to understand the concept of anger if when I say that I am angry this is always and necessarily on the basis of my observation of my own behaviour.

One *learns* how to characterize one's own feelings, and the feelings of others, in the same way. It could not be said that a child had mastered the use of words to refer to his own mental states unless his use of those words coincided appropriately with the rest of his behaviour. That is, the criteria of feelings, the meanings of emotion-terms, are given by certain forms of behaviour directed on to objects. But 'behaviour' here is not used in the way the behaviourist uses it, that is, to refer to mere mechanistic movements; it refers to that of which only a *human being* (or an animal) is capable. In short, the meaning of the terms I use to identify and describe my own feelings is given by the background of normal human behaviour.

To put the point another way, Wisdom (1952, pp. 226–35) writes of the asymmetrical logic of psychological statements, by which he means that the position of the person experiencing an emotion or a sensation, for instance, is not symmetrical with that of anyone else. Someone else's statement that I am in pain has to be made on the basis of my behaviour, including my verbal behaviour, whereas my statement that I am in pain has not. Moreover, as long as I understand the concept, I cannot be mistaken when I say that I am in pain, whereas others obviously can be mistaken in attributing pain to me. It is important to recognize that this asymmetry lends no support to the dualistic, subjectivist notion that body and mind are separate entities, that thoughts and feelings are purely private, and that only I can have infallible knowledge of my own experiences. That conception, as we have seen, makes no sense. My present point is that psychological terms applied to a *human being*, as contrasted with a conjunct of physical stuff and mental stuff, have this asymmetry. The meaning of 'I am in pain' is learned by the *public* criteria given with language. Therefore, contrary to what the subjectivist assumes, meaning cannot be purely private; neither can there be two kinds of meaning, in this sense, the private and the public, since 'I am in pain', said by me, is true if and only if 'He is in pain', said by an observer, is true. This asymmetry lends no support to the notion that only I can be certain, or can know directly, that I am in pain, whereas others can have only a degree of indirect probability. On the contrary, if, for instance you see someone hit by a falling rock, and he clutches his head, groans, bleeds, and so on, you can be as certain as you can be of anything that he is in pain. Moreover, as has been pointed out often enough, it makes no sense, in normal circumstances, to say 'I know I am in pain', since the attribution of knowledge is contrasted with doubt and uncertainty, and one could make no sense of the suggestion that one might doubt or be uncertain whether one were in pain.

In brief, then, what the asymmetry amounts to is that mental experience is that of a human being, and he is obviously in a different relation to it from anyone else. He has the experience and thus might be said to be the subject of it. But that is not in the least to say that the experience is subjective, in the sense that its identification is not answerable to objective criteria. A person can ascribe terms like 'pain' and 'anger' to himself only if he has learned the objective criteria for their correct use in a public language. His experience is certainly not subjective in the sense that its characterization is a matter solely of his private perception of 'inner' mental states.

The meaning of the terms I use to identify and describe my own feelings is given by the *background of normal human behaviour*. A human being can hide his emotional feelings and pretend to have such feelings; he can recognize the feelings of other people; he can be wrong about his own emotional feelings, or he can be right despite the contrary assertions of others. All these possibilities depend upon the fundamental fact that he is a human being, neither a conjunct of body and mind, nor simply a physical body. He learns the language of a society, and he responds to others as human beings who think, and have emotions. He does not see them as physical bodies, neither does he attempt unintelligible inferences to purely private, subjective feelings and thoughts. He *sees* that someone is angry, frightened, or thoughtful, because he has learned what it is for *human beings*, including himself, to be angry, frightened and thoughtful. To repeat a theme, individual thoughts and feelings are determined by the *conversation* that we are.

Feeling and Medium

As we saw in Chapters 6 and 7, the possibility of individual creativity and expression depends upon the existence and a grasp of the appropriate disciplines and social practices. The criteria for what feelings are, in the case of the artist, also depend upon such disciplines and practices. To take an analogous case, some years ago when I was learning to ski I reached a stage where I was struggling, largely in vain, to master parallel Christis. I succeeded, to some extent, only in tantalizingly brief and evanescent moments. One day, after assiduous practice, I felt that I had succeeded, and at the bottom of the slope I exclaimed to a friend: 'At last I know what it feels like to do parallel Christis.' To which he replied: 'Oh no you don't. I saw you coming down.'

The point is that there are public criteria for feelings. Whatever my kinaesthetic or aesthetic feeling, it obviously could not have been that of parallel skiing. Moreover, the possibility of the feeling depends upon the existence and the learning of the activity. Similar considerations apply to the feelings expressed by the artist. The feeling is an artistic feeling, expressible only in that artistic medium, and it would make no sense to suppose that it could exist independently of that public medium.

There are subjectivists who accept that if artistic meaning is 'in the mind' there can be no criteria, or answerability to rationality, and there are those who do not recognize the subjectivist consequences of their positions. These latter, for instance, assume that there is no problem about 'externalizing' or 'objectifying' into public media or symbols the 'purely private', 'subjective', 'felt life', 'in the mind'. If by such statements they mean that the *meaning* of what is publicly expressed is given by a private feeling or idea which exists prior to and independently of the public medium, then, as we have seen, such a notion makes no sense. In effect, they are helping themselves to objective public criteria for artistic feeling and meaning to which their own theory does not entitle them. A major source of this tempting position is that it is so often confused with the obvious fact that one can have artistic feelings and ideas which are not publicly expressed. Paradoxically, in view of their concern, often, to provide a justification for the arts, their misconception arises from a *failure* to recognize sufficiently the importance of the concept of art.

An example will illustrate my point. Eisner, in 'The role of the arts in cognition and curriculum' (1981), (a topic on which he has spoken often, and has written a book) commendably recognizes the crucial place of cognition with respect to the justification of the arts in education. As I have emphasised, a sound conception of mind is necessary for any coherent account of the philosophy of the arts, or of the arts in education. Roughly, Eisner's justification consists in trying to show that art contributes importantly to mental development. But while one applauds the attempt, Eisner gets himself hopelessly out of his depth in philosophical difficulties of which he is unaware. That he is unaware of the complexities involved is made abundantly clear in his opening sentence: 'My thesis is straightforward but not widely accepted.' In fact, on the contrary, the subjectivist conception of mind on which he relies *is* widely accepted, but on examination it can be seen to be not only very far from straightforward, but radically confused, and educationally disastrous. Eisner, in this paper, significantly entitled in an earlier version 'Representing what one knows', espouses three fundamental subjectivist misconceptions which are an inevitable consequence of insufficiently recognizing the importance of the *medium*, whether linguistic or artistic.

(1)   Eisner shares the prevalent mistaken assumption that meaning, whether linguistic or artistic, is given by reference, or at least answerability, to *images*. For instance, he writes (pp. 18–19):

> it is easy to see how concepts such as dog or chair, or red or blue depend upon sensory information. But what about concepts such as 'justice', 'category', 'nation', 'infinity'? I would argue that these words are nothing more than meaningless noises or marks on paper unless their referents can be imagined . . . Unless we can imagine 'infinity', the term is nothing more than a few decibels of sound moving through space. I do not mean to imply that every time we hear a word we conjure up an image. We have so automated our response mechanisms that this is not necessary. But when I say, 'The man was a feckless mountebank' the statement will have meaning only if you know what 'feckless' and 'mountebank' refer

to. If you do not then you turn to a friend or a dictionary for words whose images allow you to create an analogy. . . Concepts, in this view, are not at base linguistic, they are sensory. (pp. 18–19)

There are two connected assumptions here, (a) that meaning is reference, (which is a version of what I earlier called the 'naming' view of meaning, which is very common, has led to many confusions, and which, as in Eisner's case almost invariably leads to, or is inseparable from, an unintelligibly subjectivist conception of meaning), and (b) that meaning necessarily depends, at least ultimately, on reference to images. With respect to (a), to assume that linguistic terms always name or refer is, at the very least, to adopt a very limited and distorting conception of language. While it may be initially plausible for words like 'dog' or 'chair', it loses even initial plausibility for words such as 'if', 'but', 'and'. What, for instance, does 'if' refer to? Even when a word does refer, the referring cannot intelligibly be regarded as its meaning. For example, on the meaning-as-reference conception the term 'prime minister' would have to change its meaning every time there were a change of prime minister. Those imbued with the naming, or denotational, view of meaning usually try to overcome this obvious problem by resorting to the notion that the meaning of such words is given by their naming not the person or thing, but the *idea* or *image* of it. In this way, the naming view of meaning almost invariably leads to or is part of the unintelligibility of subjectivism. The important point to recognise is that it makes no sense to *equate* meaning with reference, even in those cases where a word is used to refer. It is equally important to recognise that there are various uses of language other than the referential, such as the expressive, hortatory and exclamatory. It is highly misleading, and reveals a complete failure to recognise its hugely varied possibilities, to assume that language functions in only one way. (I have considered this issue more fully elsewhere [Best, 1974, pp. 15–21].)

We can see, then, how (a) above, leads to (b), i.e. how a misconceived assumption that meaning-is-reference leads to the subjectivist supposition that the reference is to 'inner' mental ideas or images.

The widely prevalent assumption that meaning is given by reference, or the possibility of reference, to an image is fundamentally mistaken. For instance, even in the cases mentioned above, where it may be initially plausible to equate meaning with reference, it can easily be shown that the concurrence of an image is neither necessary nor sufficient for meaning. If I have no image at all, or have an image of a bandaged arm because I was once bitten, whenever I hear or use the word 'dog', that does not *in the least* imply that I do not know the meaning of 'dog'. On the contrary, whatever image I may have, or even if I have and can conjure up none, if I *use* the word correctly, then that shows that I *do* know its meaning. So an image is not necessary for meaning. Conversely, even if I should always have an image of a dog, whenever 'dog' is used, that does not in the least imply that I know its meaning. On the contrary, even if I always have such an image when I use the term, yet I *use it incorrectly* in general, then that shows that I do not know its meaning. So an image is not sufficient for meaning. A mark or sound which would otherwise be meaningless is not endowed with meaning by the concurrence of an image. For example, if the sound of a sneeze conjures up an image of Ann, who is prone to sneezing, there is no question of meaning at all here, and certainly the sound of a sneeze does not mean 'Ann'.

Incidentally, to use Eisner's own example, how could one have an *image* of infinity? The very idea makes no sense, but that does not imply that the word 'infinity' has no meaning. But, according to Eisner we have had an image of infinity so often that our response has become 'automated'. Just try forming an image of infinity even *once!* The absurdity of the notion is so immediately obvious that it reveals conclusively how completely Eisner is in the unquestioned — even unquestionable — grip of the subjectivist doctrine. For even his own example involves such obvious absurdity that it can only be the distortion of his subjectivist theory of meaning which blinds him to that absurdity.

It is clear, then, that Eisner is deeply infected with subjectivism, since he assumes that meaning is given by a private introspection of 'inner' mental images. I hope I have, already said enough to expose that notion not only as senseless, but as disastrous educationally. The criterion of knowing the meaning of a term is the ability to *use it correctly in various linguistic contexts*. In practice we all know very well that someone knows the meaning of a word only if, in general, he uses it correctly. So why on earth do we create the intractable difficulty of locating meaning in the mysterious realm of people's purely private 'inner' minds? Taking that view one could *never* know whether anyone understood the meaning of *anything*, since it makes no sense to suggest that one could somehow get into his private mind to find what he means by it. To repeat, the depth of the difficulty lies *on the surface*. We all know that the way to discover whether a child, for instance, understands the meaning of a word is to see how he *uses* it. So, again, why are so many trapped in a theory which makes understanding meaning totally impossible, or rather, senseless? The answer to that question, of course, is that almost all arts educators, and many more, are so totally immersed in the subjectivist doctrine that they are oblivious even of the most obvious absurdities and self-contradictions of it.

Of course this is not in the least to deny the intelligibility of the notion of mental imagery. That is, talk of mental imagery is not necessarily unintelligibly subjective. In some art forms, mental imagery can sometimes be a fruitful source of artistic inspiration. But it is clear from what he writes that Eisner's theory is hopelessly subjective. We have uncovered another common guise of subjectivism — one which is, perhaps, particularly prevalent in the visual arts.

The issue may be clarified by contrasting images with sensations. Some are tempted to believe that sensations are purely private, but clearly there are objective criteria for the attribution, for instance, of pain. These criteria are both verbal and non-verbal. That is, that someone is in pain is shown either by what he says, or by the way he behaves in certain circumstances — for example, wringing his hand when he has hit his thumb with a hammer. By contrast, in the case of mental imagery, the *non*-verbal drop-out, for there are no non-verbal, non-artistic etc. criteria. That is, almost the *only* criteria for the existence and character of mental images are language, arts, and other cultural media.

It is the language, art form, or other public medium of expression in which it is or could be *articulated*, which is a criterion for the existence and character of a mental image. Thus, for example, there could be no sense in attributing imagery to creatures, such as animals, without language and art forms. Consequently, to make linguistic and artistic meaning depend ultimately upon 'inner' mental *imagery*, as Eisner does, is to be committed to subjectivism. This subjectivist misconception is, indeed, entirely the wrong way round. It makes no sense to suppose that meaning is given by imagery: it is rather the converse, that the meaning of the imagery is given by the social medium in which it can be formulated. The central issue for my thesis is that the concepts, and thus the feelings with which we are concerned, could not exist prior to and independently of the public medium, of language or the arts.

It may be worth adding that it is a mistake, which may tend to subjectivism, to equate imagination with having images. Imagination sometimes involves having mental images, as in 'Close your eyes and imagine the Eiffel Tower'. But children who are asked to imagine that they are Red Indians do not need to have images to comply. Their imagining can be revealed in the way they act, and play.

(2) Eisner assumes that meaning, understanding and education can be achieved solely by sensory experience. This common misconception is seriously misleading for the arts, language and education generally. It is parallel to the confused notion which we considered earlier that emotional feelings can be equated with sensations. Simone Weil gives the example of two women who receive letters during the war, informing them of the deaths of their sons. One can read, the other cannot. The former, on looking at her letter, faints with shock, while the latter, on looking at an identical letter, is completely unconcerned. The sensory experience of each is the same. The differences of emotional response can be attributed only to the former's *understanding*. Similarly, two people watching a game of chess, one of whom understands it and one of whom knows nothing of chess or any similar game, may have the same sensory experience. The difference between them is that only one understands the game.

Certainly the senses are *necessary* in order to learn language and artistic meaning, but that certainly does not imply that linguistic and artistic concepts *are* sensory. It is difficult to know what it could mean to say that one *senses* the meanings of verbal terms. If by saying that concepts are at base sensory Eisner means, as he seems to mean, that sensory experience is *sufficient* to provide us with concepts, then this is obviously mistaken. Concepts are intrinsic to language, art forms, and other cultural practices. They are acquired in learning how to engage in those activities. They certainly cannot be acquired solely through the senses.

The point can be brought out in a different way by asking the question: 'Can a man who has been blind since birth have a concept of colour?' If concepts were sensory experiences then obviously he could not. Yet a blind man can use colour-words correctly in various contexts, and could, for instance, recognize inconsistencies in other people's uses of such words. He cannot have as complete a grasp of colour concepts as most normally sighted people, but this is because there are various *uses of colour-terms* of which he is incapable. Nevertheless, a blind man could have a far better grasp of colour-concepts than a man with perfect vision who is severely mentally retarded. This again emphasizes the point that meaning and understanding are not solely a matter of sensory experience. The difference between the two men is that the blind man, although incapable of the relevant sensory experience, has learned the public medium of language and thus has learned, to a limited extent, how to use colour-words.

It is misleading in this context to write of 'sensory information'. If sensory experience were sufficient to give concepts, then they would be independent of the public media of language and the arts. Yet, as the example reveals, concepts depend for their existence upon such public media. Thus Eisner's view is the wrong way round. It makes no sense to claim, as he does in the quotation earlier, that 'concepts are not at base linguistic, they are sensory'. On the contrary, to put it briefly, they are not 'at base' sensory, they are linguistic.

An important educational consequence is that if we wish to help students to extend their conceptual horizons it is certainly not sufficient simply to offer them extended sensory experience. It is necessary to help them to a richer *understanding* of the media which give sense to experience.

(3)   Eisner writes (1981): 'Somehow an individual who wishes to externalize a concept must find some way of constructing an equivalent for it in the empirical world.' (p. 22) His thesis is that concepts are inaccessibly subjective, but that we find ways of expressing them publicly. The clearest short expression of this thesis is to be found in the abstract of his paper where he writes:

> Humans not only have the capacity to form different kinds of concepts, they also, *because of their social nature*, have the need to *externalize* and *share* what has been conceptualized. To achieve such an end, human beings have invented *forms of representation* [which] are the means by which *privately held conceptions* are transferred into *public images* so that the meaning they embody can be shared. (My italics)

This classic example of the confused subjectivist doctrine regards mental phenomena, such as thoughts and feelings, as existing independently of their possible forms of expression. It is assumed, and explicitly stated here by Eisner, that human beings had the thoughts — 'privately held conceptions' — *prior* to, and therefore independently of, the existence of language, and that they *invented* language *subsequently* in order to share those thoughts with others. But this makes no sense at all. One cannot know or understand anything, even privately, unless there is something to be known and understood. One cannot have thoughts of the relevant kind, whether private or public, unless there is *already* a medium, such as language or art form, in which to formulate them. To put the point with possibly oversimple brevity, the use of language, or the work of art, *is* the thinking and feeling, *not* a representation or symbol of it.

It can clearly be seen that this fundamentally misconceived philosophy of mind is the root of many of the confused and misguided educational theories we have examined. For according to this subjectivist doctrine the medium (language, the art forms) are mere *extraneous* forms of expression, quite independent of the ideas and feelings themselves. Hence Witkin (1980) as we saw, assumes that these media get in the way of, distort, the supposedly 'direct', 'pure' feelings. Again I refer to the light dove, in the quotation from Kant at the beginning of Chapter 6. Just as the light dove confusedly wants to be rid of the resistant air for *real* freedom to fly, so the subjectivist craves the unintelligible ideal of a complete vacuum for the formulation of feelings and ideas. Hence the influence of the 'free expression' school of thought. Yet in the complete absence of language, the arts, and other media, there could be no thoughts and feelings of the relevant kind. Human beings would be immeasurably impoverished: they would be reduced to the level of animals in their thoughts and feelings.

Eisner clearly believes that forms of representation are required merely to *express*, private, subjective 'inner' conceptions. Yet, as we have seen, it makes no sense to suppose that knowledge or concepts could exist, even privately, if there were not already the relevant objective public institution. The importance of the point can hardly be over-emphasized in a discussion of feeling and understanding in the arts, since it underlines the fundamental importance of the *forms of art*. Without the art forms the individual could not *have* the relevant understandings or concepts and therefore he could not *have* the feelings.

The point can be brought out in another way. Eisner states that, because of his social nature, man invents, or decides to create, forms of representation and communication in order to share with others his inaccessibly private concepts. How is this achieved? Eisner says that, in each case, we invent 'a socially arbitrary sign whose meaning is conventionally defined to convey that meaning. Thus words and numbers are meaningful not because they look like their referents but because we have *agreed* that they shall stand for them' (1981, p. 21) (my italics). But since, in Eisner's subjectivist view, all these conceptions are purely *private*, how could people *agree* on what the words and numbers shall stand for? The supposition makes no sense. Worse still, for this doctrine, how could there be *words* and *numbers* in the first place? This is a classic case of the radical confusions and self-contradictions of subjectivism. Eisner is here contradicting himself by presupposing in his explanation precisely what he is supposed to be explaining. As I pointed out earlier, imagine holding a committee meeting in order to invent language, or to agree on meanings. It would be a bizarre meeting, since no one could communicate with anyone else. On this subjectivist view there could be no words or numbers, but only unintelligible marks or sounds. The notion of *words* and *numbers* entails that there are *already publicly shared* meanings, with objective criteria for correct use. That is, unless there is already a shared language of communication, there is no sense in the supposition that a group of men could get together to decide what these 'socially arbitrary' signs shall mean. Although this confused subjectivist thesis is explicitly stated by Eisner, I should emphasise that this form of subjectivism, even if not explicitly stated, is very common indeed among not only arts educators, but psychologists, linguistic theorists, and many others. Hence it is worth the risk of labouring the point to expose as clearly as possible its fatal defects. Remember that, according to this subjectivist thesis, each person is at the outset, as it were, logically locked within his own 'inner' mind: his thoughts are totally private, completely inaccessible to anyone else. Yet he is supposed to agree with others, each of whom is *also* locked inescapably in his private mind, on meanings. But to be able to agree on meanings entails that people can *already* communicate with each other, and thus that there are already *shared* meanings.

This becomes very clear if we contrast language with a code. A group of people can agree among themselves that certain code-signs shall have certain meanings. But this can take place only where there is a language which is already understood among them. Clearly it makes no sense to suppose that language itself could be invented in the same way since the enterprise is supposed to begin without *any* possibility of shared meanings, and thus communication. No one else could ever know my completely private thoughts and feelings, and obviously I cannot *tell* others what I am thinking and feeling since there is no language of communication. Yet the notion that language itself is a code is surprisingly common. For instance, Argyle (1975) writes: 'Communication of all kinds can be looked at in terms of a sender who encodes and a receiver who decodes, so that a signal has a meaning for each of them', and 'In discussions of communication it is usually supposed that there is an encoder, a message, and a decoder' (p. 5). This again is a classic example of subjectivism. It implies that what is expressed in language exists and is specifiable independently of language. There are two related fallacies here:

(a) Acquiring language cannot be a matter of learning to translate purely private, subjective concepts since there could be no criteria for knowing what the private concepts of other people were. Nothing could count as a translation since there could be no way of knowing what concept was being translated, because one could never get to the supposedly purely subjective, private mind of another in order to discover what he meant by it. To repeat a point which cannot be overemphasised, criteria have to be objective, publicly available. So on Eisner's conception of concepts as private, subjective, 'inner' entities, it would be unintelligible to talk of the criterion of the correctness of a translation even for oneself.

(b) As we have seen, it makes no sense to suggest that certain feelings and thoughts are possible for beings without language. Thus it cannot intelligibly be supposed that what is expressed in language are independently existent, non-linguistic thoughts and feelings. Without language such ideas and feelings could not even *exist*. Clearly this point is very closely related to (a), since the feelings with which we are concerned necessarily involve understanding of language, the arts, and other cultural practices.

It is fundamentally to misunderstand the character of language to regard it as a code, since the notion of a code necessarily presupposes the language which gives it meaning. Similarly, it is unintelligible to suppose a correlation between purely private subjective concepts or feelings, and the language, art form, or other 'form of representation' in which they can be expressed. This reveals the crucial relationship between the concept of mind and the concept of language and the arts. It becomes clear what a fundamental misapprehension of mind, language and the arts is involved in the common subjectivist supposition, explicitly stated by Eisner, that 'Somehow an individual who wishes to externalize a concept must find some way of constructing an equivalent for it in the empirical world'.

To regard concepts as 'privately held' is to deny any possibility of language, forms of art, or other 'forms of representation'; it is to deny the *medium* without which such concepts could not be formulated, and therefore could not exist. It removes any intelligibility from the notions of agreement, shared use, or understanding. Moreover, it can give no sense to the possibility of mental and personality development, in the sense of the enormously varied and extended range of understandings and feelings which become possible for an individual *only* by learning overt cultural practices such as language and the arts.

That Eisner helps himself to a notion of shared meaning to which he is not entitled by the terms of his own theory, and that such shared meaning must be taken as presupposed to any notion of understanding, is most obviously revealed in his writing, in the quotation earlier, that if you do not know the meaning of 'feckless' and 'mountebank' 'then you turn to a friend or a dictionary for words whose images allow you to create an analogy'. On the basis that concepts are purely subjective, private, sensorily derived images it would be pointless turning to a friend, since it would be impossible to know what purely subjective private concepts he had. The appeal to a dictionary is an even more obvious concession that a public language must exist as a precondition of understanding. On the hypothesis of concepts as private, subjective images there could be no sense to the notion of a dictionary, still less of understanding what is in it.

In order to bring out the point in another way I shall freely adapt an example given by Wittgenstein (1953). Suppose that each of a group of people has a box with something in it which is called a 'froonwappa'. No one can look into anyone else's box, and everyone says he knows what a froonwappa is *only* by looking at *his own* froonwappa. It would obviously be possible for everyone to have something quite different in his box. Indeed it might even be constantly changing. The thing in the box clearly can have no place in the language at all; not even as a *something*, for a box might even be empty, i.e. 'a froonwappa' might mean 'an empty space'. Thus one can 'divide through' by the thing in the box; it cancels out, whatever it may be.

This example shows very clearly that meaning cannot be a matter of introspective examination of private, subjective, 'inner' mental experiences or images.

Symbolic Meaning

To his credit, Louis Arnaud Reid recognises that on a subjectivist basis there can be no justification for the arts in education. He recognises that it is necessary to argue the case for objective justification of artistic judgments. Yet the influence of the prevailing subjectivist/metaphysical doctrine is so strong and pervasive that he is unable to escape it, even when he believes he has done so. It takes some probing to reveal this underneath the guise. It is important to do so, since Reid's views continue to be influential for some arts educators, and it is a particularly interesting exercise in unmasking some of the common guises of the subjectivist/metaphysical doctrine, since Reid was never able to recognise it himself.

Here, I shall consider just two clear indications of his unrecognised subjectivism. The first is his inability to recognise anything as a theory of meaning which does not involve symbolism. As an initial indication, let me cite a paper of his (1980, p. 169) in which he accuses me of inconsistency in repudiating a general symbolic *theory* of meaning, while accepting that meaning can *sometimes* be symbolic. What I wrote was (1978, p. 132): 'I hope I shall not be misunderstood as denying that movements *can* be symbolic. Obviously they can. What I am denying is . . . that movements are *always and necessarily* symbolic, and it is this which uniquely endows them with meaning.' Where is the inconsistency? If I were to say: 'Grass is not always and necessarily green, but obviously grass can be green', would Reid accuse me of inconsistency?

This may appear to be a mere slip by Reid, but, considered in relation to what transpires next, it seems clearly to indicates that Reid is so immersed in a symbolic theory of meaning, that he is unable to consider the possible validity of an alternative view.

Reid's apparently unrecognised preconception that all linguistic and artistic meaning *must* be symbolic becomes even more apparent in another example later in the same piece. I had argued that artistic meaning is necessarily related to socio-historical context. Reid (p. 170) objects that this contention is inconsistent with my earlier repudiation of symbolic theory since it 'suggests that consideration of different symbolisms is important'. But it suggests this only if one *accepts* a symbolic theory of meaning, and I could hardly more explicitly have repudiated it! Reid's preconception, that meaning entails symbolism is so deeply ingrained that he appears to be unable even to *consider* a view which *distinguishes* between meaning and symbolism. Notice that he produces no argument in defence of his assertion. He begs the question against me by accusing me of *inconsistency* because I both insist on socio-historical context, and reject symbolic theory. In short Reid simply *assumes* that it *must* be self-contradictory to talk of meaning which is *not* symbolic. That a philosopher of Reid's experience could make such a mistake is a clear indication of the grip of the subjectivist/metaphysical doctrine, which is so dominant that Reid is oblivious of his immersion in it.

Let me emphasise again that this is not simply a trivial matter of pointing out what in my view are fallacies in Reid's thinking. What matters, crucially, is to be able (a) to *recognise* this as a guise of subjectivism, and (b) to understand why it is so confused.

In relation to (b), I have already indicated in my repudiation of Eisner's theory of meaning why symbolism is part of the confusions of subjectivist metaphysics. Briefly, symbolism is normally referential, i.e. talk of symbolic meaning invites the question 'Symbolic of what?'. Thus symbolic theories are one of the most pervasive examples of the 'naming' (denotational) theories of meaning which were refuted earlier, in relation to Eisner. Such theories almost inevitably lead to, or are part of, confused, subjectivist theories of mind. (I have considered naming (denotational) theories elsewhere (Best, 1974, pp. 15–21). Symbolic theories of artistic meaning are not only ultimately incoherent, but they lead inevitably to a denial of the *unique* meaning of each work of art, since in terms of the theories there is no reason why there should not be more than one symbol (work of art), referring to, standing for, the same meaning (wherever and whatever that is supposed to be) And this, of course, is where such theories often resort to unintelligible metaphysics. (I discuss symbolic meaning more fully elsewhere [Best, 1978, Chapter 8].)

However, there is sometimes a slippery attempt to defend symbolic theory by denying that symbolism *is* referential. Thus, a work of art is said to be a symbol, but not a symbol *of* anything, so that 'X is a symbol' merely amounts to, i.e. is precisely the same as, 'X *has meaning*'. At the least, this is a very confusing usage, and is almost bound to be assumed to be referential — otherwise why assert that the meaning is *symbolic*? Why not simply say that a work of art has meaning? In short, the term 'symbolic meaning', in this sense, is completely vacuous. Inevitably, these two supposed meanings are conflated, so that to deny that X has *symbolic* meaning is taken to entail a denial that X has *any* meaning.

One consequence of this conflation is an attempt to have one's cake and eat it. Thus some authors are so deeply imbued with the conviction that artistic and linguistic meaning *must* be symbolic that they struggle to retain a *substantial* content (i.e. to avoid this vacuity) for the notion of symbolism, while trying to avoid the embarrassingly unintelligible metaphysical consequences of its referentialism. That is, (a) they cannot conceive of meaning as other than symbolic, (b) 'symbolic meaning' in a referential sense incurs intractable metaphysical problems, (c) yet, it is recognised that to deny a referential sense implies that 'symbolic' meaning is vacuous — it means no more than 'meaning'.

A classic statement of a philosopher enmeshed in this irresolvable confusion can be seen in this quotation from Suzanne Langer (1957):

The art symbol . . . *is* the expressive form. It is not a symbol in the full familiar sense, for it does not convey something beyond itself. Therefore it cannot strictly be said to have a meaning; what it does have is import. It is a symbol in a special and derivative sense, because it does not fulfil all the functions of a true symbol. Its import is seen in it; not like the meaning of a genuine symbol, by means of it but separable from the sign.

This passage reveals the intractable problem for symbolic theories. A work of art has meaning, therefore it must be symbolic; yet it cannot have meaning, i.e, it cannot be symbolic, because that would entail that the meaning is separate from and somehow projected into or embodied in the work. The tension is created by a conviction, on the one hand, that art has meaning, yet a recognition, on the other hand, that it cannot have meaning if, meaning is equated with *symbolism*, and therefore a separation of form and content. (I discuss this issue, in relation to Langer and Reid, elsewhere [Best, 1974, pp. 179–92].)

The elaborate paraphernalia of symbolic theory *obscures*, rather than explains, artistic and linguistic meaning. It is one of the commonest, most plausible, yet most pernicious manifestations of the subjectivist/metaphysical doctrine.

Once again, much of the confusion is created by the presumption that to find artistic meaning one has to delve *deeply* into what *lies behind* the work of art. In fact, as I have said before, the *depth* of the problem is that it lies *on the surface*. Thus, not only is a general symbolic theory of artistic meaning unintelligibly confused, in its inevitable resort to the subjectivist/metaphysical doctrine, but it also seriously belittles and trivialises the *work of art itself*. Symbolic theory locates the meaning *elsewhere, away* from the art object, since the meaning is given not by the work of art, but by what it is supposed to symbolise. In fact, as we all know *very well indeed*, when we want to discover the meaning, for instance, of a complex work of art, the notion of delving into metaphysical regions, or occult 'inner' subjective processes, never even remotely occurs to us. What we *do*, is to engage in a careful concentration on the details of the *work of art itself*, sometimes helped by the perceptive comments of others. Even given the dominant influence of the doctrine, it really is surprising that *artists*, at least, should for so long have embraced symbolic, subjectivist, metaphysical theories which take away the emphasis from the work of art itself.[1]

Subjectivism Again

Reid's conception of language reveals even more clearly his subjectivist pre-conceptions. Consider what he writes, in which he irrefutably convicts himself (1980, p. 169): 'While conceiving, or "having ideas", is on one side a *private and mental operation*, the concept or idea (say of football or the Prime Minister), the *object* of the conceiving or thinking is shareable and in that sense public' (my italics). It is not clear what he means by this. There are two possible explanations, both of which, as I shall show, are inescapably subjectivist. The most likely interpretation is that the phrase 'the concept or idea (say of football or the Prime Minister)' refers back to 'a private mental operation'. In that case Reid is saying that concepts or conceivings *are* only private mental occurrences. That is, he appears to be claiming that the *object* is shareable and public, but that the *concept* of the object is inaccessibly private and mental, and thus *subjective*.

Based on this view, it would be unintelligible for the concepts to be of the *same* objects, since all concepts, understanding, or knowledge would be totally individual, private, subjective. In order to make this absolutely clear, consider again the example I gave earlier of the froonwappa in the box. Using Reid's conception, it would make no sense to say that we could be talking of the *same* object, since no one could have *any* idea what a 'froonwappa' might be. It might not be an object at all! It could even be an exclamation! Therefore, it would make no sense to suggest that one could ever know what anyone else meant, or understood, by his reference to an object. Worse, it would make no sense to suggest that he was *referring* to *any* object at all and the whole of language, understanding, and meaning would be wholly, inaccessibly subjective.

A less likely interpretation of Reid's sentence is that, in his view, although *concepts* are shareable and public, it is the 'conceiving' or 'having ideas' of the concepts which is inaccessibly private and subjective. This is equally vulnerable to the same criticism of incoherence. For, it would therefore make no sense to suppose that there could be *shared concepts*, just as, on the more likely interpretation, it makes no sense to suppose that the concepts could be of the same objects. In either case, the supposed 'mental' element (the 'conceiving' or 'having ideas' on the latter interpretation, or the 'concept' on the former) is *inaccessibly private* and *subjective*. In which case there could be *no grounds whatsoever* for assuming that we understood anyone else — indeed there could be no *sense* in the notion of understanding anyone else, or of communication, since, in this subjective, solipsistic world each person's 'ideas', 'conceivings' or 'concepts' would be *inaccessible* to anyone else. What seems to give some initial plausibility to this kind of view is the assumption that each person can *tell* the others about his private, subjective concepts. Yet to suppose that telling others is possible is to presuppose that which the subjectivist is explicitly denying, namely that concepts are *not* private, but public and shareable. That is, one can tell others about one's ideas *only* if they are derived from a public, objective, shared language. And it is precisely that which Reid is implicitly denying in his subjectivist account of meaning.

Indeed, on this subjectivist account, language and meaning would be impossible *even for the person himself*, since where concepts or ideas are purely private, there could be no independent check on whether he meant the same by his use of the term each time he used it. That is, there could be no distinction between *seeming* to be correct, and *being* correct.

Notice that it is no use saying, 'But there can be shareability here *to some extent*, since their private concepts are of the *same* public object'. For talk of 'the same object' makes sense only *in terms of shared concepts*, and it is precisely this notion to which Reid is not entitled, and which, in fact, he is explicitly denying.

Thus, although Reid objects to being labelled a subjectivist, I submit that in this passage (as in others) he is caught red-handed. He is further convicted by his explicitly stated view that the feelings expressed in art, abstractly and analytically regarded, 'are on the side of the *subject*, not the object'. The arguments earlier in this chapter decisively refute that subjectivist conception.

Reid, in my view, is a classic example of a subjectivist who tries to avoid intractable philosophical problems by simply *postulating* that the purely private 'inner' concepts are of the *same* object, and are thus shareable. But that makes no sense. There could be no grounds whatsoever for saying that one was ever referring to the same object, or even referring at all, or to any object. Reid helps himself, without justification, to an objectivity which he commendably recognises to be essential, for any intelligible account of artistic meaning, and especially for the arts in education. What he, like Eisner and many others, fails to recognise is that his whole subjectivist/metaphysical theory completely rules out any possibility of meaning in the arts. It therefore also rules out any justification for the arts in education.

The Given: Language and the Arts

Any intelligible account of the concepts and feelings expressible in language and the arts has to take the medium of expression as what has traditionally been called in philosophy 'the given'. The given is that to which *ultimate* appeal is made in explanation, and which gives sense to reasons, explanation and justification. For example, as we have seen, it makes no sense to suppose that language was invented or created *in order that* men could communicate concepts or express their social nature. It is rather that men have the kinds of concepts they have, and the social nature which is peculiar to men, *because of language*. It is language which allows men to possess those concepts and to have that social nature. In this sense, contrary to what Eisner supposes, concepts *are* at base linguistic. That could sound like a trivial tautology. In this context it is to make the point that we cannot look *outside* language for an understanding of what it is to possess the concepts expressible in it, any more than one can look outside chess for an understanding of chess moves. Of course, as I emphasised in Chapter 2, language cannot coherently be regarded as independent of the natural ways of acting and responding which impregnate linguistic meaning, and give sense to the utterance of words. These natural forms of behaviour, not images, are the *roots* of language and the arts. Nevertheless, the superstructure of language and the arts, which has developed and draws its sustenance from those roots, provides the possibility of a vast and varied range of feelings, thoughts, understandings, and intentions which would otherwise be impossible. This is perhaps the most crucial educational implication of the rejection of the subjectivist/metaphysical conception, and its replacement with what, in relation to it, is the revolutionary approach of this book.

One learns how to use and understand language rather as one learns how to play chess. However, this analogy may be misleading, for whereas chess may have been invented it is unintelligible to suppose that language and the concepts given with it could be invented. To repeat an example, imagine a committee set up to invent language, so that men and women could communicate with each other. There would be some bizarre committee meetings, since no one could communicate with anyone else! Remember that, on this subjectivist view, no communication is possible *at all* — not only in language, but in any other way, since the concepts and feelings are supposed to be purely private and totally impenetrable by and incomprehensible to anyone else. The supposition that men invented language is clearly absurd. To put the point paradoxically, the only way in which language could be invented would be if there were *already* a language in which to do the inventing.

The supposition of the invention of language is patently nonsenical, even though this supposition is very prevalent, both explicitly and implicitly. The subjectivist notion of the autonomous mentalist/individualist logically *entails* that absurdity. That it is so obviously absurd, even on cursory reflection, underlines yet again just how completely almost all arts educators are in the grip of the subjectivist conception — so much so that the great majority of people are oblivious of it. It cannot even be regarded as an *assumption*, it is rather the unquestioned — effectively the unquestion*able* — foundation of thinking about the arts, and many other crucial aspects of the human condition.

It is important to avoid the danger of trivialising this crucial issue. Some people have assumed that my criticisms in this respect of theorists such as Eisner, Witkin, Louis Arnaud Reid, are mere quibbling over terms such as 'invent'. I hope I have said enough already to expose the fallacy of that charge. For, as I hope I have shown, the notion that humans could invent language and the arts is an inseparable part of the whole subjectivist/metaphysical doctrine which almost inevitably infects talk about the arts, and poisons attempts to argue for the vital contribution of the arts to education. That is very far from a trivial matter. On the contrary, it is by far the most important issue for all those seriously concerned for the arts in education and society.

Indeed, it is important to notice that this kind of criticism of philosophy as verbal quibbling, is *itself*, usually, another of the guises of the senseless but pervasive subjectivist doctrine. The common distrust and trivialisation of language, among so many arts educators, is usually a clear indication that they regard language as a mere message-carrier of private, subjective, 'inner' ideas, which exist independently of language. On this view, it is not the particular use of particular words which matters, but rather the supposedly private, 'inner' subjective ideas, feelings, 'concepts' which are separate from but symbolized or expressed *by* those words. It becomes very obvious that, in this sense, the charge of verbal quibbling is itself a symptom of the unintelligible and disastrous subjectivist doctrine.

Of course there *can* be mere verbal quibbling, and there can obviously be clearer and more effective ways of expressing oneself, verbally and artistically. But this cannot be because the 'inner' subjective idea already exists independently of the linguistic or artistic medium in which it is formulated and is potentially expressible. It is rather that what is already, perhaps vaguely and inadequately, formulated, is open to improvement. And *that* is to say that a vague and inadequate *idea or feeling* can be improved to become a clearer or more effective idea or feeling. There is no sense in the notion of a linguistic or artistic idea or feeling which is independent of *any* formulation in the respective medium.

It is a great pity that arts people are so often suspicious or dismissive of language, for, in the most important sense, language and the arts are doing the same thing — *hugely* enlarging the possibility of human *experience. Not* enlarging merely the possibility of the symbolism or *expression* of feelings, thoughts, ideas, but enlarging the possibility of the *feelings, thoughts and ideas themselves*. The educational implications, for the arts and language, are both obvious and of *immense* significance.

This brings out the full force of the relation between mental development, and the arts and language, for to put it as starkly as possible, it is not that man creates language and the arts, but that *language and the arts create man.*

Concepts and Feelings

An analogy will illuminate the issue. MacIntyre (1967) argues that one important reason why Christian practices have retained some tenuous general hold in some Western societies, despite the widespread rejection of doctrine, or rather, more significantly, the general assumption that such practices are irrelevant to ordinary life, is the lack of an alternative vocabulary or practice with which to respond to the major crises or events in men's lives, such as death. I am referring not to an *intellectual* inability to work out satisfactory formulae, but rather to the situations in which, faced with actual deaths, there should be formulae which would have emotional and moral relevance and significance. Perhaps the most fundamental and urgent question we have to face is: 'What is the meaning and significance of the life of someone we have loved, or whom we love?' How can this significance be expressed, since, in the absence of a possibility of expression, one feels that there can be no such significance? MacIntyre (p. 70) writes:

> If you read contemporary theology carefully, its content amounts to this, that we are not to take literally what people in past ages said about Hell or Purgatory. Instead we are to treat these as informative metaphors, or myths. The degree of insistence that we are not to take these doctrines literally appears to be a recognition that what was said will not do any more, but at the same time there is nothing to put in the place of literal doctrines.

The possibility even of *raising questions* depends upon the existence of concepts, or a vocabulary, in which they could be formulated. In this case, the questions are framed in a vocabulary which can no longer provide adequate answers, since it expresses concepts and feelings which are mere etiolated remnants of practices which are no longer genuinely part of people's lives. Of course, we can cease to involve ourselves with the arts, whereas we are inevitably confronted with the problem of coming to terms with death. But if we continue to concern ourselves with the arts then, in the same way, the art forms set the limits of sense for possible interpretation, appreciation, and artistic experience and creativity.

The set of related issues which are centred on the problem of death, such as the meaning and value of human life, and what human achievement amounts to, are determined by the vocabulary in which they can be formulated. I do not mean simply that the issues could not be *expressed* without a vocabulary or set of practices, but something more fundamental, namely, that the feelings and thoughts, could not even *arise.* For the notion that there could be such feelings, thoughts, and concerns if there were no medium in which they could be expressed is unintelligible. The point is made in Edward Bond's play *The Sea* (1973), where Hatch is dimly aware that the *mores* of post-Victorian society are dangerously inadequate to cope with the changes which he vaguely senses to be encroaching menacingly upon it. Lacking a vocabulary in which his fears can be formulated, his groping desperation leads him to inane delusions of invisible forces from outer space. It is significant that the play starts with the drowning of a character who, although he never appears except as a body washed up on the shore, dominates the play by confronting the effete social ways of thinking and talking with the need to respond to death in the community.

The analogy with the problem of responding to death is particularly illuminating because in this case it is surely wildly implausible to imagine that, with the loss of the old religious customs, people could simply get together and *decide on* or *invent* some new ways of marking the significance of a human life, except, of course, as a development of conceptions or practices which are *already* valued as being endowed with the requisite gravity. Not anything could count as an expression of the meaning of a human life, and that is to say that not *anything* can count as one's *feeling* about the meaning of a human life, and the death of a loved one. This tension, or fragmentation, is inevitably reflected in the prevalent reluctance to think about death, or the meaning of life.

Ian Robinson, in Chapter 2 of *The Survival of English* (1973), argues that the change of language in the New English Bible amounts to a drastic reduction in *experience*. Part of his point is the same as a main theme of my argument, namely, that there is a misconception involved in the notion that different *forms* of expression are merely different ways of expressing feelings and concepts which are *independent* of those forms. Specifically, Robinson argues in convincing detail, in a chapter which is well worth reading, that the New English Bible cannot intelligibly be regarded, as is often claimed, as a modern *translation* of the *same* concepts and experiences expressed in the earlier version. The change of language involves, in subtle but highly *significant* ways, changes in *what* it expresses. In this sense the language gives and is not distinguishable from the experience. Except in a crude sense, which would miss its full religious significance, there is no intelligible distinction between the language used and the possible mental/emotional experience; the loss of the language of the earlier version, that is, the lack of the *use* of this language, incurs the loss of possible *individual* experience. 'Religious English is the style of our common language that *makes religion possible* (or not, as the case may be)', (p. 55; my italics). Moreover, given the centrality of this kind of language to our concepts of the value and meaning of life, 'the New English Bible is a diminution of our *whole* language' (p. 60), and thus of our possible depth of feeling and experience, since 'the state of a language depends on everybody who uses it and is indistinguishable from *their* state' (p. 62). This again underlines the fundamental importance of recognising that personal identity, in terms of the character of individual thoughts, feelings and actions, is constituted by what I called earlier 'the *conversation* that we are'.

Whether it is possible to translate the same feelings and concepts into another language depends partly on what is meant by 'language'. If it were possible for there to be a language in which precisely the same feelings and concepts, rooted in precisely the same ways of life, were expressed in different signs or sounds, then an exact translation would be possible. But if by a different language one means that at least to some extent the concepts and ways of life are different, then clearly no exact translation which involves them would be possible. Robinson shows how these particular changes of language necessarily involve changes of concept, or understanding, and thus of experience. Similarly, what is expressible and imaginable, and thus what it is possible to *experience* in an art form, is determined by the vocabulary in which it can be formulated. And by that I mean such factors as the limits of the particular physical medium, and the school of thought within which an artist is working.

Subjectivism and Understanding

There are those whose conception of mind is subjectivist, yet who implicitly trade on what they are explicitly repudiating by accepting that there is artistic meaning, i.e. that artistic feelings and ideas *cannot* intelligibly be subjective, but, on the contrary, are *objective*, in the sense that they can be shared and understood. Phenix (1964, p. 167), for example, writes of a dancer's movements 'They make visible the subjective life of persons by a series of symbolic gestures', and Langer (1957, p. 26) writes that 'felt life' is objectified in a work of art, and in this way 'The arts objectify subjective reality'. These quotations by themselves *may* not necessarily commit the authors to the subjectivism I am criticizing, although it is difficult to see how else they could be construed. I quote them to bring out another important issue. If, by 'subjective' they mean that the 'life' or conception is independent of the medium then, as we have seen, such a thesis makes no sense. If, on the other hand, they mean that it is possible to formulate ideas and feelings which *need not* be overtly expressed, then that is correct as long as it is recognized that such a possibility presupposes the existence of an objectively available public form of art.

If, by saying that art is feeling objectified, or that the arts objectify subjective reality, one means that there are, to a large extent, shared criteria for what counts as the expression of feeling in an art form, and if one means that reasons can be given to support one's contention that a work falls under a particular description of it as expressing a certain feeling, then, while that is correct, one wonders why these authors make this point about the *arts* particularly. For it is clear that feelings *in general* are *already* objectified. That is, quite apart from the deep and serious misconception that the peculiar province of the arts is to objectify independently existent non-artistic subjective feelings, this implies that there are no objective criteria for non-artistic feelings. Yet clearly there are criteria for what counts as sadness, fear, anger, and so on. Such criteria are learned in learning language. In short, the feelings expressed in art are no more and no less objectified than any other feelings.

How Can a Feeling Be in an Object?

The objection may arise that there is an asymmetry here, for whereas human beings clearly do express feelings, how can works of art do so? Reid proposes what is still a very common and tempting thesis (1931, pp. 62–3):

> How do perceived characters come to appear to possess, for aesthetic imagination, qualities which as bare perceived facts they do not possess? How does body, a nonmental object, come to 'embody' or 'express', for our aesthetic imagination, values which it does not literally contain? Why should colours and shapes and patterns, sounds and harmonies and rhythms, come to mean so very much more than they are? The

embodiment of value in the aesthetic object is of such a nature that the value embodied in the perceived object or body is not literally situated in the body. The joy expressed in music is not literally in the succession of sounds. Our question is, How do the values get there? The only possible answer is that we put them there in imagination.

In a similar vein, as we saw in Chapter 3, Ducasse (1919) writes: 'The feeling is apprehended as if it were a quality of the object' (p. 177); and Perry (1926): 'It seems necessary at some point to admit that the qualities of feeling may be "referred" where they do not belong . . .' (p. 31)

In fact, there is not only a symmetry but an important connection between the feelings expressed by people and those expressed in art. To bring out what I mean, consider a point made by Reid in a more recent work (1969, p. 76). Discussing the problem of content and medium in the arts he writes that there is a similarity to the way we 'see' character in a person's face. In the context of his general thesis his inverted commas imply that one does not *literally* see someone's character, since it is possible literally to *see* only physical things like flesh. Yet this raises the problem of how a purely physical thing like a human body can express nonphysical, mental, 'inner' feelings — which is precisely parallel to the problem of how a physical work of art can express feelings. We have uncovered another guise of subjectivism.

Reid says that he is aware of the intractable problems inherent in Suzanne Langer's dualism (body and mind as separate entities), or subjectivism. He also says that he has recognized the defects of his earlier 'two-term' theory. Yet, this very admisson makes it clear that in fact he is still trapped by subjectivist preconceptions. Consider what he writes later:

> To feel happy, or angry, at ease or in anxiety, is neither mental only nor physical only, but psycho-physical. The aspects are indivisible and convey the ideas of meaningful embodied experience.

It is true that when we see character, or emotion, in a person's face or actions we are not attending just to the purely physical in the behaviourist's sense, but it is of the first importance to recognise that we are not attending to *two* indivisibly united things either. To see character in a person's face is not to see the mental embodied in the physical, it is to *recognise* that character in the face of a *human being*. To ask how the feeling, or the life-experience, gets into the art-object is, similarly, to go wrong at the outset, for the very formulation of the question makes the fatal presupposition, of the two entities. Although Reid insists that these entities are 'indivisible', however closely they are tied together, to think in terms of two entities inevitably leads to a metaphysical answer to the question. 'How do we *know* that the feeling, or meaning, is embodied in this physical artefact?' Reid: 'Embodiment can receive all that expression has to offer it; then the creative transformation occurs, the *fiat* of embodiment.'

This is the language of metaphysics at its most intractably confused. How can we *know* that these two entities, the supposed subjective feeling, and the physical work of art, have come together? How can we *know* that a subjective feeling is expressed in a physical work of art? Supposedly only by the archetypally mysterious, metaphysical 'fiat of embodiment'. Reid has no choice but to resort to such incoherent notions as a 'fiat of embodiment', known only by a supposedly 'basic intellectual act' of intuition, because he cannot escape the web of the subjectivist/metaphysical doctrine.

It is the *question*, inevitably arising from the subjectivist conception, which is the source of the whole confusion — the question: 'How can non-physical feelings and character be expressed in a physical object like a face?, or 'How can non-physical feelings be expressed in a physical work of art?' Such questions *reinforce*, they do not *question*, the subjectivist doctrine; even to *attempt* to answer them is to be trapped within the parameters of that doctrine. This is a classic example of a situation common in philosophy, where it is the *question*, with its loaded pre-suppositions, which is so dangerously misleading.

There are not *two* entities, however inextricably united. There is only *one*, a human being, or a work of art, both of which can, for instance, be sad or joyful. An analogy may be helpfully illustrative. We do not have *two* entities or elements, a table, and a shape, with an intractable metaphysical problem of how the shape got into the table.

No theory which assumes two kinds of entity, one mental, one physical, however closely united, can solve this problem, in the case either of feelings expressed in the arts, or character or feeling expressed in a person's face. One cannot give a coherent account of the expression of feelings if perception is limited to physical bodies or objects in this sense. The crucial point is that we are not concerned, in either case, with *physical* objects, in that sense. The symmetry between the two cases can be brought out by reference to the notion of the 'given', mentioned above, for the given is not a physical body but a *human being*; the given is not a physical object but a *work of art*. One does not 'see' the character in a person's face, one *sees* the character in a person's face. One does not refer a feeling into a physical artefact where it does not belong, one sees the feeling expressed in the art object. One does not apprehend the feeling *as if* it were a quality of the object, one *sees* the expressive quality of the art object.

The intractable nature of the problem is created by a confusion of objects, or kinds of explanation. For example, Reid says that the joy expressed in music is not literally in the succession of sounds. It is true that no physical or chemical examination will reveal joy in a succession of sound waves, but it is precisely *that* way of posing the problem which makes it impossible to offer a coherent solution. For if one looks for the feelings (or meanings and values) expressed in art in that way one will have either to conclude that there cannot be any, since they cannot be found, or to postulate subjective non-physical entities lying behind, or imaginatively referred or projected into, as if they were qualities of, the physical stuff. This last notion is, of course, simply another formulation of, and largely underlies, the common subjectivist assumption that 'Beauty is in the eye of the beholder', and 'Beauty is no quality in things themselves; it exists merely in the mind which contemplates them'.

The problem is created by moving from 'The joy is not literally in the succession of sounds' to 'The joy is not literally in the music', or by regarding these two sentences as equivalent. This is a case of crossing conceptual wires, rather like asking for the weight in grams of heavy sarcasm or light entertainment. A largely contributory factor here is the scientism of our age which too easily seduces one into assuming that the only things which *literally* exist are physical entities which can be scientifically examined and quantified. Of course, a physicist could examine a Beethoven symphony to determine its constitution in terms of sound waves, but it would obviously be an absurd confusion to think that this could have any relevance whatsoever to questions about its meaning or value as *music*.

Thus, what Bosanquet regards as the central problem of the aesthetic, namely, how a feeling can be got into an object, is created by the presuppositions implicit in the *question*, which are underlain by the deep general misconceptions of the subjectivist conception of the relationship of mind to body. For to formulate the question in those terms both manifests and conduces to subjectivist confusion. It is rather like asking: 'How can what is really nothing more than a carved piece of wood be a king in chess?' There is no temptation here to assume a separate occult quality of 'kingship' metaphysically lying behind, or projected on to, a piece of physical wood. For those who know what chess is, it is not normally seen as a piece of wood, but as a chess-piece. Similarly, a written word is not literally, simply physical marks on a paper, but a *word*, which is given its sense and identity by the cultural practice of language.

Once the perspective is changed and we recognize that the given is a *human being*, or an *art object*, respectively, the problem evaporates, for there is no longer any question of how a feeling can be in a physical object. A physical body is not the kind of thing which can have feelings, but a human being is; a physical object is not the kind of thing which can express feeling, but a work of art is. The feeling is a quality of the art object; that is the kind of thing an art object can be. There are not two entities, a physical object and a feeling, there is only one, a work of art which may have an expressive quality. Similarly, one does not try to carry out incoherent inferences to a non-physical entity of sadness, in some intractably mysterious way located 'inside' a physical body. One *sees*, for instance, because he is sobbing, that a human being is sad. In learning the language one learns that such behaviour by a human being is a criterion of sadness, just as in learning to understand an art form one learns what are the criteria for the feelings expressed in it.

It is important to make it quite clear that, in sharp contrast to the view attributed to me by McAdoo (1987, p. 314), I emphatically do *not* regard the objectivity of artistic judgments as 'dependent on inter-subjective agreement'. On the contrary, a main theme of the whole argument of this book is to show that such 'inter-subjectivity' is unintelligible. It amounts to begging the question. For it makes no sense to suppose that there could be *agreement*, if each of us were locked inescapably in a private, 'inner' subjective world, or a world of individual personal associations.

It can now be understood why it was necessary briefly to outline philosophy of mind in general, since the misconceptions about understanding, meaning and the expression of feeling in the arts, are manifestations of deeper, underlying and remarkably tenacious confusions about the concept of mind. The immense difficulty of eradicating the pervasive and mischievous fallacies of the subjectivist doctrine is, to a very large extent, that of *recognising it clearly*. As we have seen, Louis Arnaud Reid is a classic example of an able philosopher who was unable to reconsider the foundations of his position because he failed to recognise that his view *is subjectivist*. His subjectivist or dualist theory of artistic meaning, in terms of 'meaning as embodied' is an almost inevitable consequence of his underlying, subjectivist/dualist theory of the body/mind relationship. The quotation above reveals clearly that he believed the character of a person to be a separate, non-physical *entity*, which is somehow embodied in his physical face. With that kind of view it is hardly surprising that, in a parallel way, he regarded artistic meaning as a non-physical entity which is somehow embodied in a physical artefact. Reid presents a clear example of how confusions about the body/mind relationship inevitably lead to confusions about artistic meaning and value.

It can also be seen why analogies have been drawn between the arts and language. Indeed, in important respects it is misleading to refer to them as analogies. For while it is mistaken to regard an art form *as* a language, there is an opposite danger of overlooking their close relationship and crucial interdependence. Both language and the arts are expressions of conceptions of life and value. The character of the individual thoughts and experiences of individual human beings is determined, except at the most primitive level, by the culture of a community. And by culture I mean that *inextricable amalgam* of social practices, language and art forms which give man his conception of the meaning and value of life. It is in that highly significant sense that language, art forms, cultural practices actually *create* the character and identity of human beings. The immense responsibility and rich possibilities of those of us involved in education, at all levels, are clear, daunting and exciting.

Note

1   From an educational point of view Rod Taylor's excellent book in this series (1992) provides examples which convincingly refute symbolic theories of learning. His students' studies reveal penetratingly careful analyses of features of works themselves. *Sometimes*, to a limited extent, as in the case of Amanda (*The Visual Arts in Education*, p. 106 *et. seq.*) this involves suggested symbolic meaning, e.g. of *some* of the particular flowers which Millais included in his *Ophelia*. But *most* of the analysis is not of symbolic meaning, e.g. 'startling luminosity of colour . . . ' (p. 108). Critical studies, as Rod Taylor has shown frequently in his pioneering work, are concentrated on the particular features of particular works. They are not concerned, even if the hypothesis made sense, with what those works symbolise. Once again, this approach reflects common practice among good arts teachers.

Chapter 9

Artist and Audience

In this chapter we shall examine some further apparent problems for the notion of the rationality of feeling. In particular, we shall discuss whether reasons given for the feeling or intention of the artist, and for the response of the spectator, respectively, can be relevant to questions of artistic meaning. The common tendency to deny their relevance has its source in the subjectivist assumption that the relevant feelings and intentions exist 'in the mind', independently of the work of art. Such an assumption also reveals a failure to recognise the ineliminable significance of the *art form*, without which it would make no sense to say that the feelings and intentions could even exist.

The Rationality of Feeling

A central theme of this book is that artistic experience is fully cognitive and rational, in that the understanding of the work of art, which identifies the feeling-response to it, is answerable to reason. That is, it is possible in principle that the understanding, and thus the feeling, can be changed by reasons for a different understanding of the work. However, this does not imply that one always reasons one's way to a feeling. On the contrary, if that were always necessary it would indicate an *inability* fully to appreciate the arts, and a limited capacity for emotional feeling generally. Such a misunderstanding may partly underlie the tendency to deny that reason has a place in artistic experience, and to assume that reasoning is inimical to feeling. Robert Browning's sonnet XIV makes the point:

> If thou must love me let it be for nought
> Except for love's sake only. Do not say
> 'I love her for her smile — her look — her way
> Of speaking gently — for a trick of thought
> That falls in well with mine, and certes brought
> A sense of pleasant ease on such a day' —
> For these things in themselves, Beloved, may
> Be changed, or change for thee — and love, so wrought,
> May be unwrought so.

Of course love is not achieved rather like reaching a conclusion from a reasoned argument. One would suspect the sincerity or the capacity genuinely to love of someone who said that he loved because the beloved satisfied certain desirable criteria. Such considerations induce some philosophers to deny that reasoning has any place in some emotions, and especially love. Yet although it may be inappropriate to talk of the justification of love, there is undoubtedly a sense in which one can give reasons in explanation of why one loves or likes someone. Browning could have referred to her smile, her look, her way of speaking gently, and so on. Moreover, there is no sharp distinction between justification and explanation in this sense. A further parallel with the arts is that one may create the possibility of love or liking for a particular person by reasoning. This could be achieved by showing someone else a different conception of, a new way of seeing, a person. It may be that reason has a less central role in such a case than in the arts, but it certainly has a place.

What it is about the person which moves us cannot be adequately captured in words, but that is not to say that no reasons can be given. (This question is importantly related to the *particularity* of the response to works of art, and to people, which will be considered in Chapter 11.) Similarly, one of the motives for denying the place of reason in the arts is the recognition that what is expressed in a non-verbal work of art cannot be comprehensively captured in words, and what is expressed in a verbal work cannot be captured in other words. But this point should not be exaggerated. First, as we saw in Chapter 3, reasoning, in the sense of bringing someone to a different conception or understanding, should not be limited to the verbal. A musician could demonstrate a different interpretation of a piece by playing or singing it with particular emphases; a dancer could demonstrate the significance of a particular sequence of movements to the meaning of a dance. Secondly, from the fact that not *everything* can be said about the non-verbal arts in words it certainly does not follow that not *anything* helpful can be said. On the contrary, verbal reasoning is a *principal* way of learning to appreciate both verbal and non-verbal arts. It is strange, and sad, that so often people in the arts are so suspicious of, and even hostile to, verbal language. This may be largely a reaction against the persistent, deeply confused, and educationally restrictive philosophical assumption that all knowledge is propositional, with the consequent attempt to distort artistic knowledge to make it fit the theory. But, to repeat, every teacher of the arts knows very well that verbal language is a principal way of helping students to understand all the arts. There are numerous examples, but, to take just one, there is an excellent programme on Radio 3, entitled 'Record Review', in which a perceptive critic considers different recorded versions of the same piece of music. One can learn a great deal in this way — learning in *words*, which deepens and extends one's *feelings*, for a non-verbal art form.

Each extreme is absurd. Of course artistic experience cannot be comprehensively expressed in words (or other words). Yet of course verbal language can be very helpful in contributing to one's understanding of and therefore response to the non-verbal arts.

Understanding and Feeling

Another way of bringing out the crucial importance to artistic feeling of understanding and rationality is to point out the consequences of denying it. For to deny the central importance of rationality and understanding is to take away any sense in the notion of the *appropriateness*, of artistic feeling, even within wide parameters of possible differences of opinion. And if there is no sense in the appropriateness of the feeling to the object, i.e. if *any* feeling is supposed to be equally 'appropriate', as it would be on a subjectivist conception, this would, at best, reduce 'artistic' response to the kind of response of which an animal would be capable. That, of course, would mean that there was no sense at all in the notion of 'artistic appreciation'. Bambrough (1979, p. 99) draws a similar distinction in relation to morality:

> . . . even a complete vegetarianism may be based on a mere revulsion like that of the insular Englishman against frogs: but in that case, by the very fact of no longer allowing for argument, it disqualifies itself from being a moral position and becomes instead a mere reaction, to be sharply contrasted rather than closely compared with any typical moral attitude or opinion.

It is the *object* of the revulsion which is the crucial distinguishing feature. For example, as we saw in Chapter 2, Swift suggested in *A Modest Proposal* that the twin problems of insufficient food and overpopulation could easily be solved by eating babies. One's reaction, as he expected, is immediate revulsion, but this, unlike the revulsion Bambrough refers to, is a moral one. So it is not simply *revulsion* which distinguishes the two kinds of case, but the *character* of it. And the character of the revulsion is identified by the object at which it is directed. The distinction is, for instance, between (a) when the object is that which was recently a living creature, by contrast with (b) when the object of the revulsion is simply the texture of meat. The important distinguishing feature is that in the case of moral revulsion it is possible to bring others to *understand* it. For example, where someone does not share this response one may refer to the slaughter of animals and show him live animals. In this way he may be brought at least to understand the revulsion, and perhaps to feel it for himself.

A confusion of a parallel kind contributes to subjectivism in the arts. To use an earlier example, I may respond with sadness to a joyful Mozart rondo because it was my dead mother's favourite piece of music. This is subjective, in the sense that it would be quite out of place to give reasons for the inappropriateness of the response. That is, *understanding* of the *music* may be irrelevant to it. The feeling just happens to be related to the music by association, since another piece might have been her favourite. Such a response is not part of artistic appreciation; it is not related to features of the music, and notions such as understanding and appropriateness to the character of the music play no part.

That kind of case tends to be confused with the particularity of the response, that is, where the response is to a *particular* work of art. I shall refer to that question shortly, and discuss it more fully in Chapter 11. It is also confused with the important emphasis on the personal nature of artistic response. Briefly to recapitulate what was said in Chapter 4, that an artistic judgment is necessarily personal, in the sense that each person must experience the work for himself, is not in the least to deny the relevance of appropriateness and understanding. While an artistic judgment could not count as such unless the individual had made it as a result of his own experience, it equally could not count as an artistic judgment if questions of understanding and appropriateness were irrelevant. As we have seen, a precondition of being able to respond to an art object is that one should have understood the relevant art form, and that includes a grasp of its criteria of appropriate response. Once again, in order to avoid misconception, it is worth considering the case of one's own reflection about a work of art, where one works one's own way to an understanding of it, and thus to an emotional response to it.

The comparison with morality can be pressed further. Reasoning one's way to a moral repudiation of the killing of the innocent is not simply *unnecessary*; it is rather that if it were deemed necessary, that would be a significant indication of a *lack* of a certain moral commitment. Nevertheless, even in such a case, reasoning is not necessarily out of place. For example, where a child is born severely deformed, or where someone is suffering severe pain from an incurable disease, rational discussion may well ensue about whether it would be morally right to terminate innocent life. Moreover, some of the firmest moral feelings which people have can be changed or modified by reason, as in the case of deeply ingrained prejudice, or one's conversion to, or coming to reject the validity of, a deeply held religious belief.

There is a further parallel. It is sometimes said that the media or conventions of art are mediating influences on artistic responses. In a similar vein, it is also sometimes said that the purpose of convention in art is to distance one from the object, and thus to reduce or eliminate emotional response. We shall discuss some of these issues in Chapters 10 and 13, but it is worth saying now that if these notions imply that emotional response cannot be *immediate*, then they are mistaken. As in the distinction between the two cases of revulsion, the distinguishing feature between artistic and non-artistic responses is not the immediacy of response in the latter case, but the character of the *object* — which *is* the character of the response. A response to a moving musical, theatrical, or dance performance can be as immediate as any non-artistic response.

Of course it is true that an inappropriate and exaggerated emphasis on reasoning can be inimical to spontaneous, immediate feeling, but that *is far* from saying that reasoning is necessarily inimical to spontaneous feeling. On the contrary, it would be impossible to *have* such spontaneous feelings in response to the arts unless one had learned to understand them — very often as a result of reasoning. Paradigm cases in the arts are those in which a great deal has to be learned in order to appreciate that they *are* paradigms, and in order to be able to respond fully. For instance, in such cases there may be various possible interpretations — what has been called the 'creative ambiguity' of some of the greatest works of art.

My objection to the prevalent Myth of the Two Faculties, or Two Realms, which was discussed in Chapter 1, is not only philosophical but educational. It is to *caricature* the arts to assume, as is so persistently assumed, that understanding and rationality are irrelevant or inimical to artistic appreciation and creation. It makes no sense to suppose that artistic feelings, whether of artist or spectator, could even *exist* independently of rational understanding. To regard the arts as exclusively the province of feeling and imagination *as opposed to* reason is to endorse the subjectivist conception of mind which, so far from repudiating, perpetuates the traditional and current dismissive regard for the arts in education. For too long there has been a disastrous failure to understand the contribution of reasoning to the emotions generally, and to the feelings involved in artistic experience in particular, and this failure continues to handicap the case for the arts in education. What is required is a clear recognition of the necessarily *cognitive and rational* character of emotional feelings, and in particular those involved in the creation and appreciation of the arts.

Understanding is not, of course, necessary for all emotions. Obviously some emotional responses, such as many kinds of fear, are instinctive. Animals, for instance, are capable of fear and other emotional feelings. But, in an enormous and varied range of cases it makes no sense to suppose that feelings would be possible for any creature which did not have an understanding of certain cultural practices, with their implicit objective criteria of value and appropriateness. For instance, competence in the use of language is a necessary condition for a whole range of emotions, such as remorse about one's behaviour a few months ago, fear of continued economic inflation, and dismay about the likely result of the next general election. Nothing could count as fear of a happening in the distant future, or regret about the distant past, if there were no language. Learning a language, and with it what counts as reason and understanding, is necessary for the possibility of experiencing such feelings. As we saw in Chapter 6, the same applies to the arts.

It has been objected that my thesis is a form of elitism, since I am arguing that only those who have learned to understand an art form can have the relevant feelings. The objection is confused. In a *social* sense, the thesis is not in the least elitist since, on the contrary, I want to offer to *everyone* the chance of extending horizons of understanding, and thus the possibility of an extension of feelings. In an *educational* sense, I am simply saying, that those who have been educated in certain ways have advantages over those who have not. If *that* is what is meant by 'elitism' then every educational activity is elitist, and it would be of no value if it were not.

Tolstoy's confused insistence that true art should communicate itself easily to all mankind would disqualify his own works, and, if it makes sense at all, would reduce the arts to banality. That no great work of art can be easily understood by all is an *inevitable consequence* of there being so much to be learned in and through the arts.

There is often confusion, leading to unjustified pejorative allegations, about elitism, so it is important to be clear about it. It is certainly *not* elitist to insist that education gives possibilities of experience of which students would otherwise be deprived. Neither is it elitist to insist that some experiences are better than others. Without those two convictions no education would be possible at all. That is, if we do not sincerely believe that our students and future citizens will be *better* off when they have learned what we are offering in education, then we are not educating at all.

The Artist's Feeling

It is often assumed that there is a special problem about the relation of the artist's feeling to the art object. The source of the greatest misconception on this issue is again, the underlying influence of subjectivism, in this case the assumption that the feeling is an 'inner' mental event independent of the art object. A remark by Collingwood (1938) can be used to illustrate the important points. He wrote: 'Until a man has expressed his emotion, he does not yet know what emotion it is. The act of expressing it is therefore an exploration of his own emotions' (p. 111).

In one sense there is a mistake here, since I can know that I am angry, for instance, before or even without ever expressing it. However, more important, it may be true that knowing what I am feeling, and knowing what I am *inclined to do*, are inseparable. That is, unless there were a background of a general conceptual connection between feelings and the way they are expressed, no sense could be made of the notion that an individual could know what feelings he himself is having. As we have seen, one learns how to characterize one's own feelings as one learns to characterize the feelings of others. Similarly, it is possible to know that one has an artistic feeling which has not been expressed, but only because there is an artistic medium in which such feelings can be articulated, and are expressible.

More important issues are raised by Collingwood's second assertion, that the act of expression is an exploration of the artist's own emotions. Again a qualification is needed, since this may give the impression that such emotions could exist independently of the art form, whereas, as we have seen, they depend for their very existence on the existence of the medium in which they can be formulated. What is important here is to recognise the distinction between having a feeling and knowing what that feeling is. Enough has already been said to show that it makes no sense to suppose that a feeling could be purely private, in the sense that it is impossible, in principle for anyone else to have 'direct' knowledge of it. According to that subjectivist misconception only the person himself can have infallible knowledge of the character of his own feelings. Yet since the meaning of emotion-terms is rooted in behaviour, including verbal behaviour, it cannot be the case that one is *necessarily* in a better position than others for identifying the character of one's own feelings. For example, much of a psychoanalyst's task is trying to help his patients to recognize the character of their own feelings, for instance, of jealousy or envy, which they have failed to identify accurately. In the case of the arts, it is possible for the artist to *have* a feeling which he cannot, or cannot adequately, identify or describe. The exploration of the precise *form* of expressing it *is* the exploration of its identity and character. That is, *what* the feeling *is*, is discovered by the artist himself, in the act of creating the work of art. It makes no sense to suppose that the feeling is an independent mental event. Discovering how to express it in the artistic medium *is* discovering the artist's feeling.

Moreover, the act of expression, at least often, involves an exploration of the medium, and thereby confers a greater or confirmed grasp of its expressive possibilities, and with it a greater possibility of *having* the feelings. This raises the question of what I meant when I said that there is an important sense in which the emotion of the artist cannot intelligently be regarded as distinct from the work of art. First, it should be remembered that we are concerned with an *art* object, not simply a physical object. Even so, it sounds odd to suggest that what the artist experienced was a painting. Nevertheless, if that object, or kind of object, did not exist then neither could that emotion or kind of emotion. The clearest and most appropriate illustration is that of a highly particularized emotion directed not on to a *kind* of object, but on to a particular object. (This kind of case will be further discussed in Chapter 11.) For instance, consider the case of my feeling of affection for my former College in Cambridge. In one sense the College and my feeling are distinct, since the College could have existed without the feeling. But this particular feeling could not exist if the particular College had not existed. This emphasizes the point that the relation is logical or conceptual. On a subjectivist basis the emotion would just happen to be related to the College, and its character would be discovered by introspection. In that case, it would be logically possible, despite the fact that I have various mementos of the College, regularly attend reunions, visit it frequently and speak of it with affection, that I could discover by introspection that that particular affection was not for the College but was for walking in the Lake District. Such a supposition is, of course, senseless. (For those with a philosophical background it may be worth pointing out that I do not deny that there are also causal factors, and that I neither wish nor need to take sides on the issue of whether reasons can be construed as causes.) The appropriateness of the example is that, in the arts, we are concerned with particular emotions characterized by particular works.

The problem of the relation between the object and the emotion in the arts is parallel to that between thoughts and words. If you ask what are my thoughts on a certain issue, I may refer you to an article I have written. In this case there is little temptation to say, analogously: 'But what went on in you was not marks on pieces of paper, or printed words.' My thoughts are *identified by* the printed words. Without the medium of verbal language such thoughts could not exist, even unexpressed.

A philosophy undergraduate, struggling with a problem, may say that his thoughts on the issue are clear 'deep down' but that he is simply having difficulty in expressing them. But, in general, there is no such thing as a clear idea which cannot be clearly expressed. The qualification is that it is possible for there to be a case rather like that of inability to find the right word, although one is clear about what one wants to say. Nevertheless, in general, if the expression is confused, so are the thoughts 'deep down'. Normally, the struggle for clarity of expression *is* a struggle for clarity of thought.

There are two issues here: (a) it makes no sense to suppose that one could have the particular feeling or idea unless one had to a relevant extent mastered the art form; but (b) does it make sense to say that one may have a clear idea or feeling which cannot be expressed? We need to distinguish between a *specific* feeling or idea, and a *clear* one. An artist may have a *specific* idea for which he may struggle, in the manipulation of the medium, to find a precise expression. A notable example is that of the series of preliminary sketches, leading up to the finished work, in which Picasso expressed his feelings about the bombing of Guernica. It is highly probable that he did not have the specific idea prior to working through his sketches, but only a relatively vague one which was refined in his experimentation with them. But it is possible that the final version clearly expressed or captured the original specific but unclear idea. The idea could not have been *clear*, even to *him*, until he had found the precise expression for it.

The distinction can be brought out in terms of choreographing a dance. The choreographer, searching for a particular piece of music, may listen to several pieces, some of which may be quite near to what he wants. At last he hears one which is just right. How are we to describe this? His idea may have been specific since he was able to recognize the precise piece of music immediately, but it could not have been clear, since he himself did not know precisely what it was.

To repeat, this does not imply that it is always impossible to have clear but unexpressed thoughts and ideas, although that possibility is severely limited, and it depends upon a grasp of the cultural practice, the art form, with its implicit objective criteria. Thus Collingwood's remark would have to be amended to something like: 'Until a man knows how he would express it, he does not yet know precisely what emotion it is.' There are, then, two possibilities:

(a) An idea or feeling which is only relatively specific, in that, for instance, the artist may be aware that there is only a fairly narrow range of expressive possibilities, and can certainly say that some possibilities are inappropriate. Within that range he needs to explore and experiment to find the precise one he wants. He will *make* the idea or feeling both specific and clear in *working it out in the medium*.

(b) As a highly exceptional case, an idea or feeling which is specific, since the right expression can be recognized, but which cannot be clear to the artist since he is unable to say or identify precisely what he wants, or otherwise to formulate it clearly.

Consider my analogy with the philosophy undergraduate. The most likely case is as (a) above. However, it is possible, but only *as an exceptional case*, that he may have an idea which is specific but not clear. He may repudiate every other formulation, and give good reasons for denying that it expresses his thoughts, until he is offered precisely the formulation which he accepts. One would describe him as having had an idea which was specific but not clear; what he is offered makes clear what was already a specific idea.

Reasons: The Artist's Intention

It is a common practice, in discussion of the meaning of a work of art, to refer to what is believed to be the artist's intention in creating it. That is, reasons given for the artist's intention are assumed to be equivalent to reasons for what it means. However, it is an inevitable consequence of the dominant subjectivist doctrine that this assumption is entirely unjustified, or rather, makes no sense. For if, as the subjectivist believes, an intention is a private, 'inner' mental event, it would make no sense to suggest that one could refer to it. This is most obviously the case where an artist is long-dead, and has left no record of what he intended. So, on the face of it, there is a problem about the intelligibility of the common practice of giving reasons for the meaning of a work of art by reference to the artist's intention.

It would be a digression to discuss the question of intentions in detail. I shall consider it in order to reveal that the source of much of the confusion is another aspect of the subjectivist doctrine. In short, the apparent self-contradiction is *created* by the subjectivist assumption that an intention is a purely private, discrete 'inner' mental event.

It may already be apparent that the subjectivist misconception discussed above of assuming that the feeling expressed in a work of art is identifiable independently of the work, is exactly parallel to the assumption that the artist's intention is irrelevant to questions of meaning and appreciation. For both intention and feeling are construed as independently existing 'inner' mental events, known only to the artist. As in the case of artistic feeling, the intention is supposed to exist prior to and quite separately from the artistic medium in which it is expressed, or in which it can be formulated. This is why some theorists have come to the conclusion that it is a fallacy to assume that the meaning of a work of art can be equated with, or even related to, assumptions about the artist's intention in creating it. Consequently, taking their view, it is a fallacy to offer reasons for the meaning of art which refer to the artist's intention.

The best-known, and most influential, source of this view is a paper by Wimsatt and Beardsley (1962), entitled 'The intentional fallacy'. The authors make two major points: (a) we cannot usually discover the artist's intention, and (b) even if we could, it is irrelevant to the meaning of the work. Hence, they conclude, it is a fallacy to assume that the artist's intention is related to artistic meaning. In fact, as I hope is evident, the argument that this is a fallacy is itself a fallacy. We have uncovered another guise of the subjectivist doctrine.

It may be initially plausible to assert that the artist's intention cannot usually be discovered since, for instance, he may be dead and cannot be asked what he intended. It may be similarly initially plausible to assume that the intention is irrelevant to artistic meaning, since what matters is the work itself. But, the plausibility of both contentions depends solely upon the subjectivist presupposition that the intention is a separate 'inner' mental event, independent of the work, which can be infallibly known only to the artist. Enough has been said in relation to feelings, ideas and concepts to show that this prevalent subjectivist doctrine involves a fundamental misunderstanding of mental concepts. It makes no sense to construe an intention, like a feeling or a concept, as purely private, and infallibly known only to the person himself. As in the parallel case of feelings, there is a distinction between (a) having an intention, and (b) being able to identify it. This again points up the importance of cultural practices and tradition. For it makes no sense to suppose that certain intentions are possible without language, the arts and other social practices. Obviously, the attribution of the intention to make a particular move in chess could not intelligibly be made to someone who knew nothing about the game. It is obvious nonsense to suppose that such an intention could exist independently of the social activity of playing chess, although the intention need not be expressed. That is, although it is possible to have an intention without overtly acting on it or saying what it is, that possibility necessarily depends upon the existence, and one's understanding, of the publicly available medium — in this case chess — in which it can be formulated. Thus, in the cases which interest us, the possibility of keeping intentions to oneself, is parasitic upon a cultural practice, with its objective criteria of validity and value, in which those intentions can be formulated.

Having an intention should not be confused with, or taken to imply, the ability to identify it. It is perfectly possible, and indeed very common experience, to be confused about one's own intentions: it is perfectly possible, and common experience, to be mistaken about *one's own* intentions. It is a strangely persistent prejudice, perhaps especially in the arts, that the person (or artist) himself has infallible knowledge of his intentions and thus is necessarily in the best position to say what they are. As I have indicated, quite apart from philosophical considerations, it is contrary to common experience. For instance, a psychoanalyst's task is often to help a patient to recognize that he has misconstrued his own intentions. Less dramatically, we often learn that we have been mistaken about our own intentions, and it is an effort progressively to identify them more accurately and honestly. It is a central, and difficult, aspect of one's progressive struggle to achieve sincerity that one strives continuously to face truthfully the character of one's own intentions. So dauntingly often they are not what we so very much *want* to believe they are, and consequently what we *do* believe they are. The importance of this issue, with respect to how one lives one's normal life, and especially with respect to our close personal relationships, can hardly be exaggerated. It reveals again, very clearly, that philosophical issues, and perhaps especially philosophy of mind and moral philosophy, can have a powerful practical effect on the most important aspects of our lives.

The point is dramatically illustrated in Shakespeare's play *Measure for Measure*. Angelo, who had always been convinced that he was a man of cold, calculating nature, and strict moral rectitude, is suddenly overwhelmed by uncontrollable sexual passion. His shocked realisation that he is not the man he thought he was, and his recognition of his helpless ignorance of his own feelings, intentions and character, are brought sharply into focus in one of the most moving and thought-provoking scenes in the play when he asks: 'What *dost* thou? or, *What* art thou, Angelo?'

As this play brings out very clearly, in relation not only to Angelo, but also to Isabella, our capacity for self-deception is considerable. It is remarkable how unaware we are of our ignorance of the character of our own feelings and intentions. Self-knowledge is extremely difficult to achieve, largely because we tend to assume that it is so easy to understand oneself that we remain confidently unaware of the difficulty. The question: 'Who am I?' is one of the most important, yet one of the most difficult, questions of our lives. Yet without the *constant* search for an answer to that question one cannot be a sincere person and one may unwittingly be harming others. Thus the question of the *intrinsic* nature of the character of oneself is of overriding importance. As Simone Weil puts it (1968): 'The substance of our life is composed of fiction. We fictionalise our future; and unless we are heroically devoted to the truth, we fictionalise our past, refashioning it to our taste.' (p. 61) The point underlies an incisively perceptive recommendation by an anonymous medieval religious writer: 'Swink and sweat until thou knowest thyself, and then, I trow, thou shalt know thy God.'

Necessarily, in general, what I say about my own intentions coincides with what others say about them. That is what makes sense of the notion of learning how to use expressions of the form 'I intend to do X'. There would be no sense in the notion of learning the use of intention-language on a subjectivist account. On the contrary, what does make sense of it is that I learn to characterize my own intentions in the same way, and at the same time, as I learn to characterize the intentions of others. It makes no sense to assume, as the subjectivist does, that an intention is necessarily or normally independent of what is *done*. That is, the intention with which an action is carried out cannot intelligibly be construed as normally or necessarily a preceding or concurrent 'inner' mental event. There are not *two* events, but only *one*. To refer to an action as being done with a certain intention is to say what *kind* of action it is. This is not to deny that some intentions can be formulated in advance, or that sometimes they are not carried out. When I lift my cup to drink tea, that is an intentional action, but it is rarely if ever preceded or accompanied by a formulated intention to do so. I simply lift the cup intentionally, and I am usually thinking or talking about something else. Nevertheless, I can, in advance, form the intention to go on holiday in Brittany, or to telephone my brother tomorrow evening. And sometimes I do not carry out what I intend.

Again, it can hardly be over-emphasized that the difficulty is to rid oneself of subjectivist presuppositions, that is, of assuming that the notion of an intentional action or product involves *two* separate entities. To repeat the point made in Chapter 8, we have neither a conjunct of mental stuff and physical stuff, nor merely physical stuff, but a *human being*, whose feelings, thoughts and intentions are to an overwhelmingly large extent conferred by the language, arts and cultural practices of society. A human being, when he has learned the discipline of a medium, can keep his intentions, given by it, to himself, or he can carry out intentional actions in that medium. There can be conflicts of criteria in that what a person says about his own intention may conflict with what observers say about it. There can be no *general* answer to the question 'Who is right?'.

The most important point is that it is what a person *does* which is the principal criterion for what his intention is. It is almost a truism in philosophy that the principal sign, or criterion, of wanting is trying to get. Similarly, a principal sign or criterion of intending is what is *done*. If someone strikes out because he has been attacked or insulted, we do not need, even it it made sense, to attempt to conduct an 'inference' from that 'external' behaviour to a supposed 'internal' purely private, subjective 'intention'. That is, his *action* is a criterion, i.e. necessarily a reason, for attributing to him that intention. And in many cases, such as this, there is not even any room for doubt. His action *is*, unquestionably, his intention. To repeat, in that context such behaviour *is* a criterion of his intention. This point was well illustrated in a talk I once heard by Ron Geesin, an artist who creates the most extraordinary sounds out of the most ordinary by an ingenious use of tape-recorders. After he had played one of his pieces, a member of the audience asked him what he had originally intended to produce. He looked puzzled for a moment, and then, gesturing to the tape-recorder, he said that *that* was what he had intended. The questioner was not satisfied, repeating that he knew that was what was eventually produced, but what had been his original intention. Ron Geesin looked even more puzzled for a time, then burst out: 'That was my intention. You've just heard it.'

In this kind of case there need be no further answer, and further questions would make no sense. The work of art is normally what *identifies* the artist's intention. To assume, in general, that the intention can be identified independently of the work is fundamentally to misunderstand the concept of an intention. There is a logical relation between the intention and the form of its expression. Of course the work is not always what the artist intended, any more than, in other contexts, one always and necessarily achieves what one intends. Once when visiting an artist friend I expressed admiration for an unusual piece of pottery. He laughed and confessed that its unusual shape was the result of an accident in firing. Nevertheless, this kind of case is *necessarily the exception*. I can intend to do only what I believe I can do, thus although I may wish, I cannot *intend*, to fly like a bird. Consequently, unless one normally achieves what one says one intends, it could not count as an intention.

Since one is not necessarily the best judge of one's own intentions: the question may arise: 'What about a conflict of criteria, where the person says that his intention was X, while others who know him well say that it was Y? How can we discover what he really intended?' There can be no *general* answer to this kind of question. One has to consider the strength of the conflicting reasons in each case. In some cases there may be no clear answer. As we saw in Chapter 3, the fact that reasoning is involved does not necessarily imply that a decisive resolution of different interpretations or conceptions can be achieved, and this applies equally to intentions — one's own, and those of other people.

To interpret a work of art *is*, normally, to interpret the artist's intention. Whether or not one takes into account the artist's *stated* intentions, perhaps implicitly in the title, depends upon the particular case. The stated intention is neither necessarily decisive nor necessarily irrelevant, although in view of the artist's intimate connection with the work, it would normally be a factor to which one would give serious consideration.

The highly imaginative choreographer, Alwin Nikolais, said at a conference some years ago that it often takes him five years to discover what he intended in the dances he creates. He achieves this largely by means of careful reflection about what perceptive critics write. To refer back to a term I used in Chapter 5, the artist's intention is a central criterion of the meaning of the work of art. By that I mean that, normally, what one takes to be the artist's intention is necessarily a reason to be taken importantly into account in one's interpretation of the work, and conversely.

One cannot say simply that the work *is* his intention since there can be other criteria, such as the explicit repudiation by the artist of what others say about his intention. Thus there is room for debate about the extent to which other factors should play a part in interpretation of the work. Nevertheless, the work is the principal criterion for what the artist intended. Works of art are normally the intended creations of human beings, and they are necessarily formulated in the public media of art forms. The supposition that works of art could, in general, be purely fortuitous occurrences would make no sense, since it would take away any sense from the notion of a work of art. The crucial point is that the sense is given by an intention which is necessarily normally formulated in an artistic medium. 'Happenings' and *objets trouvés*, to be regarded as art, are necessarily parasitic on, or extensions of, a concept of art whose sense is given by works which are normally intentionally created. It is significant, too, that *objets trouvés* are *intentionally* selected. Analogously, merely by chance, cracks in a brick wall might form a meaningful word, but the meaning is derived from a medium in which, normally, words are used *intentionally* to communicate. It would make no sense to suppose that word meanings could normally be given by purely fortuitous cracks in brick walls.

It transpires that the common practice of assuming that giving reasons for the artist's intention *is*, normally, to give reasons for the meaning of the work of art is entirely justified. Doubts about the intelligibility of it arise from the subjectivist fallacy that intentions are independent, 'inner' mental events, about which others can never have 'certain' or 'direct' knowledge.

Reasons: The Spectator's Response

The other side of the same subjectivist coin as the contention that it is a fallacy to regard reasons for the artist's intention as relevant to artistic meaning, is the contention that it is a fallacy to regard reasons which cite the response of the *spectator* as relevant to the meaning of a work of art. This supposed fallacy is known as the affective fallacy, and its best-known proponents are again Wimsatt and Beardsley, in a paper of that title (1960, pp. 21–39).

According to this view, artistic appreciation should be concerned solely with phenomenal features, such as coloured patches, and thus to describe a work of art in affective terms such as 'moving', 'inspiring', 'joyful', and so on, is to talk not of the work itself, but of one's response to it. To repeat, this time it is not the feeling or intention of the artist which is regarded as independent of the work, and therefore irrelevant, but the feeling of the *spectator*.

An initially plausible argument for this view is that since people have different emotional responses, what counts as the meaning of a work of art would vary if affective terms were to be regarded as constituting a legitimate part of artistic appreciation. But a similar argument applies to perception of phenomenal features, since people vary in their ability to discriminate. This kind of argument, if taken to an extreme, would completely eliminate any possibility of meaning, or saying anything whatsoever about a work. The distinction drawn in Chapter 4 between the individual and the subjective is again important here. That individuals vary in their abilities is clearly no reason for denying the objectivity of mathematics and the sciences, or that linguistic terms have objective meaning.

That one is giving reasons for its meaning by the use of affective terms does not in the least imply that one is not talking about the painting itself. There is a distinction, as we saw earlier, between a response which just happens to be related to the work, perhaps because of association, and an *objective* response, which one might characterize in affective terms but for which one could offer reasons by reference to features of the work. These would count as reasons, of course, only if they were grounded in the concept of art, the culture, and perhaps a particular school of thought or approach.

There is an important distinction to be drawn here. When involved in artistic appreciation one is not normally consciously concerned with how *others* respond to a work. Certainly, as we have seen, individual response is central. But this should be distinguished from the mistaken contention that affective terms cannot be legitimately applied to works of art. It should also be sharply distinguished from the important point that the meaning or intelligibility of the use of affective terms is rooted in a general uniformity of response. For example, one might apply the term 'moving' to a convincing performance of King Lear's agonized grief at the death of Cordelia. One could give reasons for the legitimacy of the application of the term 'moving', for instance, by reference to Lear's having learned as a consequence of his harrowing experiences that, contrary to his initial belief and despite his harsh treatment of her, Cordelia was the only daughter who genuinely loved him. Moreover, if only the message revoking her death had arrived minutes earlier, her life would have been saved. In answer to the question 'What is the justification for calling the scene "moving"?', one's reasons would consist not in referring to the reactions of other people but in citing the circumstances in the play and the convincing way in which they were portrayed. If the question were *then* asked 'Nevertheless, given those circumstances why was it a moving scene?', one could make no sense of the question. For the intelligibility of the original question, and of the justification for the application of the term, is *given* by the fact that people *are* normally moved by such circumstances. This emphasizes again the importance of the issue discussed in Chapter 2, that artistic appreciation, artistic meaning, and the sense of reasons given for judgments, are rooted in the ways in which people naturally or instinctively respond.

Similarly, unless there were general uniformity in colour-judgments there could be no meaning to colour-terms. Yet it is possible in both cases that even the whole group could be mistaken on exceptional occasion. Everyone could be wrong in a particular colour-judgment, just as all the knowledgeable could have an inappropriate affective response to a particular work of art. The relation between the meaning of affective terms, as of colour-terms, and the response or judgments of people, is by no means simple and straightforward. But in both cases it depends ultimately upon a certain uniformity of response.

There are, then, two points here: (a) there are affective qualities in works of art, and the attribution of them can certainly be supported with reasons; (b) the meaning, or intelligible application, of affective terms depends ultimately upon a general uniformity of response among those who understand the art form.

There are two major points which arise from this and the preceding section.

1　To deny the relevance of questions of the artist's intention, and of the affective response, is to presuppose a clear, sharp and unproblematic distinction between what the work *means*, and what is *extrinsic* to it. That is, it is to presuppose that the question of what is and what is not extrinsic to it is *independent* of the question of the meaning of the work. But this is confused, for the question of what counts as intrinsic and extrinsic is *part of*, and inseparable from, the question of how the work should be understood or interpreted. For example, the question of whether or not we should accept, or at least seriously consider, as a valid reason for its meaning, the account given by Berlioz of what he was expressing in the *Symphonie Fantastique is* the question of what it means. Our conception of a work may be in intentional or affective terms, and to rule out such discourse as extrinsic is to beg the question of what is and is not extrinsic; it presupposes an incoherently oversimple conception of artistic meaning. Artistic meaning is complex and impossible to demarcate sharply. Hence it makes no sense to suppose that a definitive *general* distinction can be drawn between what is and what is not relevant as a reason for the meaning of a work of art. Such a distinction can be drawn only in particular cases, and even then it may be difficult.

2　A medium of expression, such as a language or an art form, necessarily requires both an expresser and a receiver. That is what it means to be a public medium or cultural practice. It makes no sense to assume, as the subjectivist assumes, that the feelings and intentions expressed in art are discrete 'inner' mental events which could exist independently of the art form, and thus that the question of what was the artist's intention is normally distinct from the question of the meaning of the work he has created. In one respect at least, the misconception of the anti-affectivist can be seen as the other side of the same coin, for to deny the relevance of the response is equally to fail adequately to recognize the central significance of the *art form*, and that an art form is necessarily a *public* medium of expression. Thus there has to be the possibility of some degree of match between what the artist has expressed in the work, and the response of at least some of the audience. As in linguistic expression, the match may not be exact. To insist on the possibility of some degree of match is entailed by saying that an art form, like language, is a *social*, shared, practice. This is a central aspect of the notion of personal identity which is an underlying theme of this book, and which is aptly captured in the phrase 'the conversation that we are'.

However, there is an important difference between these two points. While the intelligibility of application of affective terms depends upon a general uniformity of response, in any *particular* case the actual response of any individual or even a whole group may not be relevant to the question of the meaning of a work of art. By contrast, there is a logical relation between what the artist intended and the meaning of a work in any particular case. That is, while the question of the artist's *intention* is *always* relevant to the question of the meaning of a work, this is not true of the affective response to a work.

The Education of Feeling

The argument of this chapter underlines again that emotional feelings can be learned, both in the arts and generally. The education of feeling in the arts consists in giving reasons for, and encouraging people to recognize for themselves, different conceptions of a work of art. A different understanding of a work will constitute a different object of the emotion, and thus a different feeling. Progressively recognizing the validity of reasons for more finely discriminating conceptions of the arts gives the possibility of a progressive development of more finely discriminated feelings.

Some people are prepared to accept my thesis only up to a point. They concede that expressive meaning is partly a matter of a logical relation between the work and feeling, but, they are inclined to say, there are also subjective aspects. To this I would reply that to the extent that they involve subjectivity, no sense can be made of learning, and thus there could be no place in the arts for the education of feeling.

It is important to emphasise again that the term 'subjective' is usually very unclear, and may be used with at least four *very* different meanings. If by saying that the arts are partly subjective one means that personal involvement and feeling, and individual differences, are central to the creation and appreciation of the arts, then, so far from being incompatible with my argument, that is a *main theme* of it. By contrast, there are three other meanings of 'subjective' which are often confused with the foregoing and which continue to do serious damage to the case for the arts in education. By far the commonest, and that which poisons almost all discussion about the arts, refers to the purely private realm of 'inner' mental events, which it is a main aim of this book to expose as making no sense, in any of its many manifestations. The second meaning of 'subjective' does make sense, within limits, and it refers to the idiosyncratic. Thus, if I have a sad response to a joyful Mozart rondo because it was my dead mother's favourite piece of music, that is subjective in the sense that it is inappropriate to the qualities of the music, and the notion of giving reasons to bring about a changed response through understanding is out of place. The qualification, 'within limits', is necessary because, of course, if all or most responses were idiosyncratic in this sense, then this meaning of 'subjective' would collapse into the former one, that is, it would make no sense. Neither, of course, could there be any sense in the notion of being idiosyncratic, since there would be no notion of appropriateness by contrast with which anything could intelligibly be said to be idiosyncratic.

This is certainly not to oppose the idiosyncratic in art where this means something like the highly individual or unusual. The kind of response to which I am referring as unacceptably confused is that which is inappropriate to the character of its object. An idiosyncratic response would be appropriate to an idiosyncratic work of art. The kind of idiosyncratic, or subjective, response which I am opposing cannot intelligibly be regarded as part of artistic appreciation. It is an important part of the individuality of involvement with the arts that experiences in life generally may give the possibility of deeper feelings in response to art. But those feelings must be *appropriate*, and the sense of the notion of appropriateness involves *understanding*. That is, deeper feelings will be inseparably bound up with deeper conceptions of works of art.

The third meaning of 'subjective' I have mentioned earlier in the book. On this meaning 'subjective' is equivalent merely to personal liking or preference. The conception that the arts are subjective in this sense, though very common, is also thoroughly confused philosophically, and disastrous in the damage it does to the arts in education. (As we shall see in Chapter 12, it is related to, or part of, the prevalent use of the term 'aesthetic' to refer both to the arts and to non-arts objects and experiences. It is crucial to be clear that there are *two separate*, but *sometimes* overlapping, concepts — the aesthetic, and the artistic.) For if, for instance, appreciation of a work of art is merely a matter of whether one likes it or not, it is difficult to see how it could be argued that the arts are important, in education and society.

We should remain *very* clear, to avoid confusion, that all these meanings of 'subjective' are usually run together, so that it is often unclear what is meant by the use of the term.

Chapter 10

Two Attitudes:
Detached and Involved

There are broadly two different kinds of approach to artistic appreciation. Usually they are not explicitly distinguished. The proponents of each sometimes tend to assume that theirs is what *really* counts as artistic appreciation, and that the other approach simply misses what is important. I shall refer to them as the detached and the involved attitudes. There is no sharp distinction between them. Although at the extremes they are very different, they are not always clearly distinguishable. The detached attitude includes a predominant concern with structure and technique, but is not limited to such a concern. For instance, one might recognize the emotional meaning in a work without experiencing the relevant feelings. Similarly, one may adopt a relatively detached attitude to other people, and in some professions, such as medicine and the law, this is, to some extent, necessary.

By contrast, one may respond with feeling to both works of art and people. One may alternate between these attitudes. For example, at a concert of choral and orchestral music one might sometimes read the score, following chord progressions, or selecting for attention the part of a particular voice or instrument. Sometimes, closing the score, one might immerse oneself in the expressive qualities of the music, no longer consciously aware of structural or technical aspects. During a long work such as Bach's *St Matthew Passion*, one might alternate several times between these attitudes. Similarly, one's interest in a play or novel may be centred on the development of the plot, structure, style of writing, acting-techniques, or the significance of the language used; or one may instead identify with some of the characters or situations portrayed. This is, indeed, one of the reasons why one so often wants to see a superb performance of a play or dance more than once. For example, as I write, I have recently seen Trevor Nunn's brilliant production of Shakespeare's *Measure for Measure*, at The Other Place, Stratford upon Avon. The performance was so riveting, and one was so immersed in it, that I went to see it a second time partly in order to try to analyse how such powerful effects were produced. For instance, there was a remarkably convincing portrayal of the difficult part of Angelo. Among many other perceptive and imaginative details, the actor presented Angelo as sycophantic at the beginning, in his obsequious attitude to the Duke. This made very good sense of his later authoritarian rigidity, and of the yearning passion and humanity which underlay it. I wanted to see just *how*, technically, he had achieved such a brilliantly insightful characterization. But that was only one of the aspects of the production which I wanted to consider from a detached point of view. There are numerous examples of these two attitudes in the appreciation of all the art forms.

It is often assumed that genuine artistic appreciation consists *really* in only one of these attitudes. This is an assumption made, at one extreme by romantic, or traditional expressionist, theorists, and at the other extreme by formalists. Each regards either emotional identification, or detached critical appraisal, respectively, as the *only* legitimate form of art appreciation. The expressionist extreme censures the formalist's supposedly unimaginatively sterile, dissecting, cold and impersonally rational missing of the *real* point of art; the formalist extreme censures the expressionist's supposedly heart-on-sleeve, sentimentally romantic, uncritically imaginative and irrational missing of the *real* point of art. The expressionist, who is rightly convinced of the central importance of feeling and personal involvement, sometimes wrongly assumes that he has to repudiate rationality and critical appraisal; conversely, the formalist who is rightly convinced of the central importance of rationality and critical appraisal in the arts sometimes assumes that he has to repudiate feeling and personal involvement. The source of the conflict is their shared conception that feeling and reason are incompatible, and even inimical to each other. That deeply fallacious presupposition has, I hope, by now been thoroughly exposed as one of the most disastrously confused aspects of subjectivism. The narrow conception of rationality and of feeling which is inherent in it is the major source of prevalent distorted conceptions of artistic experience. Each protagonist holds too restricted a view of the possibilities of artistic experience, for *both* attitudes are appropriate and enriching, and even complementary.

The current tendency among artists and critics towards an exclusive concern with the formal is an understandable reaction against the excesses of romanticism, which more readily appeal to popular taste, and are manifested, for instance, in the sentimentalism of many films, television programmes, popular songs and the reproductions of paintings sold in large department stores. But, of course, it is not simply a reaction. It would reveal a failure to understand much contemporary art if one were unaware that it consists to a large extent in extending the grammar or vocabulary of the art form. That is, it is extending the expressive possibilities of the art form, just as an extended vocabulary extends the possibilities of linguistic expression. For example, Schoenberg considered that Wagner had extended the possibilities of tonal structure to their limits, so although he was influenced by expressionist music, and initially wrote in that idiom himself, he reached the point where he felt he had to abandon the framework of key signatures and tonality altogether. This was a grammatical exploration, since Schoenberg considered that the tonal idiom was largely exhausted, and that new possibilities were required. So he experimented with the twelve-tone composition. In serial music a tone-row is established, and the composer can invert, or transpose it, or invert the transposition , or create a retrograde series, or a retrograde inversion, and so on. This allows forty-eight possibilities.

These approaches to music, and the modern idiom generally, would on the whole be regarded as manifestations of the detached attitude. They are structural explorations. A tone-row is difficult to recognize, and requires some technical expertise to follow the composer's manipulation of it, particularly on the first few occasions of listening. Without the ability to recognize, at least minimally, such compositional adroitness, the music may be of little interest or meaning. This shows again the fallacy inherent in the assumption that a criterion of the value of a work of art is ease and generality of communication. Schoenberg expressly believed that great music can be understood only by a listener educated and experienced in the art form and particular idiom.

Similar formal explorations frequently occur in the other arts as, for example, in Picasso's abandonment of chiaroscuro, and his 'conceptual' distortions of the human figure as a result of his conviction that the traditional idiom had been almost fully explored. Picasso's innovations opened the way for others, as Schoenberg's had in music. Hence Paul Klee, Mark Rothko and Piet Mondrian, to name but a few, are highly experimental, using colour and line in unusual juxtaposition, simply for its own intrinsic interest — indeed, Klee is sometimes referred to as a modern Leonardo da Vinci. One could cite similar examples across the range of modern arts, such as Samuel Beckett, Barbara Hepworth, James Joyce, Alwin Nikolais, Ingmar Bergman. In each case there is a strong interest in grammatical problems, in extending the formal, structural possibilities, *per se.*

However, although these approaches are manifestations of the detached attitude to the arts, it is, as I have already hinted, a confusion to suppose that the two attitudes are necessarily opposed to each other. For grammatical explorations may *create* expressive possibilities which could not otherwise exist. As we have seen in earlier chapters, artistic feelings are necessarily cognitive, and rational: one cannot *have* artistic feelings without understanding. That understanding is of a particular art form within a whole cultural context. Thus an extension of the conceptual, formal possibilities, of the structural framework of an art form, is an extension of the possibilities of feeling. Analogously, the grammar and vocabulary of a language set limits, although not rigid and timeless limits, to what words can mean, to what can be expressed, and to what can be thought, felt, and experienced. For example, it would make no sense, normally, to say that one could experience pride in a cloud. There are logical limits, set by the normal uses of the term, to what can count as an object of pride. Similar considerations apply to the arts, although there may be greater flexibility in this sphere. There is a range of emotions which are expressible within a particular style and, as Wollheim points out (1970, p. 80): 'it is virtually impossible for us to imagine the expression of a state which falls outside this range being accomplished within the style. The supposition of an optimistic painting by Watteau, or a tortured or tempestuous group by Clodion, verges upon absurdity.' The innovations, in extending the formal possibilities, are extending the range of what can be formulated in the medium, and therefore of what can be felt and expressed.

Although one may sympathize with a strong reaction against the excesses of expressionism, as, for instance, in Stravinsky's assertion that music by its very nature is incapable of expressing anything, it is a misconception to exaggerate it. Those whom I shall loosely call the Romantics may err too far towards uncritical personal involvement, but the current tendency is often to err to an opposite extreme. For example, there is a prevalent acceptance of a view most notably propounded by Kant that the aesthetic attitude is essentially one of disinterested contemplation, requiring 'distancing' for detached critical appraisal. In this vein Scruton (1974, p. 130) writes: 'It is a purpose of convention in art to overcome emotional involvement.' But although there is a point of substance here, there is also a confusion. First, as we have seen, the conventions, so far from overcoming, are inseparable from, the feelings which are a legitimate and appropriate part of artistic expression and appreciation. It is true that part of one's understanding of the art form of drama is revealed by the fact that one does not run up to the stage to save Desdemona. But it is a confusion to assume that this implies the necessity for distancing and detachment, in the mistaken belief that artistic appreciation, properly so called, requires the *overcoming* of emotional involvement. On the contrary, in many cases it would be a mark of one's *failure* fully to appreciate a work if one were *not* emotionally involved. The artistic conventions do not *overcome*, but rather *determine the character of*, the emotional involvement.

What I mean by that is, for instance, that one does not respond to a situation in a play in exactly the same way as one would in real life. The object towards which the emotion is directed, and which determines what response it is, is a *fictional* character. One responds not to Mary Smith, who is playing the part, but to Desdemona, the character in the play . This once again emphasises the crucial, ineliminable importance of the cultural practice which is the root of artistic understanding, and therefore response. *That* kind of response is, given by an understanding of a particular cultural tradition and concept of art. So it is deeply confused to regard it as the same kind of response, only requiring 'distancing', and the *overcoming* of emotional involvement. The relation between life and art is the main theme of Chapter 13. Here I want simply to emphasize that emotional response to art is *different* in important respects from emotional response in life, and it is a confusion to regard the former as a diminished version of the latter.

The Inuit people who, attending a performance of *Othello*, were appalled to see what they took to be the killing of people on a stage, experienced an *inappropriate* emotional response because, having no grasp of the concept of drama, they *misunderstood* what was going on. Once they discovered that people had not been killed, and were shown what happens in such a drama production, without any understanding of what is involved in drama they would simply find the whole thing thoroughly silly. It would be a confusion to conclude that an understanding of the concept of drama would give them detachment, distancing and thus an overcoming of emotional involvement. On the contrary, if the play were well performed, those with the relevant understanding might well reveal their appreciation of the performance *by* their emotional involvement. One might be tempted to make the point by saying that such spectators, as compared with the Inuit, could be *equally* involved emotionally, but, of course, that might be misleading in implying a comparison on the same scale, whereas the point I am emphasizing can be better made by saying that the scales are different. To repeat, there is a difference in the *kinds* of emotional feeling, hence it may be misleading to suggest that they can legitimately be compared on the same scale in terms of emotional intensity.

The formalist who exaggerates or misconstrues the significance of understanding and rationality to the point of *excluding* emotional involvement reveals a deep *mis*understanding of the concept of art. For an *adequate* understanding of what is involved in the concept of art reveals the *character* of appropriate artistic emotional response. It certainly does not reveal an overcoming of emotional involvement — indeed, quite the contrary.

There is another misconception inherent in the contention that artistic appreciation is essentially detached. In Chapter 4 it was shown that an artistic judgment is made as a result of personal experience, and is partly an expression of one's personal feeling about or attitude to the work. The experience of an emotionally expressive work on which any adequate judgment is made will often require a personal identification with it. To repeat, even in such a case, I am not saying that an exclusively detached attitude could not even count as artistic appreciation. What I am saying is that this would amount only to a limited appreciation of the work. Only if this is accepted can one make any sense of the revulsion one feels for sentimental art, since one is implicitly invited to identify with, and thus experience on one's own behalf, feelings which one recognizes to be insincere.

Sentimentality

To say that sentimentality is insincere is not to imply that it is intended to deceive others. One may deceive oneself. The point is brought out by D.H. Lawrence (1936):

> Sentimentalism is the working off on yourself of feelings you haven't really got. We all *want* to have certain feelings: feelings of love, of passionate sex, of kindliness and so forth. Very few people really feel love, or sex passion, or kindliness, or anything else that goes at all deep. So the mass just fake these feelings inside themselves. Faked feelings! The world is all gummy with them. (p. 545)

The point becomes clear when we consider music, which can be sentimental although the question of deception, in the ordinary sense, cannot arise. Ian Robinson (1973, pp. 39–40), for instance, cites Brahms as a composer who is 'when he seems most serious, insincere because sentimental', in that he 'worked off on himself' feelings, for example, of affirmation and serenity, that he had not really got. This issue is related to the quotation from Wilde in Chapter 6, about the intellectual and emotional life of ordinary people:

> Just as they borrow their ideas from a sort of circulating library of thought . . . and send them back soiled at the end of each week, so they always try to get their emotions on credit, and refuse to pay the bill when it comes in. (In Chapter 6)

To work off on oneself feelings one hasn't really got *is* to get emotions on credit, and because they are not genuinely felt, there is no bill to pay. One is, as it were, *playing at* having feelings, and one can withdraw from the game. This is one of the pernicious effects of television. People may be superficially moved by the plight of the starving or homeless portrayed in a documentary. That the feeling is spurious is revealed by their ability to enjoy a comedy programme which immediately follows. Television inoculates against deep, sincere feelings by progressively dulling the sensibilities, by providing such a constant stream of faked, shallow, 'gummy', sentimental feelings that any potential for discrimination and intensity of feeling becomes permanently blunted and lost.

Ian Robinson (1973, pp. 39–40) endorses Lawrence by saying: 'all real insincerity is self-deceiving rather than trickery'. Yet, while this is an important aspect of sentimentality, there is an even more important one. For to call his feelings sentimental may not be to say that someone is working off on himself feelings which he has not really got, but, far more seriously, it may be to characterize the feelings which he *has really got.* That is, it may not be a case of 'unconsciously suppressing knowledge of the rottenness within' (ibid., p. 9) but that a person with only trite understandings or forms of expression, is a person who is capable of only trite feelings. Those *are* the confines of his emotional feelings, the limits of his personality, the restrictions on himself. This shows the *crucial* relation between the cognitive/rational, and the emotional, in general. For simply to accept uncritically the trivialising wash of cliché gushing forth from, for instance, the popular press and television is to restrict one's understanding, and consequently one's *feelings*, to the level of triviality.

This is why I am convinced that the *most* important contribution of education is to extend horizons of understanding, and to encourage students to continue to do so for the rest of their lives. For, as I have emphasized, to extend the possibility of emotional experience necessarily *requires,* is *inseparable from,* an extension of *understanding.* Beckett's *Happy Days* illustrates the point. Winnie, buried in a growing mound of cliché, which limits her thoughts and feelings to the banal, can exclaim, of each of her days: 'Another happy day.' So restricted are her conceptual horizons that *this is* what happiness *amounts to* for her. These are the narrow and superficial confines of her understanding, and therefore the narrow and superficial limits of her feelings of happiness. Feelings given by far richer and deeper understanding are completely beyond her horizons, outside the possibility of her experience. There is a painting by Francis Bacon of a distorted figure sitting on a bare chair, in a bare cell, with a single bare electric-light bulb above him. The whole atmosphere is redolent of a police-state or concentration camp. His resigned, contorted face stares dejectedly, hopelessly at the windowless walls of his cell. There is no possibility of escape, as he stares fixedly forwards. Yet, behind him, there is an open door. For him, the door may as well be locked and barred, because he is completely unaware of it.

There are numerous examples of ways in which a frighteningly large proportion of people are permanently limited in their conceptions and feelings, and thus permanently excluded from possibilities of a far more fulfilling life, by the grounds of values and understandings set by advertisements, television, and the popular press and radio. Thus the most pernicious sentimentality is where a person really *has* got trite and superficial feelings: such feelings are what *count* as the *only* genuine responses to, and therefore understanding of, life for him. In such a case he may indeed pay the bill to the full, as have many soldiers, in many wars, for sentimental, superficial feelings of nationalism or jingoism which were sincerely yet uncritically held, but which were specious and tragically mistaken. Hence, of course, the motive of some of the poets of the First World War was precisely to expose the sentimental 'old lie' that it is glorious to die for one's country. As we saw in Chapter 7, it took a creative struggle to change that conception, and thus to change the relevant feelings.

The arts, some art forms in particular, have an immensely important responsibility, and contribution to make, in this respect. To anticipate an issue which will be further discussed in later chapters, the arts can open up for us fresh, unexpected perspectives on a wide and varied range of situations in life generally, and in this way they can give greatly extended possibilities of feeling. Other disciplines, such as history, can also do this. But the arts have a much wider and more varied scope. Almost, if not quite, *any* aspect of life can be the subject of art. Coriolanus, in Shakespeare's play, exclaims: 'There is a world elsewhere'. It is a crucial contribution of the arts, especially in education, that they can make available to us worlds of feeling and experience elsewhere.

Involved and Detached Attitudes: Complementary

Adopting the involved attitude does not in the least imply the abjuring of critical reasoning. On the contrary, as I hope is now clear, the development of expressive and responsive feelings necessarily *requires* the development of critical abilities.[1] This is part of what is meant by saying that the feelings involved in artistic experience are inseparable from understanding and rationality. Artistic feelings are necessarily identified by modes of understanding. Thus critical reasoning is certainly not the exclusive province of the detached attitude. On the contrary, as I hope I have made abundantly clear, the feelings characteristic of the involved attitude are rational in kind. The distinction between the two attitudes marks a distinction between *kinds* of reasoning. For instance, the kind of reasoning which is part of the detached attitude may be concerned with the formal structure of a work rather than the emotional response which is appropriate to it.

It is not the case that for every work of art one can adopt either of these attitudes. Sometimes only one of them may be appropriate. Nevertheless, in many cases it is only by adopting both that one can fully appreciate, or perhaps be fully possessed by, a work. In order fully to appreciate a work, in many cases, one can and should alternate between the detached and the involved attitudes. Even when fully involved one may be aware of, for instance, the artist's mastery of his medium, and one may want to experience the work again in order to concentrate more upon his technical expertise, partly to see how such a powerful impact was achieved.

The distinction may not always be sharp or clearly recognizable, but it is important, and central aspects of artistic experience can be missed if there is an exclusive preoccupation with one at the expense of the other, or if it be assumed that only one of them is legitimate. That there are two attitudes which are in some ways very different no more implies that only one of them is legitimate, or is *really* artistic appreciation, than the fact that one may respond emotionally to a verbal utterance implies that one cannot *also* consider its grammatical structure or vocabulary. A parallel loss of richness of experience would be incurred by anyone who adopted only one of these attitudes to language. An exclusively involved attitude, if that were possible, would preclude the extension of conceptual understanding which is necessary for the possibility of extending the relevant emotional experience; an exclusively detached attitude, centred, for instance, on logical or grammatical aspects of language, would equally incur loss of emotional experience. In the case both of the arts and of language, a failure, in relevant circumstances, to employ and develop *both* attitudes incurs the loss of a dimension of central importance. It may tend, at one extreme, to susceptibility to sentimentalism; and at the other extreme, to shallow intellectualism. Fully to appreciate the arts one needs both detached critical appraisal, and the educated emotional capacity to involve oneself in a personally meaningful way.

Personal Association

To revert to an issue raised in Chapter 4, the personal involvement which is central to artistic experience should not be assumed to consist in personal associations. As we have seen, this common and plausible assumption is another of the guises of the subjectivist doctrine. I shall briefly consider a clearly articulated argument in favour of that subjectivist assumption.

In his interesting review (1987) of the earlier version of my book, McAdoo's subjectivist presuppositions are apparent when he states starkly that the 'evocation of personal associations . . . is, after all, what we *mean* by "personal involvement".' What I mean by 'personal involvement' will be further explained in Chapter 13, but I hope it is already abundantly clear, from Chapter 4, and this chapter, that in fact this subjectivist conception, of personal associations in general, can make no sense of the notion of personal involvement with the arts.

That McAdoo's argument is underlain by subjectivist preconceptions is evident in several places, notably, for instance, where he writes (p. 145): 'In so far as Best's objectivity, for all its open-endedness, seems to rely upon a conception of the aesthetic object as something independent of any personal way in which we may constitute it, it is difficult to see how he can posit a rational place for personal response . . .' Some confusion here is created by McAdoo's continued use of terms such as 'aesthetic' object etc. That is, despite my *rejecting* as confused, the prevalent conflation of the aesthetic and the artistic, he continues his discussion of my views in terms of it. For example, he writes in his paper (1987, p. 311): 'It is a necessary feature of *aesthetic* (*sic*) experience not to be engenderable through rules alone' (my italics). But what, for instance, of mathematics, and proofs of theorems in Euclidean geometry? It is certainly possible to engender an *aesthetic*, but not an *artistic*, experience through an elegant proof of such a kind. As I show in Chapter 12 the very common failure to distinguish the aesthetic from the artistic is often itself a manifestation of, or at least conduces to, subjectivism about the arts.

What is far more important in the quotation above is McAdoo's failure to understand my argument. For, in contrast to the way in which he misconstrues me, my argument is that personal response IS seeing the objective features of the work. Personal response is not, as subjectivists assume, something which can be identified independently of the work. On that view, as we saw in Chapter 8, there can be no sense in the notion of personal response in artistic appreciation. We considered equally unintelligible subjectivist conceptions in Chapter 9, where the subjectivist construes the artist's intention, and the spectator's response, respectively, as independent 'inner' mental events.

There are two possible conceptions of personal associations: (a) of the unintelligible kind, where such associations are supposed to be purely private, 'inner' subjective mental events, and (b) of the intelligible kind, as in my example of personal associations with a Mozart Rondo, or a mushroom-shaped cloud. Both conceptions are invalid as an account of the personal involvement characteristic of artistic appreciation because each construes the personal response as identifiable *independently* of the work itself. What I am arguing, throughout this book, is that the only intelligible account of personal response is that it just *is* the appreciation of the objective qualities in the work of art, under what I have called the involved attitude.

It is because McAdoo is still immersed in subjectivist preconceptions, of the kind expressed in the Myth which was discussed in Chapter 1, that he is convinced that my 'objectivist' argument can leave no place for personal involvement. Personal involvement in George Eliot's *Middlemarch*, in Dostoievsky's *The Brothers Karamazov*, and *Crime and Punishment*, in Jane Austen's *Persuasion*, in some of the brilliant dance performances of *London Contemporary Dance Theatre*, in the plays of Shakespeare, Beckett, Ibsen, Chekov, in the paintings of Turner, Bacon, Fra Angelico, in Michelangelo's sculptures, in the work of Wilfred Owen and some of the other war poets, *is* exclusively, a matter of seeing objectively the values *in the works themselves*. We do not need to posit either a separate accompanying subjective mental event or a personal association as that which constitutes the personal involvement. The personal involvement *is* the seeing of the objective features. And this is another way of saying that there are *not*, as supposed by the Myth, two distinct things, on one hand the objective/rational understanding, and on the other hand the subjective feeling. On the contrary, what we have is the *rationality of feeling* — that is, the artistic feeling IS rational and cognitive. The feeling *consists in* the understanding of the objective features of the work.

To repeat an example I used in Chapter 1, after King Lear's harrowing experience in the storm on the heath, because of a deeply moving emotional experience he learns what he had never been aware of in his days of power. How are we to describe this? Was it his changed understanding which changed his feelings, or was it his feelings which changed his understanding? To put the point in either way is highly misleading, in its subjectivist implication that the understanding and the feeling are *distinct*, if closely related, mental events. It would be correct to say that Lear's change of feeling is an *expression* of his changed understanding; his new understanding is a *criterion of*, and *identifies*, his feeling. That is, it would make no sense to attribute to Lear that feeling without his characterising his understanding of the situation in the way he does. There are not two things — understanding and feeling, but only one, a feeling which *is* rational and cognitive. This, I think, is what Lucian Freud is striving for when he says 'I would wish my portraits to be about people, not like people. Not having the look of the sitter, *being* them. Whether this can be achieved depends on how intensely the painter understands and feels for the person or object of his choice'.

McAdoo's commitment to the Myth is also revealed in the following quotation (p. 313): 'What also needs questioning about the 'objectivist' position is the appropriateness, *on every occasion*, of the detached, observational attitude that goes with it . . . there are times when an excited response may yield a more valid appraisal than a calm, detached one . . .' (my italics). This is a clear expression of the Myth of the supposed inevitable opposition between, on the one hand, objectivity, rationality, conceptual knowledge, understanding, and on the other hand, feeling, imagination etc. It is that conception of objectivity which, throughout this book, I am repudiating. To repeat, the objectivity, the rationality, of artistic experience necessarily *involves* feeling. Nowhere have I denied, nor would I deny, the importance and appropriateness, perhaps especially in an educational context, of spontaneous, excited response to the arts. On the contrary, that is one of the richest aspects of artistic experience, and if there were never excited, spontaneous personal responses then that would amount to a failure of *understanding*. And certainly this would be a serious educational failure. To repeat, my thesis is that artistic responses are *cognitive and rational in kind*, whether spontaneous and excited or not. McAdoo continues to assume that objectivity and rationality necessarily imply a cool, detached attitude. I hope that this book and this chapter in particular have demolished that view. Nevertheless, I am grateful to McAdoo for taking my argument seriously, and for articulating clearly a difficulty which many people will experience in understanding the radically different conception of artistic experience for which I am arguing.

As we have seen earlier, it is *possible* to adopt a relatively detached attitude, to the arts and to people. But, at the very least, to have only or predominantly the detached attitude, if that were possible at all, would involve severely limited artistic experience, and personal relationships, respectively. With respect to the latter, the point is well illustrated in Swift's *Gulliver's Travels*, in the chapter on the visit to the country of the Houyhnhnms, whose personal relationships *are* completely of the detached kind. It is a frightening chapter, which brings out the difficulty of making sense of the notion of personal relationships as we know them, if human beings were similarly capable of only the detached attitude.

Another closely related, analogous case is that of morality. If someone were *systematically* to make cool, detached moral judgments, even in the most extreme cases of injustice, cruelty, unnecessary suffering etc. that would, *ipso facto* reveal, at least to some extent, a failure of *understanding* of the relevant situations. Or, it would cast doubt on whether they were, in fact, *moral judgments*.

The subjectivist doctrine, presupposed by McAdoo, sees the major problem as a dichotomy: How, he asks (p. 314), *can* the *personal* involvement which frequently I insist is central to artistic experience be reconciled with my equally frequent insistence that artistic features are *wholly in the work*. It will, I hope, be clear that the problem is *created* by the subjectivist, dualist preconception with which McAdoo approaches the question of artistic response and appreciation. The personal emotional response is not merely subjectively associated with, contingently related to, and *accompanying*, one's understanding of the objective features of the work, for that conception can make no sense of artistic experience. On the contrary, there is no such dichotomy, so we are not faced with the unintelligible problem of how the objective and the subjective can be brought together. There is no tension between an insistence on *personal response* as central to artistic appreciation, and an insistence that artistic appreciation is exclusively given by one's understanding of features which are *wholly in the work*.

Personal artistic response IS seeing features which are wholly in the work; it IS one's understanding of objective artistic qualities.

Note

1 Rod Taylor's work (1992) provides excellent examples. See, for instance, the *obviously* intense emotional involvement of Amarda's critical reasoning (see pp. 106–112 of his book).

Chapter 11

The Particularity of Feeling

A work of art is something which is unlike anything else. It is art, which, best of all, gives us the idea of what is particular.

. . . it is due to feeling (friendship, love, affection) that one human being is different from others. To label, classify someone one loves, that is impious.

. . . It is due to feeling alone that a thing becomes freed from abstraction and becomes something individual and concrete. So, contrary to what is commonly believed, the contemplation of particular things is what elevates a man, and distinguishes him from animals. (Simone Weil, 1978, p. 59)

One of the most important, yet most widely misunderstood characteristics of many emotional feelings, both in the arts and in life generally, is their particularity. Emotion-terms, such as 'anger', 'fear', 'love', 'sad', etc., are applied to a range of varied feelings which fall within the broad category of each. Very often the general term is appropriate, because fine discrimination is unnecessary. But sometimes crucial aspects of a feeling are missed if we do not recognise its *particular* characteristics — some of which are *unique* to that feeling. As will be clear from the preceding argument, this failure to recognise possible particularity of discrimination also incurs a potential loss of *experiencing* finely discriminated feelings.

It is important to recognise that the feelings expressed in and experienced in response to the arts are particular in this sense. Although they can be, and often are, described in general terms, such as 'sad', this misses the particularity which is such a crucially important characteristic of artistic feeling. However, although our main concern in this book is with artistic feeling, it is worth pointing out that particularity of feeling is perhaps even more important in other aspects of life, such as, especially, personal relationships.

Although there are important parallels and illuminating analogies between language and the arts, a significant difference between linguistic and artistic meaning is that whereas there are synonyms in language, it would reveal a failure to understand the nature of the arts to suppose that what is expressed in one work of art could be expressed in another, or, indeed, in any other way. Since my argument applies indiscriminately to expression and response, these and related terms will be used interchangeably.

A Spectrum: General to Particular

As we have seen, according to subjectivism an emotional feeling is a discrete, 'inner' mental event, which is independent of external circumstances. It is a clear consequence of that view that there could be no limits to the objects at which the emotion is directed, and thus, for instance, one might be afraid of absolutely *anything*. Clearly that is an absurd supposition. For example not anything could be an object of fear, since one can be afraid only of objects of a kind which are believed or understood to be threatening or harmful in some way. Hence, unless there were a special context, one could make no sense of the supposition that someone was afraid of an ordinary currant bun. This would make no sense because it could not be regarded as dangerous. If recognized as such, an ordinary currant bun is outside the limits of sense of the concept of fear — those limits are constituted by the belief that the object is harmful or threatening. Nevertheless, these limits of what makes sense leave open the question of what is the object of fear on any particular occasion. To take another example, in normal contexts it would make no sense to speak of pride in a cloud. To make it intelligible, that is, to bring it within the limits of sense of the concept of pride, there would have to be a special context such as that of a scientist who has created a cloud for rain-making purposes. For, roughly, one can be said to be proud only of what one thinks of as an achievement. Within those limits it is possible to change the object of pride without changing the feeling of pride. For example, the scientist may equally be proud of a book he has written.

At first sight this seems to raise a problem for my argument about the particularity of artistic and other emotion feelings. For it would seem that emotions are always of a kind, in that the object of an emotion such as fear, and therefore the feeling *itself*, (since it is the kind of object which identifies the feeling, i.e. determines what feeling it is) is always substitutable without incurring a change in the emotion. That is, there can be many *different* objects of the *same* feeling, in this case fear. I shall consider this problem with some care, mainly to bring out as sharply as possible my argument about the crucial notion of particularity of emotional feeling.

The argument that emotional feelings are always *of a kind*, and therefore general, and substitutable, is clearly expounded by Beardsmore. If he were right, of course, it would show that since artistic feelings are *particular*, they cannot be emotional, but most are of some other kind. This is how he puts his case, in an interesting article (1973):

> ... emotions like fear or grief (are) directed *towards objects of a certain kind* and not towards particular objects. The creaking of my stairs at midnight may awaken in me a nameless terror, but one reason why it is possible for a terror to be nameless is that in the circumstances it need not matter whether the creak is brought about by an escaped leopard or by an axe wielding psychopath. In either case the terror may be the same.

He concludes that responses to works of art cannot be emotional since it makes no sense to suppose that one could have the same response in relation to two different works. His point, then, which raises a problem for my thesis about the particular emotional character of artistic and other feelings, is that objects of emotion are always *of a kind*, and thus *substitutable*, rather than particular. This objection depends, however, upon an oversimple, if common, conception of emotional feelings. For, contrary to what Beardsmore believes, particularity is an important and frequently overlooked aspect of emotional feelings, not only in the arts but also in other central areas of human experience.

Emotions can be placed along a spectrum with, at one extreme, those feelings which are relatively general and undifferentiated, and at the other extreme those which are highly particular. Placing on the spectrum depends upon the range of possible objects on to which typical behaviour may be directed, and which identify what feeling it is. Thus feelings at the general extreme may be identified by a diverse range of objects. For example, if someone were afraid of people, his feeling would be directed on to any of the great variety of kinds of people. And clearly he would still have the same feeling of fear for any one of the numerous people. That is, the object of his fear would be substitutable. One could substitute Frank for Eddie and he would still have the same fear — of people. Another example at this extreme would be fear of reptiles, where, again, *any* reptile could be the object of the same feeling.

Towards the centre of the spectrum the feelings are more particularized in that there are fewer possible objects of each. Fear of aggressive people would come into this category, for although there are various possible objects of this feeling, since different people can be aggressive in various ways, the possibility is obviously considerably more limited than in the case of fear of people in general. Substitution is still possible, since any aggressive person could be the object of such a feeling. Similarly, fear of snakes is more particularized, has fewer possible objects, than fear of reptiles.

At the other extreme of the spectrum are those highly particularized feelings each of which can be experienced and identified in *only one way*. It would make no sense to suggest that such a feeling could be directed towards any other object since, apart from its relation to *this particular object*, the emotion could not intelligibly be said to exist. An example might be fear of a particular person with a peculiarly sneering and sarcastic manner, or, more obviously, love or friendship for a particular person. In these cases the emotion is directed on to and is identified by only one object. (Caution is required about what counts as a particular emotion in this sense. For example, consider: 'He is afraid of Pecco, Jenny's aggressive dog.' This would not count as a highly particularized fear since the fact that it is Pecco, and Jenny's dog, adds nothing to our understanding of the kind of fear he feels. The fear would be the same in relation to any aggressive dog.) The feelings expressed in works of art are at this extreme. For example, to speak of the sadness of Mozart's Fortieth Symphony is to speak of a feeling which can be identified only by that piece of music. To change the particular form of the expression, whether within the same artistic medium, or into another, would be to change the *object* of the emotion, and consequently the *feeling itself*.

A qualification is required. Clearly, the response to a work of art could be specified in a general way, for example as 'sad', or, according to the theme of the work, it could be specified with varying degrees of particularity. It could be placed at any point on the spectrum according to the way in which it is specified. That is, it will always be possible to redescribe a 'particular' response in more general terms. This does not, however, undermine my thesis since it will not always be possible to identify more precisely an emotion characterized in general terms. Fear of a snake would not normally be so described that it could be placed at the 'particular' extreme. By contrast, it is quite normal for characterizations of responses to people and places to be at this extreme. In the case of a work of art, it will always be possible to provide a specification of the response which will locate it at that extreme.

Beardsmore, it may be remembered, contends that emotional feelings are always *general*, in that the object of an emotional feeling is never *particular*, but is substitutable. Since he agrees with me that what is expressed in a work of art is highly particular and therefore is *not* substitutable, he concludes that artistic feelings cannot be emotional. I shall show that his own example, which he cites supposedly in support of his view that emotional feelings in life cannot be particular, is nearer to the particular end of the spectrum than he supposes.

Beardsmore (1973, p. 352) takes an example from Orwell. It concerns a Belgian journalist:

> . . . like nearly all Frenchmen or Belgians, he had a very much tougher attitude: towards 'the Boche' than an Englishman or an American would have. All the main bridges into the town had been blown up, and we had to enter by a small footbridge which the Germans had evidently made efforts to defend. A dead German soldier was lying supine at the foot of the steps. His face was a waxy yellow. On his breast someone had laid a bunch of the lilac which was blossoming everywhere.
>
> The Belgian averted his face as we went past. When we were well over the bridge he confided that this was the first time he had seen a dead man . . . For several days after this, his attitude was quite different from what it had been earlier . . . His feelings, he told me, had undergone a change at the sight of '*ce pauvre mort*' beside the bridge: it had suddenly brought home to him the meaning of war.

Beardsmore says of the journalist (p. 360):

> He had to be shown what death was like. And his experiences changed him, not by contradicting anything which he had previously regarded as a fact, but by replacing the picture which he had held of the death of an enemy with a new picture, by showing him what a soldier's death is really like.

This experience was certainly a profound emotional one, and it could be identified only by reference to its object, namely, the dead soldier lying beside the bridge, and so on. But is it true, as Beardsmore suggests, that *any* dead soldier might have brought about the same change in what the journalist felt on seeing the soldier, and hence that there was some degree of substitutability in the situation? On the contrary, this example, so far from undermining my thesis, actually supports it. For the journalist's emotional response would be placed towards the 'particular' end of the spectrum, since nothing as general as 'grief', or 'sadness', or even 'the sick realization of the meaning of war' could adequately characterize his experience. In some sense it was bound up with that *particular set of circumstances*. For, although some aspects of the situation might have been alterable without a change in the journalist's feeling, it is at least possible, and even likely, that some aspects were of ineliminable importance. For instance, one such aspect is, surely, the fact that on his breast someone had laid a bunch of the lilac which was blooming everywhere — perhaps, and this might well have occurred to him, one of the allied soldiers. Moreover, it is surely significant that Orwell mentions not only the bunch of lilac, but that lilac was blooming everywhere. The contrast no doubt brought home to him all the more powerfully the meaning of war, and thus was constitutive in an important way of the object of his feeling about the incident.

It might be objected that the impact was created by the fact that this was the *first* dead man the Belgian had seen, in which case any dead soldier would have had the same effect. But there are limitations to the possibility of substitution here. For example, what if the dead soldier had been a Belgian, or, especially, the journalist's father or brother? Given his attitude, his emotional reaction would almost certainly have been very different, and this might be revealed in an attitude of even more bitter hatred towards the 'Boche'. In this imaginary case it is highly improbable that he would have acted in the way that Orwell described in the actual case:

> when he left he gave the residue of the coffee we had brought with us to the Germans on whom we were billeted. A week earlier he would probably have been scandalized at the idea of giving coffee to a 'Boche'.

To say that his feeling would almost certainly have been very different is to say that my imaginary case of the very different sort of dead soldier (e.g. his father or brother) would have constituted a very different object of his feeling. So it is certainly not true that *any* substitution of the object, i.e. *any* dead soldier, would have identified the *same* feeling. (What the feeling *is* is identified by one's *conception* or belief or understanding of the situation.)

Leaving that example aside, it is not difficult to imagine a situation in which someone thoroughly hardened to the brutalities of war might suddenly have his feelings jolted by a particular case, such as the sight of a dead soldier with a bunch of violets placed on his breast by an enemy soldier. In this case not any dead soldier in any situation could be said to identify the same feeling. The feeling could be identified as the same only if the object were understood in a relevantly similar way. And what would count as a 'relevantly similar way' here would depend upon one's conception of the incident. Beardsmore seems implicitly to concede something of this, since he says (p. 352; my italics):

> One would have to recognize that there could be no answer to the question: And what was it like, then? What death is like, was something which came out in *the* pathetic scene to which he has been a witness. Unless you had seen *the* soldier lying by *the* bridge you could not know what it was like.

His use of the three definite articles in this passage is significant. Here we have a life situation in which the emotional experience of the journalist is identified by '*the*' pathetic scene, and so on. Now all mental experience is cognitive to some extent. And it has been a main theme of this book that emotional feeling, in particular, can be identified only by means of one's understanding of the object towards which it is directed — roughly, *what* it is a feeling *of* determines what feeling it *is*. In this case, the journalist's emotional feeling could not be adequately identified apart from his conception of certain *particular* features of the situation he encountered. Without these particular features and his conception of them, the object, and therefore the emotional feeling itself, could not intelligibly be regarded as the same. And that is to concede my present point, that the limits of possible substitutability of the object are narrow in this example. (Where, for brevity, I write of the situation, it is of course always the conception or understanding of the situation which is crucial to the correct characterization of the object.)

What of the feelings situated at the 'particular' extreme of the spectrum? Is it true that there are no such highly particularized emotions in life outside the arts? On the contrary, such particularized feelings, which can be characterized only by non-substitutable objects, are a very important, though often overlooked, part of human emotional experience in life generally. Hepburn (1965, p. 192) writes of emotions which are:

> functions of an alert, active grasping of numerous features of my situation, held together as a single gestalt. In my compartment I make into one unity of feeling the train-wheels drumming, the lugubrious view from the window (steam and industrial fog), and the thought of meeting so-and so, whom I dislike, at the end of my journey. My depression is highly particularized. Or again, if one is in love, an encounter with the loved one may acquire a specific, unrepeatable emotional quality — meeting so-and-so, on that particular day, in that particular park, with that wind and those exhilarating cumulus clouds overhead. Our scale . . . is a scale of increased emotional discrimination.

Similarly, Ruby Meager (1965, p. 196) writes of the characteristics which provide rational support for her young man's judgment that Rosie is lovable:

> It is the particular form in which Rosie manifests them, and the particular way in which they are combined in her, that make just this occurrence of them together lovable . . . However precisely we discriminate Rosie's peculiar virtues in *general* terms, and without the help of pointing to her, we cannot pin Rosie down in this way, and it is just her individual manifestation of her characteristics which makes them lovable *in her*.
>
> Given a highly complex object to be evaluated for its own sake and not functionally with some general end in mind like Rosie or a symphony, it seems perfectly rational to refuse to commit oneself to generalizable evaluations of particular characteristics, however precisely defined.

The object of the young man's emotional feeling, what identifies it, or what the feeling is, is a *unique* object; it cannot intelligibly be regarded as an object, and therefore a feeling, of *a certain kind*. Indeed, it is significant that if such a substitution were possible this would constitute a good reason for *denying* that the attribution of love was legitimate. This concept of love is such that the young man could not be said to love Rosie if there were or could be another object of his feeling. This is not to say, of course, that he could not love someone else, say, Jane. But it is to say that there is an important sense in which his love for Jane *could* not be regarded as the same feeling, since the object of the feeling, constituted by the *particular* characteristics of Jane, would be different. We could speak of 'the same feeling' only in the trivial sense of a more general description which would importantly *fail* to capture the important particular details characteristic of this concept of feeling. The acquisition of what Rush Rhees (1969, Ch. 13) calls the language of love determines the possibility of experiencing the highly particularized feelings characteristic of such an emotion. And similarly, the understanding of an art form allows for the highly particularized feelings characteristic of art. This is, I think, part of the point of the following quotation from Winch (1958, p. 122):

> imagine a society which has no concept of proper names, as we know them. People are known by general descriptive phrases, say, or by numbers. This would carry with it a great many other differences from our own social life as well. The whole structure of personal relationships would be affected. Consider the importance of numbers in prison or military life. Imagine how different it would be to fall in love with a girl known only by a number rather than by a name; and what the effect of that might be, for instance, on the poetry of love.

The man who could say 'I love Rosie, but Jane would do instead' would have as little understanding of love as the man who could say 'You need not bother to read Tolstoy's *Father Sergius*, since Shakespeare's *King Lear* says the same thing' would have of literary appreciation.[1]

One could cite many other examples of such highly particularized feelings. For example, it is characteristic of the feeling involved in a lifelong, close friendship that it could be identified only by reference to numerous specific incidents which occurred over a long period of time. The suggestion of substitution in such a case would make no sense. Similarly, nostalgic feeling about places, or various feelings about incidents or phases in one's life, may be equally intimately related to particular details such that the notion of substitution, of the 'same' feeling identified by *different* details, makes no sense. I may speak of 'the Cambridge feeling', which is located by a wide variety of incidents and particular places, and people at a particular stage of their lives. The notion of substitutability, where the feeling is determined by such a complex concatenation of circumstances, again makes no sense.

If it were objected that surely *some* of these details could be altered without affecting the identity of the feeling, then one would reply that it depends upon the details. For whether in life or in art some aspects will be so significant as to constitute defining criteria of an interpretation and response, whereas others will be merely incidental.

What the Object Actually Is

One can be afraid only of what one believes or conceives to be dangerous. But what one is afraid of may not actually be dangerous. Thus there is a distinction between what the object actually is, and how a person understands it, or what he believes it to be. Someone may be afraid of an object which he thinks is a snake when it is actually a piece of rope. Anscombe (1965, pp. 166–7) gives the example of a man who aims at a dark patch in the foliage, believing it to be a stag, but in fact shoots his father. His *intention* cannot be identified in terms of what the object actually is, since he did not intend to shoot his father, even though he intended to shoot what was actually, in fact, his father.

To repeat, then, there is a distinction between what one believes or understands the object to be — what identifies one's emotional feeling — and what it actually is, although very often of course these will coincide. That is, what one understands it to be will very often be what it actually is. Yet it is important to remain clear that there is no sense in the notion of what an object really is apart from some description or other of it. Complications arise where there are differences of conception about what the object actually is. This raises an important question about the possibility of resolving differences of opinion about works of art. To bring out the point, I shall adapt Anscombe's example of a tribe which worships the sun as a god. What is the actual object in this case? It should be remembered that the actual object of an emotional feeling is not necessarily a physical object. For example, a debt can be an object in this sense. In the example of the sun, for a Western scientist the actual object is nothing but a mass of burning gas. But, as a matter of *logic*, i.e. of what makes *sense*, a tribesman could not accept that as a description of the object, since it would make no sense to suppose that he worships what he thinks of as nothing but a mass of burning gas. That is, the limits of sense of the concept of worship exclude such an object as an intelligible object of worship. In such a case there is no neutral description of the facts to which the scientist and the tribesman could refer in order to discover the character of the actual object. For the facts which determine what the object actually is are themselves determined by the set of concepts with which each is making his judgments. It may be correct for us to say that the tribesmen worship what is actually a mass of burning gas, but that is not how they conceive, or could intelligibly conceive, of what the sun actually is. Similarly, a chemist might insist that the water used in christening is actually merely H_2O, but that cannot capture its religious significance, that is, what it actually is for a Christian.

There are three kinds of case. (a) This is the kind mentioned above where a man mistakenly believes that what he saw was a stag. Similarly, someone may be afraid of what is actually a rope because he believes it to be a snake. These are simply mistakes which are, in principle, easily rectified by discovering what the object actually and uncontroversially is. (b) The examples of the sun and of christening water given above are in this category, where no appeal to what the object really is will necessarily settle a dispute between those with very different conceptions of it. (c) The cases which are central to the arts are a mixture of the above cases but much more like (b) than (a) in that where there are differences no sense can be given to the notion of what the character of a work of art actually is apart from conflicting conceptions. Of course, each conception has to be answerable to features of the art object, but within that limit indefinitely wide variations of equally valid interpretation may be possible. (I shall have to ignore the complex problem of identity, that is, to what extent different interpretations may still count as interpretations of the *same* work of art.)

There is also an important asymmetry between the case of the sun and that of differing interpretations of a work of art. The tribe speaks a different language, and they use a certain word, say 'X'. We are inclined to translate this as 'the sun', because there is some overlap between what we call 'the sun' and what they call 'X'. Asked to point to X, they point to the sun. They tell us that X rises in the morning in the east, and sets in the evening in the west, and so on. However, they also say many things about X which make no sense if taken to mean what we mean by 'the sun', some of which seem to make more sense if taken to mean what we mean by 'a god'. Obviously 'the sun' is an inadequate translation of 'X', even though some aspects of the situation give *some* point to such a translation. The two words cannot intelligibly be said to mean the same, since the employment of each word in each language is so very different. The fact that the same ostensive definitions may be used, that is, the fact that they and we may point apparently at the same thing, to explain the meaning of the words, is of little significance.

In the case of a work of art, the situation is different. Even where there are two widely divergent interpretations both critics would certainly agree, normally, on *some* description of what they are discussing. If, for instance, the work were representational they must agree to some extent on *what* it represents in order to have an intelligible base for their differences of opinion about interpretation. For example, agreement that a painting represented Churchill would have to be assumed before there could be disagreement about how it should be construed. Nevertheless, what they see when they look at the same work of art may be quite different. Yet the difference is not as fundamental as it is in the example of the sun, unless for instance, one were from another culture which lacked any concept of a work of art.

Thus the notion of what the object actually is is necessary in order for the disagreement even to arise, but no appeal to this will be relevant to solving differences about the character of a work of art. To a large extent disputants could agree on their specification of what they are talking about, yet such an agreement may be quite irrelevant to settling their dispute about how it should be interpreted.

The relationship of the foregoing discussion to my thesis is that it is the interpretation of the work of art which determines the character of the response to it. This ineliminable cognitive element, the grasping of the significance of features of the work under a certain mode of understanding, is the *particular* object of, and therefore identifies, the *particular* feeling it expresses. It is also the particular object of the feeling which is experienced as the response of the spectator or audience. The feeling expressed in, and experienced in response to, a work of art is highly particular in this sense. Matisse has said: 'The whole arrangement of each of my pictures is expressive — the positions my figures occupy, and even the space around them.'

Individuality of Response

Of course, it would not be self-contradictory to assert that a dance was performed, but that a person watching it did not experience the appropriate feeling. For instance, in the case of subtle irony, he might miss its meaning entirely. Moreover, it would be quite possible for the spectator to give every indication, at the time, of understanding and responding appropriately to the dance, while in fact failing to do so. We may withdraw our attribution to him of the appropriate response in the light of wider and later considerations — his background knowledge, subsequent reactions, and so on. This underlines again the ineliminable importance of the concept and medium of the art form, in a whole cultural setting and tradition, in characterizing responses to works of art.

This matter also emphasises again the inevitable distortion and misconception incurred in offering simple answers to the complex questions involved in philosophy of the arts. An artistic response cannot intelligibly be regarded as a discrete, definitive mental event. An explanation of an artistic response has to take into account the tradition, conventions, concept of the art form, within a whole social context of interrelated cultural practices. It may be impossible to say unambiguously what someone's, or one's own, artistic response was at the time of watching the performance or art form. The feeling, like an intention, is not necessarily something which occurs at a particular instant in time. To believe that artistic feelings, emotional feelings, intentions, are mental *events*, which necessarily have a definite time of occurrence, is to be thoroughly confused in philosophy of mind. It is part of the dangerous craving for oversimplicity which continues to wreak such damage on the arts. A spectator may have little or no grasp of the cultural tradition, art form, or school of approach, and thus, although absorbed in watching a dancer's movements he cannot respond appropriately. Similarly, a spectator cannot learn from a work unless he already has a background of some knowledge on which to build, and on which the work implicitly relies.

We have been considering the particularity of the emotions expressed in works of art, but there are also, of course, individual differences in the sensitivity, acuteness of perception, background knowledge, and so on, of different spectators. As was pointed out in Chapter 5, it is neither conceivable nor desirable that there should always be identical understanding of and response to the same work of art, since this would amount to conceiving and desiring that people should be identical. But this concedes nothing to subjectivism, in the sense that interpretation and response are purely private, and thus that *any* interpretation and response is equally appropriate, or, which is the same thing, that the notion of appropriateness makes no sense. There is a particularly strong temptation to assume that a response must be purely private and subjective in those situations where one is at a loss to offer any account of an emotional experience, in that any attempted account seems not only inadequate, but even distortingly inaccurate. In the example from Ruby Meager quoted earlier, the young man is unable to offer any adequate account of his feeling for Rosie without the help of pointing to her. But whether understanding can be achieved even in this way will depend on the person to whom Rosie's characteristics are pointed out. To cite another example, in Patrick White's novel *A Fringe of Leaves* Mrs Roxburgh, a sensitive, reflective woman who has been through a series of experiences which have profoundly changed her understanding of and attitude to life, is expected to describe them to a pompous and insensitive military commandant whose experiences of life are regimented into oversimple categories, and who consequently *is* a congeries of clichés. Mrs Roxburgh is unable to give any account of her most disturbing experience. The commandant is perplexed and irritated: 'If it made such an impression on you, I should have thought you'd be able to describe it.'

With respect to understanding spiritual qualities, Holland (1980, p. 63) writes:

> The kind of understanding open to us here is such that we can (and most often do) have it without being able to say what it is we understand. It is an understanding that is not exhausted in whatever the discursive intelligence manages to render explicit, even when someone comes out with a form of words that seems to hit off exactly the nature of the

spiritual quality before us . . . And while the feeling for the fineness of a civilization, which this understanding mainly amounts to, is not the same thing as being able to categorize it as thus and thus and does not demand the kind of analytical acumen which goes along with that, nevertheless it is tantamount to having a sense of worth, because above all else it is a matter of responding towards something wonderful . . .

However, it is of the first importance to recognize that even in such a case there are certainly descriptions which one would reject as totally failing to characterize the experience, and others which one might say come a little nearer. That alone is sufficient to make the point that the experience cannot be purely private and subjective. As we saw in Chapter 7, if an experience were purely private and subjective in the sense of being *totally* incommunicable even in principle, then there could be no sense to the notion of criteria of appropriateness, since the supposition of purely private criteria is unintelligible. That is, if absolutely *any* response could count as 'appropriate' there could be no sense in the notion of appropriate responses. And that would mean that there could be no sense in the notion of appreciating the arts. Moreover, to repeat, an appropriate response in the arts is possible only for someone with at least some grasp of the criteria of the particular medium of art. Those criteria constitute the limits of sense and appropriateness for the possibility of *individual* emotional responses.

It should be emphasized again, because the point is so important and so frequently misunderstood, that to insist that the response must fall somewhere within the scope of appropriateness does not in the least imply that there cannot be a wide variety of individual differences. On the contrary, it is to insist that there could be no sense at all in *individual* artistic appreciation if there were no limits whatsoever to that scope. The concept of art, at least in most of the societies where this book is likely to be read, would be unimaginably impoverished without the wealth of individual differences of insight and sensitivity of response.

Note

1   It has been objected that I need to qualify my insistence on the particularity of artistic response, since if the object of the response were not the character in a play or piece of music, but rather, for instance, the skill of the actor, or the interpretation of the performer, then the object could not be logically particular: exact replication is simply very unlikely. But this objection is mistaken, since in that case the particular object would be the interpretation or skilful performance, even if it were possible that precisely the same skill could be shown, or the same interpretation given, by two different actors. Perhaps the point can be made more clearly by reference to the possibility of two authors of the same novel. If the object of the response should be the *novel*, then it is particular, even though it may be possible that two different authors may have written precisely the same novel. (I am indebted to Antony Duff for this point.)

Chapter 12

The Aesthetic and the Artistic

It is remarkable that the terms 'aesthetic' and 'artistic' are still almost universally and unquestioningly regarded as synonymous, or, at least, the artistic is regarded as a sort of species of the aesthetic genus. It is remarkable because after even cursory reflection it is implausible, and because, despite that implausibility, it is rarely even questioned. The differences between artistic experience and aesthetic experience are usually so great that it is bizarre to regard them as of the same kind. The distinction may seem mere quibbling over the meanings of words. However it has had a damaging effect on policy for the arts in education.

The source of the confusion is the unclear but largely unquestioned assumption of a general metaphysical 'aesthetic', which is supposed to be instantiated in both natural phenomena and works of art. I say that it is metaphysical because it is difficult to discover anyone who offers even remotely credible *reasons* for accepting this notion of a general aesthetic faculty, attitude, kind of experience etc. Indeed, few theorists offer any reasons at all. It is merely a vague, underlying assumption. Even where the distinction between the aesthetic and the artistic is recognised to some extent, there has been a failure to mark the character of the distinctive concepts adequately, as we shall see.

It is part of the metaphysical misconception, which runs deep into the history of philosophy, that philosophy of the arts should be centrally concerned with questions of beauty. (Indeed, *significantly*, even in recent history, its misty metaphysical nature was apparent because the quest was supposed to be to discover the nature of Beauty.) In fact, a moment's reflection is sufficient to show that questions of beauty are almost irrelevant to the meaning and value of the many *arts*, even if they are relevant to one's aesthetic appreciation, for instance, of natural objects, athletic and gymnastic movements, interior decoration etc. For example, one's appreciation of Shakespeare's *Measure for Measure* would hardly include aesthetic terms at all. Such terms certainly could not be *central* to one's artistic appreciation of the play, or indeed of most works of art of any significance. Indeed, if someone were to discuss such works of art *solely* in *aesthetic* terms that would clearly reveal his *lack* of ability for *artistic* appreciation. The point has been succinctly put: 'Beauty is what the bourgeoisie pays the artist for'.

It is important to recognise clearly that there are *two*, quite *distinct*, although sometimes related concepts. To put it as starkly as possible, a central feature of an object of *artistic* as opposed to *aesthetic* interest is, roughly, that it can have a subject matter. This is extremely significant for the principal theme of this book. For, by contrast with aesthetic feelings, one's artistic feelings in response to works of art, and some of the most important reasons by which one can come to understand works of art, are frequently inseparably bound up with a wide variety of issues from *life generally*.

There are crucial educational implications, for it is the potential of the arts for deepening, extending, sensitising our understanding and feelings about an immense variety of issues in life in general which constitutes one of the most crucial contributions of the arts to education. Thus the question of the *distinction* between the aesthetic and the artistic is of the utmost importance for education. For the assumption that they are concerned primarily with *aesthetic* pleasure, e.g. with beauty, trivialises the arts.

This notion of a general aesthetic dimension is sometimes adduced in support of the artistically and educationally damaging, idea that the arts form a 'generic' area of the curriculum. (I consider this question elsewhere [Best, 1990 and 1992].)

Two common attempts to support the generic notion are as follows: (a) It is assumed that there is a general underlying metaphysical 'aesthetic', which is instantiated in both artistic and aesthetic experience. This vague assumption is usually taken to imply some sort of unspecified aesthetic unity. Rarely are any *reasons* given in favour of it, despite its implausibility. A unified 'aesthetic' is simply, and remarkably generally, assumed. The unintelligibility of some versions is apparent because it is supposed that one can recognise the instantiation of this metaphysical 'aesthetic' by a purely private, subjective process of 'intuition'. (b) There is a confused supposition that similar creative/artistic/aesthetic subjective mental 'processes' are involved in the creation and appreciation of all the art forms (and, presumably, in the appreciation of the beauties of nature). We considered that supposition in Chapter 7.

The generic notion, usually involving a vague combination of (a) and (b) has had serious practical consequences for educational policy decisions. To repeat an earlier example, in England and Wales, the Proposal of the Secretary of State for Education (August 1991) is that art and music should be offered by all schools up to the age of 14, and then 'it is our view that all schools should offer some sort of aesthetic experience in the curriculum for all 14–16 year olds'. It is difficult to know what to make of such a vague injunction. Would looking at the trees and flowers be regarded as adequate? One *assumes* that 'artistic' is meant. In that case, it would seem probable that something like the confused notion of a general faculty or attitude lies behind it, and thus that any art form, or mixture of art forms, will contribute to its development. It may not imply that, although it seems highly likely. In any case, largely because of the confusion of the aesthetic and the artistic, it is impossible to be clear what it does mean.

The Distinction

The aesthetic is generally assumed to be the genus of which the artistic is a species, in that the objects or activities which are characteristic of aesthetic interest or, as it is sometimes expressed, of the aesthetic attitude, are assumed to include works of art, but to extend beyond them to natural phenomena. But the relationship between 'aesthetic' and 'artistic' is almost always left unclear — so much so that the two terms are often used synonymously. Implicit in the views of many theorists is the assumption that the term 'aesthetic' can legitimately be applied not only to works of art but also to natural phenomena such as sunsets, birdsong and mountain ranges, whereas 'artistic' is limited to artefacts or performances intentionally created by man for aesthetic pleasure or contemplation. That is, 'aesthetic' is used of the *whole* range, including works of art, whereas 'artistic' is more limited. Thus, except in an extended or metaphorical sense, it would sound odd to speak of a sunset in terms of the 'artistic', but quite normal to assume that, with respect to a novel, poem, painting, dance, or piece of music, the terms 'aesthetic' and 'artistic' were equivalent. In one of the few explicit statements of this kind of view, Reid (1970) writes:

> When we are talking about the category of art, as distinct from the category of the aesthetic, we must be firm, I think, in insisting that in art there is someone who has made (or is making) purposefully an artefact, and that in his purpose there is contained as an essential part the idea of producing an object (not necessarily a 'thing': it could be movement or a piece of music) in some medium for aesthetic contemplation. (p. 249)

Similarly, Beardsley (1979) writes that 'an artwork can usefully be defined as an intentional arrangement of conditions for affording experiences with marked aesthetic character' (p. 729).

There is a sense in which the term 'aesthetic' can be intelligibly applied to both natural phenomena and works of art, but this is not the sense in which the artistic is a *species* of the aesthetic. On the contrary, the aesthetic and the artistic are *distinct* though sometimes related concepts. Although a work of art, like almost *everything* else, may be considered from an aesthetic point of view, that does not imply that 'artistic' can be defined in terms of that which is intentionally produced for aesthetic effect. To bring out the character of the distinction, consider another common and perhaps related conception, that there is a unique aesthetic attitude which is identifiable by reference to and developed by experience of either works of art or the contemplation of natural phenomena. For instance Beardsley (1979) writes that

> the concept of aesthetic value as a distinct kind of value enables us to draw a distinction that is indispensable to the enterprise of art criticism: that is, the distinction between relevant and irrelevant reasons that might be given in support of artistic goodness. (p. 728)

And later:

> many natural objects, such as mountains and trees . . . seem to have a value that is closely akin to that of artworks. This kinship can easily be explained in terms of aesthetic value. . . (p. 746)

This seems to me, a remarkably implausible thing to say, and we should immediately be alerted to the probability that it is based on a foundation-assumption which is, in effect, unquestionable. For how can one seriously suppose that Beethoven's *9th Symphony*, or Shakespeare's *Troilus and Cressida* are 'closely akin' to mountains and trees?

Is the supposed 'kinship' between the chestnut tree in my neighbour's garden, and Dostoievsky's novel *The Brother's Karamazov*, *easily* explained in terms of aesthetic value? Can it be explained *at all*, let alone easily? The striking thing is that it never is explained, except by vague resort to metaphysical notions such as forms of beauty etc. All we have is assertion. No reasons are given for what, on the face of it, is a very implausible claim about a supposed aesthetic kinship between very disparate objects.

As I mentioned earlier, the unintelligibly metaphysical nature of the assertion is sometimes made abundantly clear by those theorists who 'support' it by claiming that the aesthetic applies to natural objects and to all works of art, but works of art express the '*essence*' of it. Not only have I never encountered any argument for this kind of claim, but it is difficult to see what intelligible reasons *could* be offered.

Even, so far as it can be understood at all, in terms of the dubious talk of 'essences' (which, for very good reasons has now been almost totally abandoned as making little sense, within philosophy) the assertion seems obviously false. For there are some aesthetic experiences of natural objects which are, if one wants to talk in that way, so intense that nothing, and certainly not many works of art, could possibly count as having more of the aesthetic 'essence'. For example, I was recently walking on the coast of Gower, in a lonely spot, at dusk. As I faced the sea, on my right was a strikingly beautiful sunset, in a context of bizarrely shaped, black-red, menacing clouds. The flat-calm sea shone with almost painfully exquisite, textured colours. On my left, framed by jagged-jutting ominous dark cliffs, a full moon shed a melancholy shivering pathway across the sea. I found myself holding my breath, the experience was so intense. I was unable to leave, until it was so dark I had to stumble my way back.

Few works of art or performances could equal that experience for aesthetic 'essence'. One could cite numerous such instances — the almost shocking silence in snow-clad high mountains, autumn (fall) colours, swimming in a brilliantly exhilarating dawn sea, etc. But they are certainly not works of art, and it is difficult to comprehend how there could be intelligible reasons for claiming that they have a kinship with works of art in general. It certainly will not do to claim that the kinship is *easily* explained in terms of aesthetic value. It is difficult to comprehend how it could be explained *at all*.

But, of course, most importantly, I am conceding too much even to discuss this implausible contention in such terms. For it is bizarre to imagine that one can, in general, compare works of art in the same category as aesthetic appreciation of natural objects. When one reflects on it, even cursorily, it is clear that there is strange conceptual wire-crossing going on, that is, that *two* concepts are being confusedly run together. For example, my *aesthetic* experience on the coast of Gower cannot intelligibly be compared with one's *artistic* experience of seeing Shakespeare's *Measure for Measure*; or Beckett's *Endgame*, or reading Dostoievsky's *The Brothers Karamazov*, or George Eliot's *Middlemarch*; and listening to a solo cello sonata by J.S. Bach, or a Mozart piano concerto. One does not, in the main, think in the same terms at all. Aesthetic terms are used, if at all, largely peripherally in relation to such works of art. There is no sense in the suggestion that aesthetic experiences such as mine on the coast could be compared on the same *scale* — 'aesthetic value' — as such works.

The distinction, although obvious when pointed out, is almost completely ignored by philosophers and arts education theorists. But let us continue to look at just a few of the ways in which the 'aesthetic' is discussed. Among those who do see *some* kind of difference, albeit on the same scale, controversy arises over whether the experience of natural phenomena, or that of the arts, is the central or paradigm case. Carritt (1953, p. 45) criticizes those writers who concentrate exclusively or predominantly on the arts since, in his view, the experience of natural beauty is of the same kind and may well be indistinguishable from it. Hepburn (1966) has a similar view, as Beardsmore (1973) in an interesting paper on this issue points out, while Urmson (1957) is an example of a writer who takes natural beauty to be the central case of the aesthetic.

Wollheim (1970, p. 112), by contrast, criticizes Kant and Bullough for taking as paradigm cases a rose, and a fog at sea, respectively:

> A serious distortion is introduced into many accounts of the aesthetic attitude by taking as central to it cases which are really peripheral or secondary; that is, cases where what we regard as a work of art is, in point of fact, a piece of uncontrived nature.

All of these writers presuppose the notion of a general aesthetic attitude. Their disagreement centres on whether natural phenomena, or works of art, are the paradigm expressions of it. As Beardsmore puts it (1973, p. 357):

> Wollheim's argument seems simple. Carritt, Bullough, Urmson, have all got it precisely the wrong way round. Our understanding of art cannot be explicable as one variety of an attitude which we adopt primarily towards natural objects, if only because the aesthetic contemplation of nature is itself an extension of an attitude established on the basis of works of art.

This view of Wollheim's position is confirmed by his offering the following illustration (1970, p. 119):

> when the Impressionists tried to teach us to look at paintings as though we were looking at nature — a painting for Monet was *une fenêtre ouverte sur la nature* — this was because they themselves had first looked at nature in a way they had learnt from looking at paintings.

Wollheim contends that the aesthetic appreciation of natural phenomena is possible only to the extent that the aesthetic attitude has been developed by means of an understanding of art forms as the central cases. Such a view is quite common. For example, Margaret MacDonald (1952–3, p. 206) suggests that to admire a garden or the lines of a yacht is to admire it as a work of art; Nelson Goodman (1969, p. 33) claims that nature is a product of art and discourse; and Karl Britton (1972–3, p. 116) argues that to appreciate the beauty of a natural phenomenon amounts to appreciating it as if it were a work of art.

However, both the thesis that the central cases of the aesthetic attitude are to be found in appreciation of natural beauty, and its antithesis that they are to be found in artistic appreciation, share the fundamentally mistaken presupposition that the aesthetic and the artistic are indistinguishable, or not significantly distinguishable, aspects of the *same* concept. Once again, it is interesting to note that this assumption of a general, overarching 'aesthetic' is not even questioned despite the implausibility of some of these assertions. That assumption is taken as a given, an unquestionable starting point. It shows the continuing influence of the metaphysical tradition. It is still extremely difficult to persuade people seriously to question it. Yet, some of these quotations are asserting positions which are so questionable that it is surprising that the general aesthetic assumption is still so widely regarded as an article of faith, and has not been exposed to rigorous criticism.

Beardsmore is one of the very few who has recognised that this notion of a general 'aesthetic' makes no sense. He points out that there is a distinction between two ways in which the term 'aesthetic' and its cognates are employed — one in relation to the arts, and the other in relation to appreciation of natural beauty (op. cit., p. 351):

There are aspects of art appreciation which cannot be understood if one thinks of our reactions to a play as a complicated version of our reactions to a rose. And there are aspects of the love of nature which make no sense if one has before one's mind the way in which people respond to paintings and sculptures.

Later he puts the point:

I can imagine a society in which men are untouched by any form of artistic activity and yet still possess a love of nature which one might call aesthetic. I can imagine this because it is to some extent true of children in our own society ... There is little enough temptation to see in a child's love of what is grotesque or surprising in the shape of a toadstool, the influence of artistic tradition. (pp. 364–5)

To his great credit Beardsmore clearly recognises, and his arguments show conclusively, that there are two distinct concepts. Moreover, he also, perceptively points to another important aspect of the conflation of the aesthetic and the artistic, namely that it incurs the danger of minimising or even eradicating the influence of artistic tradition. But in my view he has misconstrued the character of the distinction, since it should be drawn not in terms of two senses of 'aesthetic', but in terms of a contrast between the *aesthetic* and the *artistic*. There is a far more substantial question here than mere terminological difference.

Beardsmore conceives of the two senses of 'aesthetic' in terms of our appreciation of nature, and our appreciation of the arts, respectively. Certainly these are prime, paradigm kinds of case which reveal clearly that there are two different concepts. Nevertheless, that there must be more to the distinction becomes apparent when we consider numerous areas of design which characteristically, or at least often, attract terms of aesthetic appreciation but which are neither natural, in that sense of the term, nor works of art. Obvious examples are the shape of a telephone, suitcase, car and aeroplane (Concorde is a classic case): the design of a kettle, cooker and pen; the decor of a room. One can also adduce the structure of a mathematical proof and of a philosophical argument. None of these is a natural object, but each often, and even characteristically, attracts aesthetic appreciation.

No doubt the advocates of the opposing positions would argue that such examples should be construed as extended cases of a concept centred in art, or in natural beauty, respectively. Certainly there are extended cases where, for instance, one may be invited to consider what is not art from an artistic point of view. Yet that possibility cannot overcome the problem which I am now raising. To bring out what I mean here it is important to notice that, at least in many cases, a work of art can be considered from both the aesthetic *and* the artistic points of view. Therefore the distinction cannot be as *any* of these positions supposes. As a boy, I was privileged to attend a performance by Ram Gopal, the great Indian classical dancer, and I was quite captivated by the exhilarating and exquisite quality of his movements. Yet I was unable to appreciate his dance artistically since I could not understand it. For instance, there is a great and varied range of subtle hand gestures in Indian classical dance, each with a quite precise meaning, of which I knew none. It is clear that my appreciation was aesthetic, not artistic. It could not have been *artistic* appreciation since I had no understanding of the art form, and its context in Indian cultural tradition. Yet, despite that, I was quite capable of *aesthetic* appreciation of Ram Gopal's dancing.

Among the various classifications she offers of *works of art*, Ruth Saw (1972, p. 4) includes the following:

> There is another important class of aesthetically pleasing performances in which the performers are not carrying out the instructions of another artist but are acting spontaneously. Star performers in ice hockey, cricket, football and sports generally are valued almost as much for their elegance in action as for their run-making and goal-getting ability . . . Sports commentators use the terms of aesthetic appraisal as freely as do art critics.

This reveals the 'general-aesthetic' misconception, or the conflation of the artistic and the aesthetic, in another way. It is implicit in Ruth Saw's failure to distinguish between kinds of sporting activity. I have considered this question elsewhere (Best 1978, ch. 7) but briefly, there is a class of sporting activities, which would include the great majority, in which the purpose of the activity can be specified independently of the manner of achieving it, for example, football, tennis, cricket and hockey. By contrast, there is a class of sports in which the purpose of the activity cannot be specified apart from the aesthetic manner of achieving it. In this latter class the aesthetic is intrinsic to the activity. For example, it would make no sense to suggest to a figure skater, Olympic gymnast, or diver that he should ignore aesthetic considerations and concentrate exclusively on achieving the purpose of the sport, since that purpose is necessarily concerned with the aesthetic manner of performance. By contrast, it would make perfectly good sense to urge a football or hockey team to concentrate exclusively on scoring goals without paying any attention to the manner of scoring them.

Once the distinction is recognized, it can also be seen that it is misleading to assert that sports *generally* are valued *almost as much* for their elegance as for the achievement of their ends. With respect to the former, 'purposive', class of sports that is an intelligible observation, but in the case of the latter, the 'elegance', or aesthetic quality, is *inseparable* from what the performer is trying to achieve; it would make no sense to talk of a *successful* performance which was not an *aesthetically* successful performance. Indeed, certain aesthetic norms are part of the meaning of terms such as 'vault' and 'dive', for whereas not *any* way of getting over a box or dropping into the water could count as even a bad vault or dive, *any* way of sending the ball between the opponents' posts, as long as it is within the rules, does count as a goal, albeit a clumsy or lucky one.

However, the main point is that there is no support for the assumption that an object or activity is a genuine form of *art* that terms of aesthetic appraisal are freely applied to it. It is surprising that the point is so often overlooked. That a lady is elegant or beautiful does not imply that she is a work of art. Nevertheless, on the grounds simply that terms of *aesthetic* appraisal are freely applied to them, Ruth Saw concludes that sporting activities generally are forms of art. Yet in the case of purposive sports, which constitute the great majority, it is clearly merely a contingent matter whether there is even *any* concern for the *aesthetic* manner of achievement. That is, aesthetic considerations are merely incidental: aesthetic qualities are not *necessary* to successful performance of purposive sports.

As we saw earlier, Reid is at least aware that there is a distinction, and his characterization of the artistic is initially tempting. On this view, the artistic is that which is intentionally created or performed for aesthetic value. Beardsley, too, defines art in terms of aesthetic intention (see, for instance, op. cit., p. 730). But there are many counter-examples to this suggestion. For instance, a wallpaper pattern is normally designed with the intention of giving aesthetic pleasure, but it would not normally on that account be regarded as art. There are numerous other cases, some of which I cited above, such as the shape of radiators and spectacles, and even coloured toilet paper. The intention, in each case, is to give aesthetic pleasure, but none is art (which is not to deny, of course, that there may be certain unusual circumstances in which any of them could be considered as art, or as part of a work of art).

Art Form and Subject Matter

Referring back to the distinction I drew above, a much more plausible case can be made for the credentials, as forms of art, of the 'aesthetic' sports, that is, those in which aesthetic considerations are necessary and intrinsic. To show why the case does not succeed will bring out my argument clearly.

Reid is prepared to accept that these 'aesthetic' sports can legitimately be regarded as art. As he says: 'The question is whether the production of aesthetic value is intrinsically part of the purpose of these sports. (If so, on my assumptions, they will be in part, at least, art)' (1970, p. 25). Beardsley would be committed to the same view. But this is mistaken. It fails to recognize the significance of the distinction between the aesthetic and the artistic which is implicit in my example of Indian dance.

To put the point generally, what underlies my rejection of the contention that the artistic is that which is intentionally created or performed for aesthetic value is the recognition of a particularly important characteristic of the concept of art. In view of the casualties littering this field, any attempt to characterize the arts in terms of definition, or by reference to particular kinds of object or performance, is almost certainly doomed to failure. My account emphasizes a characteristic which is central to the notion of an *art form*, rather than to a work of art within that medium. That central characteristic is that it is intrinsic to an art form that there should be the possibility of the expression of a conception of life issues.[1] Certainly, this characteristic is central to many art forms, which can express a view of, for instance, moral, social, religious and political matters. My account emphasizes that crucial aspect of the arts to which any characterization must be adequate, namely, the inseparable relationship of the arts to the life of society . To take a clear example, it is reported that during the occupation of France in the last war a German officer visited Picasso in Paris, and noticed Guernica, which Picasso had painted as an expression of his revulsion at the bombing of the little Spanish town of that name by the German fascists. Impressed by the painting, the officer asked 'Did you do that?' to which Picasso replied 'No, you did'.

The objection has been raised that in sport, too, there can be comment on life-issues, as in the case of the black American athletes at the Munich Olympic Games, who gave the clenched-fist salute for black power during the playing of the national anthem. But this does not constitute a counter-example, since the gesture was clearly extrinsic to, not intrinsic to, and expressed by means of, the conventions of sport. By contrast, it is certainly intrinsic to the concept of the arts that a view could be expressed, for instance, on colour discrimination, as in Athol Fugard's plays about that problem in South Africa.

It becomes clear why Reid and Ruth Saw are significantly mistaken to allow that the aesthetic sports are forms of art. For this is to overlook the importance of that aspect of the concept of art on which my account lays emphasis, and which is *central* to the case for the vital *educational* importance of the arts. Although, unlike purposive sports, aesthetic considerations are intrinsic, there is no possibility, within the conventions of aesthetic sports, of the expression of a conception of life issues. It is difficult to imagine a performer of gymnastics, diving, figure skating, synchronized swimming or trampolining including in his sequence movements which expressed a view of war, of love in a competitive society, or of any other such matter. Certainly, if such movements were included they would, unlike art, *detract* to some extent from the performance.[2]

There are, of course, abstract works of art, where it would be a mistake to look for meanings. In such a case one may be concerned solely with, for instance, the line, colour, movement, structure, and so on, and it would reveal a failure to understand the character of the work to try to 'read' into it some relevance to life issues. Such cases do not constitute an objection to my account, since that is proposed in terms of what it is to be an *art form*. However, they do raise problems which I shall consider below.

It should be emphasised that I am offering here only a *necessary* condition of an art form — thus, for instance, journalism, preaching and political speeches would not constitute counter-examples. I am certainly not proposing a definition, but rather a necessary condition specifically to distinguish the artistic from the aesthetic. Still less does this necessary condition offer *any* support for the currently popular, but radically misconceived notion that all the different art forms constitute a generic area of the curriculum. (See Best 1992.)

A further objection which might be raised against my account is that it is merely stipulative. Certainly no philosopher can legislate the correct use of terms, and hence 'artistic' could be used synonymously with 'aesthetic'. Moreover, there could be no philosophical objection to uses such as 'the art of cooking', 'the arts of war', 'the art of loving', and, as a classic case, a book I once noticed entitled '*The Womanly Art of Breast Feeding*'. The conceptual point is that even if 'art' and its cognates should continue to be used as broadly as this, there is still a distinction between those activities which have, and those which do not have, intrinsic to their conventions, the possibility of expressing a conception of life issues. Moreover, in such a case it would be necessary to use some other term to mark the distinction. It is much less confusing to restrict 'art' and its cognates to such activities.

An example of a conflation of the two concepts, which raises questions central to the argument of this book, occurs in an interesting and important symposium on objectivity and aesthetics by Sibley and Tanner (1968). Sibley states clearly at the outset that he is concerned with 'aesthetic descriptions', by which he means 'assertions and disagreements about whether, for instance, an art work (or, where appropriate, a person or thing) is graceful or dainty, moving or plaintive, balanced or lacking in unity' (p. 31). He later adds other terms such as 'beautiful', 'elegant' and 'charming' (p. 47). As we have seen, it is certainly possible, at least in many cases, to consider works of art from an aesthetic *as contrasted with* an artistic point of view. Moreover, to anticipate part of my later discussion, I do not argue that the two concepts are *always* clearly separable, nor do I deny that aesthetic considerations often constitute a significant part of artistic judgments. So it does not follow that to consider the use of aesthetic descriptions with respect to works of art is necessarily to misconceive the character of *artistic* appreciation. Nevertheless, it is clear from Sibley's paper that he does fail to distinguish the two concepts. As a consequence he assumes that an argument about the use of *aesthetic* descriptions is an argument about *artistic* appreciation. For instance, one of Tanner's principal arguments against Sibley's case for the objectivity of *aesthetic* judgments — an argument in which he himself takes over the same conflation of the aesthetic and the artistic — is that there is not as much agreement in critical *artistic* judgments as Sibley claims: 'One has only to look at the variety of reasons for which Shakespeare has been admired to see that this is so' (p. 65).

It is significant that Sibley bases his argument for the objectivity of aesthetic judgments on an analogy with colour judgments, which he takes to be a paradigm of objectivity, arguing that the use of aesthetic descriptions is relevantly similar. But whatever the merits of the analogy in support of his argument for the objectivity of the use of *aesthetic* descriptions, such as 'graceful', 'delicate' and 'dainty', such terms cannot be regarded as central examples of the discourse of *artistic* appreciation. Indeed, at least in many cases, an exclusive or even predominant use of such terms in an artistic context would cast serious doubt on the user's capacity for genuine appreciation of an art form.

Largely as a consequence of overlooking the distinction, there is an illegitimate extrapolation from an argument about the use of *aesthetic* terms to a conclusion about the objectivity of *artistic* appreciation. This is not to deny the usefulness of an examination of the use of aesthetic terms. What I do deny is that the use of such terms can be regarded as typical of artistic appreciation. Indeed, it is a highly significant consequence of the important characteristic which is central to my account of the concept of art that there are *no* terms which could be said to be *typical* of artistic appreciation. For instance, a critical appreciation of Shakespeare's *Measure for Measure* might be concerned with such questions as the extent to which characters such as Angelo and Isabella were deceiving themselves about their own characters and attitudes early in the play; whether their learning from their experiences is central to the play, or whether the intention is rather that those reading or watching it should learn from the inability of the characters to recognize their own weaknesses; the extent and effectiveness of Shakespeare's sense of irony; the extent to which profound and perennial moral questions are raised in terms of the play. Such discussion is not even remotely *aesthetic*, but rather concerned with insight into human character and relationships, and an understanding of life situations.

The contention over the character of this play is a good exemplification of the point, for it certainly does not even remotely involve a consideration of the aptness of applying to it aesthetic descriptions of the kind of which Sibley gives instances. Instead, to give brief examples, it ranges from Coleridge's view that it is the only painful Shakespearian play, in that both the comic and the tragic parts are disgusting; to Wilson Knight's conception of it as an allegory, in which each main character has a counterpart in the story of Christ; to Empson who thinks of it in terms of an analysis of various uses of 'sense'; to Goddard's view that it expresses the corruptive effects of power on human character; to Marxist interpretations of the play as an assertion of life and love in an unjust society — hence the centre of the play is taken to be Claudio's speech to Isabella to save his life; to T.S. Eliot, who takes the opposite view, that the centre of the play is the Duke's speech to Claudio extolling death.

Such considerations reveal unmistakably that an adequate account of the concept of art must place the emphasis on a characteristic far more significant and wide-ranging than merely the way in which people apply *aesthetic* descriptions. Hence my suggestion that it is intrinsic to at least most of the arts, by contrast with the aesthetic, that they can give expression, for instance, to moral and social concerns, insights into personal relationships and character development. This is why it is impossible to compile a list of *typical* artistic judgments. Indeed, it reveals a misconception even to attempt to do so. For the arts can give expression to conceptions of the *whole range* of the human condition.

Learning and Understanding

This raises a crucial question for the arts in education, and one which clearly reveals the trivialisation involved in approaching questions of artistic appreciation by analogy with colour-judgments. For a crucial difference, of which Sibley is certainly aware, but whose significance he does not *sufficiently* recognize, is that learning, knowledge and experience are of far greater importance for artistic appreciation than for colour discrimination. Indeed, in this respect even the supposed parallel between colour and aesthetic judgments is questionable, for by contrast with the case of colours, an aesthetic appreciation of nature, for example, may be inseparably bound up with, one expression of, a conception of life which also finds expression in an attitude to moral and social matters. That is, the kind of description which one would give of an aesthetic experience of nature, unlike the ascription of colour predicates, might be significant in revealing a good deal about one's character, depth, attitudes to life, even one's religious belief or lack of it.

What I want to emphasize, however, is that although there may be some initial plausibility in arguing that, for example, 'graceful' connotes a property rather as 'red' does, the analogy with artistic appreciation is highly *im*plausible, if this is taken to imply that the terms used in artistic judgments connote properties, however loosely that term may be interpreted. That is, if the notion of ascribing a property is construed on the model of colour-judgments, then artistic judgments are so *completely* different that it makes no sense at all to imagine that they can be construed in terms of ascribing properties. Even if we were to accept Sibley's analogy, there is a significant difference between aesthetic and colour judgments, on the one hand, and artistic judgments on the other. This difference, which is implicit in much of my argument so far, consists in the fact that, in the arts, it makes no sense to suggest that learning, understanding and experience can be regarded as distinct from learning, understanding and experiencing life situations generally. It could much more easily be supposed that the use of aesthetic descriptions could be learned in isolation from such general experience of life. Moreover, with respect to the analogy, young children generally could very well have excellent colour discrimination — indeed, far better than their elders. But it is inconceivable that young children generally could be capable of equally or more perceptive *artistic* judgments than their elders.

This aspect of the concept of art is also, of course, what makes it so difficult to appreciate artistically, as opposed to aesthetically, the arts of another culture. An artistic appreciation of the dancing of Ram Gopal, to which I referred earlier, would require an understanding not simply of an independent activity but, to some extent, of the cultural traditions and ways of life of a different society. It is his recognition of the importance of this point which leads Tanner to say (op. cit., p. 72):

> One may feel, reading poetry in a foreign language, that even though one has a mastery of the vocabulary, syntax, and even to some extent the idioms of the language, one is still bound to miss much of the signifi-cance of the poetry, because the only way to grasp it is to have spoken the language from the start, living in the community that speaks it.

Subjectivism and the 'Aesthetic'

The failure to distinguish the concept of the aesthetic from that of the artistic contributes significantly to subjectivism, perhaps especially in education. It is far more plausible, although, at least in many cases, mistaken even here, to assume that aesthetic, as opposed to artistic, appreciation or experience is simply a matter of individual preference, liking, or subjective taste, which has little or no rational or cognitive content. In many cases there may be some justification for assuming that aesthetic judgments are of this nature. For example, a choice of ice cream, or wallpaper, and numerous such choices, may be made purely on the basis of subjective liking or preference. In other cases this is certainly not true. For example, adequate aesthetic judgments of many sporting activities, such as gymnastics, require considerable understanding of the activity. However, since in many cases aesthetic judgments can with some justification plausibly be regarded as expres-sions of mere subjective preference, to conflate the aesthetic with the artistic connives in the seriously damaging misconception that artistic appreciation is also a matter of mere non-rational, subjective taste. Thus, the failure to recognise the distinction between the aesthetic and the artistic contributes largely to the trivialisation of the potential of the arts in education.

Some years ago when I had published a paper arguing for the objectivity of artistic appreciation, a letter was written objecting that I was merely attacking a straw man. For, the author contended, the real issue, which has been widely debated since philosophy immemorial, is that of such explicitly evaluative judgments as 'This is a beautiful drawing'.

He was quite right that that has been the traditional quest of the philosopher for centuries. But, as I hope is clear, that quest is thoroughly misconceived. It is this persistent manifestation of the conflation of the aesthetic and artistic which is the straw man. To repeat, questions of beauty are by no means central and are often irrelevant to artistic appreciation. Imagine going to music concerts, plays, exhibitions of paintings etc., with someone who purports to appreciate these arts, and every time we ask his opinion of a work he replies with: 'It is (or is not) beautiful', or some similar comment. We ask his opinion of Shakespeare's *King Lear* and Dostoievsky's *The Brothers Kamarazov*, and again he replies: 'They are beautiful'. If this is the only kind of response he makes, it would constitute good grounds for *denying* that he is capable of artistic appreciation. It makes no sense to suppose that an exclusive concern with whether works of art are beautiful or not could count as artistic appreciation. One would be nonplussed, for example, if, after attending the performance of *Measure for Measure* to which I referred earlier, one were to be asked whether the play was beautiful. That may be an intelligible question about some works of art — for instance ballet productions. But for many it would make little or no sense. Indeed, many artists would, justifiably, regard it as an insult to their work if it were to be discussed in terms of beauty. To repeat, it has been said that beauty is what the bourgeoisie pays the artist for. Artistic appreciation is rather revealed, for instance, in the ability to discuss, recognise and propose valid and perceptive interpretations and to give reasons for what one values in a work.[3]

A related, equally common, and equally damaging assumption, is that the arts are primarily or exclusively concerned with entertainment or enjoyment, from which, unlike, for instance, the sciences, there is nothing of significance to be learned. Notices of theatre programmes, music concerts, and art exhibitions, appear on the entertainment pages of newspapers. That assumption is more likely if the aesthetic and the artistic are conflated since, I suppose, most artefacts created to provide aesthetic satisfaction, are intended to provide enjoyment. Such a notion is not only far less plausible, in the case of artistic appreciation, but involves a fundamental misconception and trivialisation of the character, and especially the educational potential, of the arts.

The Relation Between the Concepts

The aesthetic and the artistic are not always clearly, if at all, separable. In some cases it may be impossible to distinguish them. Moreover, artistic judgments often involve aesthetic judgments. For instance, in many, perhaps most, cases one's judgments of the aesthetic quality of the movements of the dancers will be *part of* one's artistic appreciation of a dance. Similarly, it is, at least often, possible to consider paintings, plays, novels, poems and pieces of music from an aesthetic, as opposed to an artistic, point of view — for instance, in terms of purely structural considerations and, respectively, the colour or sound. But such aesthetic qualities may nevertheless be relevant to artistic appreciation. An art lecturer of my acquaintance who had hung a painting he admired in a prominent position in his college was asked by the principal to move it because it did not blend with the decor of the corridor. Clearly the principal's concern was an aesthetic one, whereas the lecturer's had been with the artistic quality of the work. But that is not to say that a consideration of the background on which it should hang is irrelevant to the artistic appreciation of a painting. And in many cases it may be impossible to distinguish an aesthetic appraisal of the colours used from an artistic appreciation of the work. Again, poetry read aloud in a language which one does not understand may strike one as aesthetically pleasing, even though an artistic appraisal of it is impossible. Nevertheless, even where one does understand a poem, the sound of it when read may be by no means irrelevant to an artistic appreciation of it — the works of Dylan Thomas and Verlaine are good examples, while Gerard Manley Hopkins actually marked the syllables he wanted to be accented on reading.

In the case of music the distinction between the two concepts and the question of the relationship between them are more difficult. Nevertheless, there is a distinction similar to that in my example of Indian classical dance. It is quite possible to enjoy music aesthetically without understanding it at all. It could strike one as having a remarkable aesthetic quality, analogous to the call of a loon on a lake in a Canadian forest, or simply as a pleasing succession of sounds, analogous to the sound of the sea, or of the wind in the trees. For example, as an undergraduate I belonged to an Asian Music Circle in which many of us were introduced to previously unknown forms of music which we found immediately attractive. Yet in some cases if we had encountered these sounds in a different context they would probably have been unrecognizable to us as forms of *music*. This shows that our appreciation could not have been *artistic*. It was purely *aesthetic*.

It should be added that it may often be necessary to take into account, at least implicitly, wider factors than what someone says on any one particular occasion in order to be able to judge whether his appraisal was aesthetic or artistic. For instance, his previous and/or subsequent behaviour and judgments may reveal that he lacks any understanding of the art form, and hence that his appreciation could only have been aesthetic.

Problems

Architecture poses a problem for my characterization of art since, in perhaps the great majority of cases, buildings do not allow for the expression of a conception of life issues in the sense in which this is possible in literature, drama, dance and painting. (There is, of course, a sense in which architecture, like almost every other aspect of life, could be said to be an expression of the spirit of the age, or of a particular society, but clearly that is a different sense from the one which interests me in the present context.) But I am inclined to think that to a large extent the reason for the difficulty is precisely the reason for my doubting whether, in the majority of cases, these can count as works of *art*, although they are undoubtedly central cases for aesthetic appraisal. It would strike one intuitively as odd to refer to the activity of designing and building the majority of houses, offices and factories, for instance, as *art*, and it is certainly not normally described in that way. Where architecture is normally and naturally designated as art, as, for instance, in the case of church architecture, this would accord with my account. For the architecture of churches can certainly, and characteristically *does,* give expression to a conception of life, as becomes particularly apparent when one visits the temples and mosques of very different cultures with very different religious beliefs.

It may seem that buildings such as ornate palaces, in which there is no such expression, are counter-examples to my account. It is no part of my case to deny that there may well be uncertain, borderline cases, but a further argument can be adduced to defend my suggestion here. I should be inclined to doubt whether such buildings are at least clear cases of art, for they are to a large extent functional, that is, there is a purpose for which they are constructed which can be specified independently of the manner of achieving it. By contrast there is no means/end distinction in the case of a work of art, since *what* the work could be said to be trying to achieve cannot be comprehensively characterized independently of the means by which it is achieved. The same consideration applies, for instance, to church architecture.

There is a parallel situation in dance, since one would not normally refer to some forms of dance as art, for example, social dance and much folk dance. But it is often impossible to draw a sharp distinction. In some cases there is a broad and hazy area between folk dance and dance as an art.

A more difficult problem for my proposed account of art is posed by music. It has been said that all art aspires to the condition of music. What is meant by this remark is, I think, that in music, more than in other art forms, the inseparability of form and content is more often more immediately obvious. This is why it frequently sounds so odd to speak of the *meaning* of a piece of music (e.g. Bach's Fifth Brandenberg Concerto). Of course, this characteristic is equally, if less obviously, true of other art forms, which is why I prefer to use the formulation 'the expression of a conception of life issues' rather than, for instance, 'the embodiment of' or 'a comment upon' life issues. For these latter more readily imply that the 'meaning' could be adequately characterized independently of the medium. Yet it makes no sense to suppose that, in the arts, *what is* expressed could be comprehensively characterized apart from the particular *way* in which it is expressed.

It will not do to attempt to overcome the problem of music in the way in which I dealt with architecture, since there are numerous pieces of music in which there is no expression of life issues, but which are *paradigm* cases of the art form, whereas this is not true of architecture. I could, and perhaps I should, rest my case on the fact that there is a vast amount of music which does give such expression, for instance opera, oratorio, religious music generally, songs generally, much of Debussy, some of Berlioz (e.g. *The Symphonie Fantastique*), Sibelius, Elgar and Beethoven (the Ninth Symphony) — and there are innumerable other examples. Strictly, that is sufficient for my characterization of an art form. Yet I am uneasy that there are also so many pieces of music which are unquestionably art but in which the suggestion that there may be some expression of a conception of life seems intolerably forced and absurd.

Conclusion

For this reason, of the two major issues I have raised in this chapter, I am confident about the first, but only tentatively so about the second. I am confident that there is an important distinction between the aesthetic and the artistic which is largely overlooked, and that even where it is recognized its character has been misconstrued. My examples reveal clearly that 'aesthetic' is certainly *not* equivalent to 'artistic', and that it is a serious misconception to slide from a consideration of the use of *aesthetic* descriptions to a generalization about *artistic* appreciation.

The second major issue is my suggestion for an important distinguishing feature of the concept of art. That suggestion is not without its difficulties, but I think that it is at least a step in the right direction.[4] Some grounds for this qualified optimism are provided by the kinds of case we have considered. The salient feature of this account is clearly illustrated by the example of sport. As we have seen, as a consequence of conflating the aesthetic and the artistic it is sometimes mistakenly believed that sporting activities are forms of *art*. This conclusion is reached on the *irrelevant* grounds that *aesthetic* appraisal is characteristically used of both sport and art. This kind of view, explicit in the passage from Ruth Saw cited earlier, is implicit in the following quotation from Lowe (1976):

> Among sculptors, R. Tait McKenzie has brought a fine sense of movement
> to his studies cast in bronze. There is no question about the aesthetic
> qualities of these art works: hence they provide intrinsic clues to our
> grasp of the elusive nature of beauty of sport. (p. 167)

Ironically, this kind of argument achieves precisely the opposite of what its authors intend, in that it implicitly *invalidates* the case for sport as art. It does so by implicitly drawing attention to the *distinction* between the aesthetic and the artistic. Thus it implicitly supports, and conveniently summarizes, my own account. For whereas sport can be the subject of art, art could not be the subject of sport. Indeed, however *aesthetically* attractive such activities may be, the very notion of a *subject* of sport makes no sense. The same applies equally to the aesthetic appraisal of other phenomena, such as the beauties of nature.

This significant difference between the two concepts gives the humorous point to Oscar Wilde's description of a sunset as only a second-rate Turner.

Notes

1 I am, of course, aware that the phrase, 'can give expression of a conception of life issues' gives only a vague indication of the characteristic I have in mind. Such vagueness is unavoidable, since, to emphasize a point whose importance, especially for the arts in education, can hardly be overstated, the arts can take as their subject matter almost, if not quite, *every* aspect of the human condition.

2 I have considered the question of whether sport is at elsewhere (Best 1988).

3 To his great credit Rod Taylor is one of the first arts educators to recognise the philosophical confusion and educational danger of continuing to conflate the aesthetic and the artistic — of supposing some mystical, metaphysical overarching 'aesthetic',

4 Graham McFee (1992, Chapter 9) offers an interesting variant of this characterization.

Chapter 13

Art and Life

A question of fundamental importance to the philosophy of the arts is that of the relationship between the arts and the life of society. One's understanding of a work, and with it one's feeling about it, may be inseparable from the aspects of life which are its subject matter, or to which implicit reference is made. For example, the meaning and emotional impact of Alan Paton's novel *Cry The Beloved Country* is given by the unusual, rather biblical, use of language in which the tragic events are expressed. The novel is emotionally moving because the characters are set in a particular socio-historical context, in which almost inescapable racist attitudes inexorably determine the tragedy. Similarly, the power of many of Shakespeare's plays consist largely in the insights they provide into the human condition.

It is, of course, this central characteristic of the arts which frequently involves moral evaluation. Thus in the notorious court case, D.H. Lawrence's novel *Lady Chatterley's Lover* was condemned by some because of its supposedly immoral attitudes to sexual relationships. It is also this characteristic which led to the wry remark that Barbara Cartland's novels positively impede an understanding of the human condition. The reasons one would give for criticising or discussing sentimental, escapist romantic novels would consist very largely in showing their lack of integrity to life.

From an educational point of view the central importance of this characteristic of the arts is obvious. There is a considerable responsibility here. For, to put it crudely, just as good art, and good approaches to art, taught by high quality teachers, can have a powerfully constructive influence, so some kinds of art and approaches to art have a potentially harmful influence. Moreover, it is important to be clear that such moral implications are inescapable. Some subjectivists would like to believe that they can opt out of this responsibility — indeed, some seem to think that it is their moral *obligation* to opt out of it. They are rather like the light dove in Chapter 6 which craved the unintelligible ideal of empty space, devoid of air, in order to have complete freedom for flight. Yet it is important to recognise clearly that to do *nothing* is *itself* morally reprehensible if there should be fruitful and enriching understanding and feeling which students could achieve only if the teacher *did* something. No teacher can avoid the crucial moral responsibility of deciding what to teach and how to teach it. In relation to the arts, such decisions will frequently involve a choice of subject matter. And, of course, to decide to teach only, for example, technical skills is *itself* a great moral responsibility. For in doing so one may be *depriving* one's students of the possibility of exploring, coming to understand, issues to which they may otherwise remain blind. Of course, this is not in the least to deny the importance, sometimes, of teaching the techniques of a discipline. As we made clear in Chapters 6 and 7, one cannot be free to explore and express oneself in the arts if one lacks the requisite skills. Neither am I even denying that a teacher could teach solely technical skills. What I am saying is that, especially in certain art forms, the decision to do so would be *inescapably* a moral decision.

The demands on the teacher's objectivity are clearly considerable. For in choosing his subject matter and method of approach he must try progressively to avoid indoctrination, the imposition, even inadvertently, of his own prejudices. He must stimulate and encourage the progressive development of the student's own attitudes, conceptions, feelings.

Polarisation

The central question of this chapter can be brought into focus by considering the tendency towards a polarisation of opinions about whether it is possible, or legitimate, for the arts to express issues from life.

Those at one pole rightly emphasize that artistic meaning is partly an expression of the life of society, and because they are especially impressed by the potential influence of the arts on understanding of and attitudes to life generally, they contend that the meaning and value of the arts consist in the purposes they serve. For instance, throughout history the arts have made powerful and incisive moral and social comments. It is a recognition of just how dangerous the arts can be in this respect which induces totalitarian régimes to censor and apply stringent restrictions on the arts. This purposive view offers a clear rationale for the important notion of education *through* the arts, in that there is a great deal of enormous significance to life generally which can be learned through the arts.

By contrast, those at the opposite pole rightly point out that to insist that the value of the arts resides in the purposes they serve is to deny their *intrinsic* value. For in that case the arts are merely means to ends. For example, since moral and social ends could be achieved by other, non-artistic, means it is difficult to see that the arts have any intrinsic value. Thus many insist that the arts are autonomous, in that their meaning and value are solely intrinsic and have no reference to the life of society. There is almost inevitably a confused sliding between the two poles of the purposive and autonomist conceptions of art, even by their advocates, since there is important truth in each.

Purposive or Autonomous

Tolstoy (1930, p. 120) believed it to be a trivialization of art to equate it with beauty, since, he thought, the value of art lies in 'the purpose it may serve in the life of man'. For Tolstoy the value of art resides in its moral purpose; thus a good work of art is one which expresses morally good feelings from which morally good lessons can be learned. By contrast, the autonomist contends that it is the purposive account which trivializes the arts by reducing them to mere 'message-carriers'. Since the 'message' could be conveyed in other ways, such as sermons, political speeches, or journalism, the purposive account appears to deny *intrinsic* value in the arts. Thus, in reaction against the purposive view, many regard the arts as self-contained activities. There are several examples of this prevalent autonomism. Oscar Wilde (1966) wrote:

> As long as a thing is useful or necessary to us, or affects us in any way, either for pain or for pleasure, or appeals strongly to our sympathies, or is a vital part of the environment in which we live, it is outside the proper sphere of art. For to art's subject-matter we should be more or less indifferent. (p. 976)

He concluded from such considerations (pp. 5–6) that: 'All art is quite useless'. Hampshire (1954) appears to be endorsing an autonomous conception of art when he writes:

> The canons of success and failure . . . are in this sense internal to the work itself . . . In so far as the perfection of a work is assessed by some external criterion, it is not being assessed as a work of art, but rather as a technical achievement in the solution of some problem . . . Nothing but holding an object still in attention, by itself and for its own sake, would count as having an aesthetic interest in it. A great part of a critic's work in any of the arts is to place a frame upon the object and upon its parts and features, and to do this by an unnatural use of works in description. (p. 162)

Other examples of autonomism which were cited in the previous chapter, but which I shall repeat here to consider them in this different context, are as follows. Peter Brooke, the theatre director, has said: 'Culture has never done anyone any good whatsoever', and 'No work of art has ever made a better man'. A similar conception is expressed by Hirst (1980, p. 6) when, for instance, he says that 'the role of the arts in education is to aestheticize people', and it seems to underline the comment of 'a distinguished educational pundit' who is quoted (*Observer* 24 January 1982) as saying sharply: 'The arts are marvellous, but moral they are not'.

This is a classic example of the way in which philosophical conflict often arises. Each protagonist is so impressed by an important insight into an area of inquiry that he over-emphasizes it to the point of denying the equally important insight of the other, thus incurring an obvious mistake. This conflict is based on the shared presupposition that art is *either* autonomous *or* dependent on external purposes. Yet, on the one hand, it is obviously mistaken to deny that the arts can express and illuminate life since there are numerous works whose meaning is of this kind. On the other hand, it is obviously mistaken to insist that the arts have no meaning and value other than that of providing a vehicle for the expression of, for instance, moral and social questions.

The Arts as Autonomous

If the autonomist thesis be taken to the extreme of denying that *anything* external is relevant to the meaning and evaluation of the work of art itself, (on a narrow conception of what can count as the work itself), it can easily be shown to be incoherent. For example, it makes no sense to suggest that knowledge of French is irrelevant to critical appreciation of Verlaine's poetry, since without some grasp of the language one could not understand it even in the most obvious sense. At least in many cases, to understand and evaluate works of art requires some comprehension of the socio-historical context in which they were created. For example, to understand Chaucer's language requires some conception of the institutions of his period. Similarly, the meanings of some of the terms used by Shakespeare have changed because of social changes. One may have to learn their original meaning, given by that different social context, before one can fully appreciate his plays. It is clear that a literary work could not be regarded as isolated from the rest of life. This point about language is of far greater significance than is often recognized, since to understand a language involves an understanding of social context. In brief, to understand a poem is to understand a language, which is to understand a culture.

Even if we ignore the most obvious connection with social context, and consider non-verbal arts, a work cannot be understood in isolation from the artistic context in which it was created. For example, it would be difficult to make sense of the notion that Stravinsky's music might have been written in the twelfth century. There is an important sense in which any work of art employs a vocabulary. A discord which might be characteristic of Bartok would be either very puzzling, or perhaps of immense significance, in Haydn. It is difficult to make sense of the suggestion that a whole Haydn symphony might consist of a series of such discords. It is evident, if one considers widely disparate historical periods or geographical regions, that there is a characteristic vocabulary, mode of approach, or group of styles, peculiar to particular artistic traditions, some comprehension of which is necessary for understanding a work of art.

Artists are not, of course, restricted to the artistic context of their day. Some of Turner's later painting has similarities to and may be seen as a precursor of modern abstract expressionism. (Compare it with Constable, for instance.) And the remarkable progressions in some of Gesualdo's madrigals are in a form often used by much more modern composers. But the striking character of these cases derives its sense from the contemporary artistic context. To recognize the uniqueness of a work presupposes an implicit comparison with others.

The meaning of at least very many works of art depends upon relations with social and artistic context to such an extent that it becomes unintelligible to regard such contextual factors as 'external'. Thus the difficulty even of formulating what its thesis amounts to tells against autonomism, since it is by no means clear what is meant by the injunction that one should limit one's attention, in critical appreciation, to the work itself. It is as unclear, or incoherent, as the suggestion that one should consider the meaning of a sentence in isolation from the rest of language and life.

Response

It is, then, unintelligible to suppose that artistic meaning is independent of the rest of life. Nevertheless, there is a problem here since, as we have seen, the possibility of artistic feelings depends upon an art form in which they can be formulated. Yet since the feelings can be identified only by reference to that formulation, how can such feelings have any relation to life? The problem can be brought into focus by asking how it is that we can be moved by what happens to characters whom we know to be fictional. At first sight it may seem odd that one can be moved by characters who are merely artistic creations. Radford (1975, p. 75) proposes a solution:

> being moved when reading a novel or watching a play is not exactly like being moved by what one believes happens in real life, and, indeed, it is very different. So there are two sorts of being moved and, perhaps, two senses of 'being moved'. There is being moved (Sense 1) in real life and 'being moved' (Sense 2) by what happens to fictional characters. (p. 75)

Yet one cannot intelligibly regard the artistic case as totally independent of life, since our being moved by situations in art depends on the fact that if these were real life situations they would be moving in the normal sense.

I have sometimes appealed to an analogy with chess in order to emphasize the importance of the medium. For, just as a checkmate experience depends upon a grasp of chess, so an artistic experience depends upon a grasp of an art form. But it is an *analogy*, and thus has limits. The concept of art differs from that of chess in that meaning in the arts is much more directly related to life outside the arts. It is, of course, true that even chess is not an isolated activity; its character and existence depend upon the fact that we are beings of a kind in whose lives there is a place for the notion of a game. Nevertheless, there is a relatively sharp boundary to chess, in that the validity of a move depends on the conventions of chess, whereas the validity and value of a work of art may depend on its truth to life. In this respect the arts are more like religion than chess, since a religion which loses touch with the concerns of people in a society degenerates into meaningless liturgical aridity. Yet although social questions cannot intelligibly be regarded as independent of religion, it is important to recognize the significant difference it makes to consider them from a religious point of view. The difference is unintelligible apart from the institution of religion, just as that institution would be meaningless if divorced from social concerns.

The purposive thesis, in effect, regards works of art as transparent windows through which we can see aspects of life. According to this view there is no intrinsic significance or value in the arts since *what* one sees and responds to would be the same whether or not it were seen through the window. The autonomist reacts to an opposite extreme, for he exaggerates their intrinsic value to the point of making the arts opaque to life, which again takes away the significance of art by isolating it from the concerns of society. The metaphor has some explanatory value if, instead, we regard art as translucent. To illustrate what I mean by this, consider Radford's sceptical conclusion (1975): 'our being moved in certain ways by works of art, though very "natural" to us, and in that way only too intelligible, involves us in inconsistency and so incoherence' (p. 78). If one had no grasp of the concept of drama the activities of actors would be unintelligible. Someone ignorant of the concept, watching a play, might well react in just the way Radford suggests: 'Why on earth is John calling himself "Gloucester" tonight and pretending to be in pain? And why is Tom calling himself "Cornwall" and pretending to pluck one of John's eyes out? They did just the same thing last night so none of us will believe it.' That is, if someone were to respond to this situation as to a life situation, rather than to one in drama, his response would be inappropriate. (By a 'life situation' I mean a situation outside the arts. The reason why I use this term, rather than 'real situation', is that, as I shall argue, there is an important sense in which it is a fundamental misconception to contrast a situation in art with the real or, less obviously perhaps, with what occurs in life.) But, as we saw in Chapter 2, his inappropriate response would not reflect a failure of rationality. The work of art casts a translucent light on the situation, and that translucence is an ineliminable part of the appropriate emotional experience. To see the situation in that light requires and reveals a grasp of the concept of art. Similarly, in the example in Chapter 2 of people who have no concept of representational art, someone might say: 'How can it seriously be claimed that what is on this piece of paper is exactly *like* Mr Lowenberger? This is just a configuration of pencil lines on paper, *he* is a human being. How can they possibly be alike?'

Radford's striking conclusion, that our being moved by works of art is both 'natural' and 'only too intelligible', and yet incoherent, arises from a failure to recognize the importance of the difference it makes that this is an *artistic* experience. For if someone were to be moved by actors, not realizing that they were actors, then his response would be based on a misunderstanding.

But equally, it would be difficult to understand how someone could be moved if the dramatic situation bore no relation whatsoever to situations in life.

Part of the point I am trying to make can be brought out by considering the common use of the term 'illusion' in the arts. It is often said, for instance, that drama and dance are concerned with illusions, and in dance the term 'illusory space' is sometimes used. But if one did not understand the use of the term *in that context*, it would be highly misleading, for whereas one may be deceived by an illusion and take it for real, it is not intended that one should take the artistic situation for real in that sense. For instance, a mirage may give the illusion that there actually is an oasis in the distance, whereas in a dramatic production it is not normally intended that the audience should be deluded into believing that there is an actual murder taking place on the stage. Thus no appeal can intelligibly be made to the notion of 'illusion' in its normal, i.e. extra-artistic, use as an *explanation* of our response to and understanding of the arts. It would reveal a similar lack of understanding of drama if a member of the audience were to ask, after the play had finished, how the murdered Caesar had been restored to life for the curtain call.

Similar difficulties arise with respect to the use of the term 'pretence' in an artistic context. For instance, in an interesting and perceptive paper on this topic, Mounce (1980, p. 183) writes of the actor and actress playing Othello and Desdemona that 'when Mr. Paul Robeson pretends to murder Miss Peggy Ashcroft, we are aware of the pretence and treat it merely *as if* it were real'. But whereas it is often, perhaps usually, the intention in a pretence to deceive someone into taking the situation for real, it is rarely if ever the intention to deceive in this way about a situation in a play.

When someone pretends to be in pain, his intention is normally that others should believe that he actually is in pain. By contrast, it is not the intention that the audience should be deceived into believing that the actor playing Gloucester is actually in pain in the scene where the latter's eyes are plucked out. It involves a confusion about the character of the object towards which the response is directed, and therefore of the character of the response itself, to think of it in terms of successful pretence.

It may be objected that I have ignored Mounce's important qualification that we are *aware* of the pretence. But although tempting as an explanation of the intelligibility of our response to art, this does not solve but merely transfers the problem. For it is difficult to see how we can treat as if it were real, and thus be moved by, Paul Robeson's pretence when we are aware that it is merely pretence. To bring out this point more clearly, consider a paradigm case of such awareness of pretence, namely that of children playing at 'let's pretend'. Could it not be argued that here we do have a case where response to pretence is the same as response to the arts? I think not, for at least two reasons. (a) We are not normally, if ever, shocked and disturbed by a 'let's pretend' case, precisely because we are *aware* that this is pretence. (b) If we were moved in such a case, the parallel would have to be being moved by, for example, a cowboy's shooting an Indian, *not* by Billy's pretending to shoot Tommy. Thus it does not help to suggest that the character of artistic response is given by its direction onto the successful pretence of an actor, even if it be supposed that we are aware of the pretence.

In short, it is true that if we are *aware* of the pretence there is no question of being deceived. But it is then difficult to understand why we should be moved. That is, if we are deceived, this might explain why we are moved, but deception is clearly not normally the intention in drama. On the other hand, if we are aware of the pretence, we are not deceived, but then this fails to explain why we are moved.

Our response is not a consequence of treating Paul Robeson's pretence as if it were real. Mounce writes later (p. 184): 'Mr. Robeson might have been pretending to murder Miss Ashcroft; the audience, however, was not *pretending* to be shocked and disturbed by what *he did*' (second italics mine). But we are not shocked and disturbed by what *he did*, that is, by Paul Robeson's *pretending* to murder Peggy Ashcroft; we are shocked and disturbed by Othello's *actually* murdering Desdemona.

It might seem at first sight that some substance is given to notions such as illusion and pretence by the fact that lighting, other stage effects, and a high standard of acting are provided in order to make the situation as convincing as possible, so that the audience will respond as if to a life situation. But while it is true that in such a case the audience may respond in *some* respects as if to a life situation, it is equally important to recognize that the intention in providing effective lighting, and so on, is certainly not that the audience should respond in *all* respects as if to a life situation. For instance, it is not intended that anyone should run on to the stage to save Desdemona or call the police, or shout a warning to Othello that Iago has deceived him about Desdemona's unfaithfulness.

It is because such situations can be so convincingly portrayed that Radford has to concede that it is 'natural' for us to be moved by works of art even though he thinks that this involves us in incoherence. As Mounce puts it (1980, p. 188): 'It is evident that there are things in life that move us. This being so, why on earth is it surprising that we should be moved by representations of such things? Would it not be more surprising if we were not so moved?' It is even less surprising that we respond in this way if the situation is convincingly portrayed. Mounce points out that it is important to recognize the distinction between the cause and the object of the response, for although the *object* towards which my emotional response is directed is an *event in a play*, what *causes* the response is the resemblance in certain respects of that situation to a similar situation in life.

More important, Radford's contention that it is *incoherent* to be moved by works of art arises from a failure to recognize the point emphasized in Chapter 2 that it is the natural response which is the *root* of the concept of art. The response is ultimate; thus to talk of what is and what is not rational or coherent at *that* level makes no sense. There is no rational principle which underlies and justifies the response, it is rather that reasons given in justification derive their sense ultimately from the response. To assume that being moved by the fate of a fictional character is incoherent is itself as incoherent as averring that there is no justification for induction, or for deductive logic. One may justify particular responses *within* the arts, but the notion of justifying artistic responses *in general*, i.e. *externally*, makes as little sense as demanding a legal justification of laws.

The question can be approached by considering the use of the term 'imagination' and its cognates. As we saw in Chapter 8, Reid proposes a very tempting and widely assumed thesis:

> How do perceived characters come to appear to possess, for aesthetic imagination, qualities which as bare perceived facts they do not possess. Why should colours and shapes and patterns, sounds and harmonies and rhythms, come to mean so very much more than they are?. . . The embodiment of value in the aesthetic object is of such a nature that the value embodied in the perceived object or body is not literally situated in the body . . . Our question is, How do the values get there? The only possible answer is that we put them there — in imagination.

This is a tempting thesis because it does seem to solve the problem of the relation between art and life, in that, for instance, on this account, the situation in a play is seen imaginatively as if it were a real-life one, and this is thought to justify our being moved by it.

But the common assumption that what distinguishes artistic experience from other kinds of experience is that, in the case of the arts, imagination is necessarily required in order to respond appropriately, is at least misleading and may be simply false. If the assumption should mean that the objects of our artistic responses are *imaginary*, then this is the same misconception as that involved in the cases of illusion and pretence considered above. For in this sense, to imagine something is to take to be happening what is not really happening. Yet one does not *imagine* that Othello murders Desdemona; Othello *does* murder Desdemona. Neither does one need imagination to understand that an actor is playing the part of Othello.

If, on the other hand, the supposition is that even though the dramatic situation is not imaginary, imagination is required in order to respond appropriately to the arts, then (a) that is not always true, and (b) in any case this is not a distinguishing feature of the arts. For instance, given a high standard of acting, it requires no imagination to respond strongly and appropriately to the gouging out of Gloucester's eyes in *King Lear* — indeed, there would be something odd about anyone who did not so respond. In relation to (b), this is not in the least, of course, to deny that imagination is of considerable importance in the arts, for instance, in identifying with a character in a play and entering into his situation, in what I called in Chapter 10, 'the involved attitude'. My point is that imagination may be equally necessary to understand and respond to certain people and situations in life. Imagination may be required to enter into King Lear's situation, to respond sensitively to the position of the character in the play, rather than simply observing what happens in a detached way. But, equally, imagination may be required to understand and respond adequately to an old man in a similar situation in life.

The prevalent assumption that imagination is a distinguishing feature of artistic experience has its source in the same misconception which underlies those theories which offer explanations of artistic response in terms of illusion or pretence. That seminal misconception pervades the history of the philosophy of the arts. Yet it is difficult to see, for instance, how imagination could perform this role. For we do not imagine that one actor is murdering another, nor do we imagine that Othello murders Desdemona.

A sophisticated version of this misconception can be seen in Scruton's book *Art and Imagination* (1974). It would be too much of a digression to consider Scruton's thesis in the detail it merits, but it is highly relevant to my thesis to show that my argument raises fundamental problems for his. To put his thesis briefly, and I hope fairly, Scruton argues that the distinguishing feature of artistic response is that we respond not to a real object, but to an imagined one. In his view, the object of attention is an imagined object, hence: 'experience of a work of art involves a distinctive order of intentionality, derived from imagination, and divorced from belief and judgment.' (op. cit., p. 77): While it is true, as I have argued, that artistic experience involves 'a distinctive order of intentionality', this certainly does *not* imply that belief and judgment are out of place. Quite the contrary. It is because he believes that what is portrayed in artistic situations is *imagined* — presumably in the sense of 'imaginary' — that Scruton takes it that therefore there can be no question of whether such portrayals can be true or not, and therefore that they must be divorced from belief or judgment. That is, one cannot be said to believe or disbelieve what is portrayed in a situation which one knows to be imaginary — which is how Scruton construes artistic experience. According to Scruton, then, involvement with the arts cannot be an involvement with matters of reality and truth, because the objects of our attention are *imagined* objects. But in my view, his thesis is founded on the deeply mistaken assumption that our response to art is to *imagined* situations and people.

An important consequence of Scruton's thesis is that: 'It is a purpose of convention in art to overcome emotional involvement' (op. cit., p. 130). This is precisely because, in his view, we are confronted not with a real, true, situation, but with an *imagined* one, with which emotional involvement would be inappropriate. Thus, for Scruton, presumably, it reveals a lack of grasp of the conventions of art if one should be emotionally involved.

To repeat a point made in Chapter 10, there is certainly *some* point in this notion, but there is a more important confusion. It is true that an understanding of the concept of drama is partly revealed in the fact that one does not, for instance, run up to the stage to save Desdemona. But it is a confusion to draw the conclusion that artistic appreciation requires distancing, detachment, the overcoming of emotional involvement. On the contrary, in many cases it would be a mark of one's failure fully to appreciate a work if one were not to respond emotionally. The conventions of art do not overcome but rather determine the *character* of the emotional involvement. The object towards which the emotional response is directed, which determines what response it is, is a fictional character, a character in a play or novel. One responds not to Peggy Ashcroft, the actress, but to Desdemona, the character in the play. This may have been what Balanchine was thinking of in his reported remark, which has puzzled many in the dance world, that a ballerina is not a woman dancing, because she is not a woman and she doesn't dance.

The response to art is different in important respects from emotional response in life, and it is a confusion to regard the former as a diminished version of the latter. Mounce's writing, quoted earlier, that because we are aware of the pretence involved in the artistic situation we treat it merely *as if* it were real seems to be another manifestation of the misconception that the response to art is a diminished version of response in life. As an illustration of what I mean, consider the example I cited earlier of the Inuit people who went to see a performance of *Othello* and believed that people on stage had really been killed. They were reassured after the performance by seeing the actors still alive. Their response was inappropriate because, lacking any understanding of drama, they misunderstood what was happening on the stage. When they discovered that no one had been killed, without any grasp of drama they might well have concluded that the whole enterprise is thoroughly silly. It would be a confusion to assume that an understanding of drama would give them detachment, distancing, and thus an overcoming of, or diminished, emotional involvement. On the contrary, if the play were well performed, those with the relevant understanding might well reveal it partly *by* their emotional involvement. It may be tempting to make the point by saying that such spectators, as compared with the Inuit, could be *equally* moved emotionally. But that may be misleading in implying a comparison on the same scale, whereas the point I am making can be better made by saying that the scales are different.

Explanation

Yet even those who agree that the question of justification does not arise may still feel that there is a legitimate question to be asked about the *explanation* of artistic response. I have said that one responds in some respects as if it were a life situation. But I do not intend that as an explanation. It may be asked: 'How *can* one respond as if to a life situation when one knows very well that these are fictional characters?' It is true that the situation is in some respects similar to situations which would move us in a similar way in life. But this will not do as an explanation since nevertheless the *differences* are so remarkable that it is difficult to understand how one can be moved. For example, the action takes place on a stage; no actor appeals to the audience for help; there may be hundreds of people watching a supposedly intimate scene; we know that these are actors; and sometimes the action or dialogue may be stylised in ways which are quite unlike situations in life.

A tempting and common contention is that what explains our responses to art is that the artistic situation represents or symbolises the relevant situation in life. Representation and symbolism are, of course, possible in art. But they cannot provide an explanation in general of response to art. Adducing the notion of symbolism in this way is ambiguous. It may be possible to recognise *that* something is a symbol externally, i.e. without an understanding of the practice within which it occurs. Yet the significance of the symbolism or representation may be very different in different practices. For example, the symbolic significance of a crucifix is internal to the concept, in that it could not be understood outside the context of the religious practice in which it has its place. Thus one cannot appeal to the notion of symbolism as a general explanation of response to art.

It may be thought that what explains artistic response is the similarity of the artistic to the life situation. Yet, at least in sophisticated cases, it is clear that the sense of the claim that the situation, for instance on a stage, is like the life situation, is given by the concept of drama. For example, allegory may be quite unlike any life situation: plays are frequently performed with different sections of the stage representing different geographical locations — Shakespeare's *Antony and Cleopatra*, with its very short scenes, is often performed in this way: asides and soliloquies, revealing secret thoughts of the speakers, if audible to those in the back row of the theatre, could certainly be heard by other characters. There are many such examples where it is implausible to suggest that the similarity of the dramatic to the life situation is an explanation of why we respond as we do. In such cases the sense of the notion of appropriate response derives from its development from the root of the concept, part of which consists in a common response, i.e. in the fact we *do* respond in a similar way to situations in life and similar situations in art.

It is neither conceptually nor empirically necessary to have experience of the relevant situation in life in order to understand that in art. There is a great range of emotion concepts which are acquired through literature, stories, play-acting. Children, for instance, learn to understand people through stories well before they have met the relevant situations in life. We respond to situations in art when we have never experienced anything similar in life. Thus the response cannot be *explained* in terms of the similarity of the art to the life situation. Similar considerations apply to representation or symbolism as a general explanation of artistic response, since both imply a prior understanding of that which is symbolised or represented. It is true that in particular cases one may need a prior understanding of a situation in life, for example in cartoons, or in a lampoon of Mrs Thatcher. Yet in many other cases one can respond to artistic situations when one has never encountered anything of that kind in life. One can learn, through artistic response, about situations not yet encountered in life.

I do not wish to imply either that a grasp of the concept is a precondition of being able to respond appropriately, or the converse. An appropriate response is an *expression* of a grasp of the concept of art. The root of the concept consists partly in the fact that we do respond similarly to the similar situation in life. At a more sophisticated level there may be no such, or only a tenuous, similarity of situation.

Yet, despite what has been said, it is still, from a certain point of view, a remarkable fact that we do respond as we do to a dramatic situation which we are aware is not a situation in life. It is because the response is so remarkable, seen in this light, that some are impelled to explain it in terms of illusion, since they assume that such a response must reveal that one is confusedly taking the situation for real; and others feel that the only explanation must be in terms of imagined objects and qualities, or in terms of pretence. It is because others share the assumption that any explanation must be of these kinds that they regard the response as irrational even if 'natural'. Such assumptions, though understandable, are mistaken, for all that can be said is that our response to the arts is immediate and natural. My thesis can be brought out more clearly, perhaps, by pointing to the implausibility of the parallel, which no one to my knowledge has suggested, that there is a confusion involved in laughing at comedy.

The thesis for which I am arguing is a repudiation of traditional and still prevalent theories or philosophies of art, which offer explanations of artistic response by reference, for instance, to imagination, illusion, or symbolism. This whole tradition in my view is based upon a fundamental misunderstanding. I am denying that there can be an explanation of artistic response, where an explanation is an attempt to show artistic response to be intelligible by showing it to be an instance of a reaction of a kind with which we are familiar in other circumstances. (I am not concerned with explanations in the sense, for instance, of accounts of the evolution of art.)

I have argued that the response is natural and immediate. This is to repudiate the contention that our being moved by characters and situations in art rests on confused thinking. Our being moved in this way rests neither on incoherence and irrationality, nor on coherence and rationality. Nor does it rest on imagination, illusion, symbolism, or pretence. It rests on nothing.

Response, Reality and Symbolism

The central point can be brought out by considering the objection that it is, indeed, irrational to be moved by characters whom we know to be fictional; our emotional response, the objection runs, if it be rational, is not to the fictional characters but to the real people whom they represent, or of whom they are symbolic. Thus, for instance, according to this objection it is irrational to be moved by the plight of the poor in Dickens' novels. Where one's response is rational it is directed to those who are poor in life in relevantly similar ways. The objection agrees that a work of art may produce a change in one's feelings towards the poor, but denies that it is one's emotional response *to the work* which produces the change.

Yet, on the contrary, if one were to respond not to the fictional character portrayed in the work but to the person or kind of person in life who is in some way symbolized or represented, then that would be a failure either artistically or in appreciation. This brings up the central thesis of Chapter 11. For in such a case substitution would in principle be possible, in that the object of the response would not be the particular character portrayed. Examples will illustrate the point. Athol Fugard's play *Statements Made After Arrest Under The Immorality Act,* as the title indicates, attempts to bring out the effects of an aspect of the apartheid laws in South Africa on the personal lives of ordinary people. Yet the play seems to me to be an artistic failure precisely because one responds not so much to the characters in it as to the people in life of whom they are symbols. To too great an extent one responds to those for whom they are surrogates rather than to the characters in the play. By contrast, Athol Fugard's *Sizwe Bansi is Dead* is, in my view, more successful artistically because one *does* respond to the situation of the particular characters in the play.

It is implausible to suggest that in a novel such as J.M. Coetzee's *Life and Times of Michael K* one's emotional response could be directed towards anyone other than the central character. One becomes immersed in the series of situations and difficulties he faces in his life, and one's response is highly particular in being identifiable only in terms of its direction on to that particular character who has lived through them in his own particular way. The notion of substitution, and thus the suggestion that the response, if it be rational, must be not to Michael K but to the kind of person he represents, makes no sense. Similarly, it is precisely a mark of the greatness of George Eliot's *Middlemarch* that one *does* respond, for instance, to Dorothea, Casaubon, Rosamund and Lydgate because of the perceptive particular detail with which they are drawn. We respond to *real* characters, not symbols.

Moreover, one may retain as vivid and detailed a memory of and feeling about such characters as one does in the case of people in life. It would reveal not a clear understanding that these *are* fictional characters, but a failure fully to appreciate, by involving oneself in, the novel, if one were to fail to respond to them in this way.

It is interesting in this respect to consider what counts as an appropriate response, and what counts as an inappropriate response, reflecting a failure of understanding. In one well-known British television series there is a popular character who suffered unhappy marriages. The actor playing the part of the husband who had recently married her, on a public appearance, was taken aside by a group of miners who, shaking clenched fists, warned him to be sure she was treated right this time. Humphrey Bogart, well known for playing film tough guys, was apparently several times accosted by aggressive men who demanded that he should prove how tough he really was. This tendency to endow the actor with the attributes of the character or kind of character he plays was also illustrated by the dismay evinced by some women when his first wife revealed that an actor well known for playing James Bond spends a great deal of time admiring himself in the mirror.

Such cases reveal a failure of understanding, and to some extent a loss of touch with reality. But they connect significantly with a major concern of this chapter, namely, the sense in which what happens on stage, or in a novel or film, is real. This is brought out by the range of reactions which are regarded as appropriate. Brutus does not pretend to stab Caesar, nor does an actor pretend to stab an actor. Brutus *really does* stab Caesar. A response as to a pretence is inappropriate here precisely because of the sense in which what happens on stage is not pretence or illusion, but *real*.

To return to the objection raised above, it is of course true that one's response to a fictional character may produce a change of feeling about people in life. One's response to the fictional character Michael K may produce a new perception of and feeling for the numerous people in every country who are born into hopeless situations, and who can only try to survive social contexts which are beyond their comprehension but of which they feel a dull, vague and immutable inability to be a part. This possibility of a change of feeling towards a general situation as a result of a particular experience is by no means limited to the arts. We saw in Chapter 11, and the point will be expanded in the next section, that a particular experience in life may bring about a profound change in one's feeling about war, the competitive spirit, or those who are disadvantaged or destitute. Indeed, contrary to the thesis of the objection, it is precisely because one is responding not to a mere symbol but to a *particular character or dramatic situation* that there can be such a real and meaningful change in one's attitude to people and situations in life.

This brings out in another way a misconception in theories which purport to explain artistic meaning in terms of symbolism. To take just one example from the many, a book on drama in education contends that the meaning of characters and situations in drama is given by their being symbolic of real people and situations in life. In fact, as we see, such a notion involves a failure to recognise the power of art. If a work is successful one responds not to a mere symbolic representation, but directly and fully to a *fictional* character who is *real*.

Learning through Feeling

Although the point is commonly overlooked, for instance in the prevalent tendency to assume that education is primarily a matter of being able to assert or assent to propositions, it is of the first importance to recognize that the *most important* lessons we learn in life are such that their significance to us *cannot* be characterized in terms of having acquired new facts. This notion is central to understanding the crucial contribution of the arts to education, in that it gives substance to the notion of education *through* the arts.

It is an obvious fact that war involves death and suffering, but a particular experience might bring home vividly, because of its emotional impact, what the fact *amounts* to. This applies not only to learning through the arts. One may learn from a particular experience, whether in life or in the arts, in ways which profoundly change one's general attitude, for instance, to war or other people.

King Lear, in mental torment, buffeted, cold and drenched while wandering without shelter in a violent storm on the heath, learns what he had never realized in his days of power:

> Poor naked wretches, whereso'er you are,
> That bide the pelting of this pitiless storm,
> How shall your houseless heads and unfed sides,
> Your looped and window'd raggedness, defend you
> From seasons such as these? O! I have ta'en
> Too little care of this. Take physic, Pomp
> Expose thyself to feel what wretches feel,
> That thou mayst shake the superflux to them.

What does it amount to to say that Lear learned from his experience? Clearly it is not a matter of acquiring facts. In that sense he knew it all when he was king. He knew that the poor go hungry, have inadequate clothing and shelter, suffer various privations, and so on. These are mere truisms. His new understanding cannot be equated with the acquisition of facts. Thus he cries 'Take physic, Pomp; expose thyself to feel what wretches feel'. It is through *feeling* that Lear begins to understand the plight of the poor. That feeling arises from a particular experience, and it brings him to see what he had never before realized. It had to be brought home to him in his feeling for a particular situation. Through an involvement with a particular work of art, such as *King Lear*, we can achieve a similar understanding. This is the peculiar power of the possibility of learning through the arts, and it is the principal reason for the central importance of the arts in education.

If enough people learned to understand, in *this* sense, the plight of the unfortunate, we surely could not continue to have so many homeless while others have several palatial homes; we could not continue to have so many wealthy people, while millions starve or suffer acute malnutrition. Our 'Pomp', our political leaders and dignitaries, already know the *facts;* their failure is a failure of *feeling.*

Similarly, after the Ghost of Hamlet's father had revealed the truth of his treacherous murder, Hamlet cries: 'My tables, — meet it is I set it down, That one may smile and smile and be a villain.' Hamlet has learned a powerful lesson. But what has he learned? If, in order to answer that question we were to consider simply and solely what he has *written down*, then we might well echo Horatio: 'There needs no ghost, my lord, come from the grave to tell us this.' For of course we all know, and Hamlet knew very well *before* this deeply moving emotional incident, that some people smile and smile even though they are villains. Yet the full force of what it *amounts to* may be brought home to us by a particular incident, such as what the Ghost told Hamlet. It might strike us in our times as a consequence of being deceived and cheated by a plausibly charming salesman.[1]

In a different context Holland (1980, p. 63) makes the point: 'The kind of understanding open to us here is such that we can (and most often do) have it without being able to say what it is we understand.' Patrick White, in *The Tree of Man*, writes that revelations are never conveyed with brilliance as revealed. Wittgenstein (1967, §158) says: 'If a theme, a phrase, suddenly means something to you, you don't have to be able to explain it. Just this gesture has been made accessible to you.'

This brings up again another point of such importance that it cannot be over-emphasized, especially in an educational context, which is that the learning involved here is essentially *personal*. It will not necessarily be accessible to everyone; it depends upon the understanding and sensitivity which each individual brings to it. One learns only to the extent that the experience is a fully involved personal experience, given by one's own conception of the work, and one's own attitude to life. The principal criterion of one's having learned from it will be a change not of stable principle but in one's attitude.

This explains how it is that we can learn through an involvement with the arts, in ways which may affect our lives, without incurring the consequence, supposed by the autonomist, that this reduces the arts to mere message-carriers. In a particular case it may be impossible to imagine another, non-artistic, way of learning, for instance, such a powerful moral, social, or emotional lesson. This is largely because the arts can have such a profound emotional impact. Consider, for instance, how banal and ineffective would be any attempt to make the same point by means of factual statements. It would make no sense to say that the learning was the same. The peculiar force of learning from a work of art consists in an emotional experience which casts a new light on a situation, revealing what the analogous life situation amounts to. There are numerous examples one could give. In each case the emotional experience is given by that particular artistic form of expression. As we have seen, the object of the emotion, that which *identifies* the emotion, cannot be characterized independently of one's *conception* of the situation. Because of this cognitive content of the emotion, what one learns from it is inseparably related to the emotional response. And the emotional response is directed on to and identified by the *particular* work of art.

What is learned may affect one's life outside art, for instance in a changed attitude to other people. In *The Tree of Man*, Patrick White writes: 'You do not know a thing until you have forgotten how that thing was learned.' After visiting an exhibition of Münch's paintings someone observed that he emerged from the gallery seeing everyone for days in terms of Münch's vision. People were seen as skeletons with dried skin drawn tightly across their bones. The vividness gradually faded, and the experience became absorbed into his general conception of life. One can have a similar experience with artists such as Francis Bacon, Edward Hopper and others.

In Chapter 2, I emphasized that the roots of art are to be found in immediate, natural responses, and that this immediacy of response should not be lost as one develops rational understanding and sophistication. In this respect, as I have said, it is seriously mistaken, though it may be common among those who over-intellectualize the arts, to suppose as Scruton does that it is a purpose of convention in art to overcome emotional involvement. It is to counter such a view that Mounce, in his perceptive paper (1980, p. 192) contends that an unsophisticate who sobs at sentimental Hollywood slush is closer to the spirit of art than an intellectual who regards his intellectualism as placing him in a position superior to and inoculated from emotional response. 'The unsophisticate responds to very bad art. But the response is at least genuine. The intellectual is deficient not perhaps in what he *thinks* good but in how he responds to it — he no longer feels its magic.'

Because of the possibility of emotional experience through involvement with the arts, one can achieve insights into and understanding of life which may be more powerful than any alternative. Through the arts one can come not only to understand a situation but, by involving oneself in analogous experience, to feel what it amounts to. Gloucester, in *King Lear*, after losing his eyes, learns so much that he exclaims that it was when he had his sight that he was blind, and it is only now, when blind, that he begins to see. Similarly, it takes insanity to make Lear sane. What their having learned these lessons amounts to could not be captured simply in their being able to assert or assent to facts or propositions which they could not have asserted or assented to previously. Stated propositionally, what they learned may appear to be mere truisms. Their new knowledge, if genuine, will be shown not in statable facts but in the way they live. We can learn the same lessons through an emotional involvement with the play.

The Arts as Entertainment

There is a widespread assumption that the arts are forms of entertainment in that they are mere diversions from the serious concerns of life, from which nothing of any significance can be learned. It is remarkable that this trivializing conception of the arts should be furthered by many who are concerned with the arts in education. One source of this conception, as we have seen, is the misguided assumption that to accept that we can learn from the moral, social and other insights expressed in the arts implies the reduction of the arts to the status of mere message-carriers. Yet, contrary to what the autonomist believes, it denigrates the arts to deny that they can express incisive insights into a wide range of aspects of life. There is an important truth in Tolstoy's contention (1930, p. 120) that it trivializes the arts to equate them with beauty, and to value them in terms of the pleasure they may give rather than the purposes they may serve in the life of man. The conception Tolstoy was opposing is still prevalent: it stems partly from the conflation of the aesthetic and the artistic which was considered in Chapter 12. It is implicit in Hirst's (1980, p. 6) assertion that the role of the arts in education is to aestheticize people, and it is also implicit in the confident assertion of the 'educational pundit' quoted earlier that 'the arts are marvellous, but moral they are not'. There is still wide scope for the application of George Eliot's characterization of the artistic ambitions and accomplishments of well-brought-up young ladies in her time as 'small tinklings and smearings'.

The seriousness of the arts consists partly but significantly in the fact that what is expressed in them feeds back into life, in the insights given into the human condition and other aspects of life. When the arts lose this seriousness they atrophy. This is particularly obvious in the literary arts, drama and film, and it clearly applies to at least some of the other arts. The point has frequently been recognized by artists. For example, the Dada group tried to revitalize art by making it face reality, by making reality into art, by sharply criticizing the artificiality of the contemporary conceptions of art which, they felt, vitiated its integrity. Their concern was a moral one, that artists should concern themselves with both the harsh and the banal in human experience. They would strongly have endorsed the aphorism that beauty is what the bourgeoisie pays the artist for. They rejected the conception of art as a mere diversion having no direct bearing on the serious concerns of life. That trivialising conception, by pandering to a desire for romantic escapism, supported and connived in the social immorality to which Dada was so hostile. Art, in this sense, they believed to be an opium of the people. Yet they can also be seen as making the logical point that if art loses touch with reality it loses its meaning and becomes a substitute for life, and art experiences become merely vicarious. In this respect, as I mentioned above, the arts resemble religion, since when religious practices and doctrines become detached from a serious concern with social and moral matters they degenerate into irrelevant and vacuous liturgical autonomy.

This point that the vitality of the arts depends upon the integrity of their relation to life generally was made by Tennyson in *The Palace of Art*. He wrote this poem as a consequence of a remark made to him by a fellow undergraduate: 'Tennyson, we cannot live in art.' He imagines his having built 'a lordly pleasure-house, Wherein at ease for aye to dwell'. The choice of terms such as 'pleasure-house' and 'at ease' are already significant. He imagines it furnished with the finest art, tastefully decorated and far removed from the squalor and harshness of reality — he sounds rather like some modern academics when he writes: 'I sit as God, holding no form of creed, But contemplating all'. Yet, the palace becomes a hollow prison and the enterprise self-defeating, since the value and meaning of art become drained of all substance and vitality. A cottage in the vale becomes far preferable.

Holland (1980, p. 108) points out that the arts, like scientific and non-scientific inquiries, are susceptible to debasement:

> Enquiries trivialize themselves in subservience to exploitation, and the arts are commuted into instruments of gratification. The more they gratify

the more they falsify and they proliferate with cancerous fecundity while in this state. So it is not their popularity but the presence or absence of anything absolutely good in them and the degree of attachment people have to whatever is absolutely good in them that makes the difference.

He goes on to make a point which I have previously emphasised, that this kind of involvement with the arts must be one which concerns *each individual separately*. In a similar vein, Shahn (1957) writes:

It is not the degree of communicability that constitutes the value of art to the public. It is its basic intent and responsibility. A work of art in which powerful passion is innate, or which contains extraordinary revelations concerning form, or manifests brilliant thinking, however difficult its language, will serve ultimately to dignify that society in which it exists. By the same argument, a work that is tawdry and calculating in intent is not made more worthy by being easily understood. (p. 106)

Meaning in Art and Life

A difficulty for the autonomist thesis which has already been mentioned is that of giving a coherent account of the meanings of terms used in discussion of the arts. As quoted earlier, Hampshire writes of the art critic's 'unnatural use of words in description'. But it is difficult to make sense of the supposition that the terms used in discussion of the arts have a meaning which bears no relation whatsoever to the meanings of those terms used in non-artistic contexts. For in that case the terms used in art criticism, although they appear to be the same as those in common use, would form a recondite technical vocabulary, understandable only by the *cognoscenti*. Of course, there are terms whose meaning is given by their use in the arts, such as 'chiaroscuro', 'iambic pentameter', 'modulation', and so on, but such terms do not form the majority, let alone the totality, of the vocabulary of critical discussion of the arts. More important, for my present point, it would make no sense to say that terms such as 'sad', 'being moved' and numerous others are totally unrelated to their use outside the arts. Most of us talk about novels, poetry, plays, and so on, quite freely and without having learned any highly specialized language. As we have said above, in general, and specifically in the case of emotion-terms, a principal criterion of one's understanding of a term used in an artistic context is one's ability to employ it in normal contexts.

However, this is certainly not to say that the meanings of terms used in an artistic context are merely parasitic on normal use. On the contrary, it is important to recognize that in this as in other aspects the arts feed back into life. Through a consideration of its use in discussion of the arts, one may achieve a richer understanding of a term whose principal use is in ordinary language. It is important to remember that the meaning of a term is not rigidly fixed. It may develop nuances as it is used in different contexts. For example, the use of the term 'sincere' and its cognates in critical discussion of the arts can endow it with richer meaning when it is used outside the arts. Or, one might say, it is possible to gain a deeper and more sensitive appreciation of its meaning by considering its use in the arts. To reflect on why a poem is sincere may give one a more perceptive grasp of the concept of sincerity in general.

A penetrating paper by Leavis (1952–3) entitled 'Reality and sincerity' is a fine example. He considers three poems, *Barbara,* by Alexander Smith, *Cold in Earth* by Emily Bronte, and *After a Journey* by Thomas Hardy. Leavis dismisses *Barbara* as a characteristic piece of Victorian sentimentality, which he has introduced simply as a heuristic foil for the other two poems. He does not consider it seriously, since it 'has all the vices that are to be feared when his theme is proposed, the theme of irreparable loss. It doesn't merely surrender to temptation, it goes straight for a sentimental debauch, an emotional wallowing, the alleged situation being only the show of an excuse for the indulgence, which is, with a kind of innocent shamelessness, sought for its own sake. If one wants a justification for invoking the term 'insincerity', one can point to the fact that the poem clearly enjoys its pang . . . The cheapness of the sentimentality appears immediately in the movement, the clichés of phrase and attitude, and the vagueness and unrealities of situation . . . ' By contrast, in Emily Bronte's poem

> the emotional sweep of the movement, the declamatory plangency . . . might seem to represent dangerous temptations; but in responding to the effect of passionate intensity we register what impresses us as a controlling strength.

Nevertheless, Leavis concludes that Hardy's poem is more sincere. Unlike the others it is not declamatory, and, although Emily Bronte's poem is striking,

> when we go back to it from Hardy's the contrast precipitates the judgment that, in it, she is dramatizing herself in a situation such as she has clearly not known in actual experience: what she offers is betrayingly less real . . . Glancing back at Alexander Smith we can say that whereas in postulating the situation of Barbara (he can hardly be said to imagine it) he is seeking a licence for an emotional debauch, Emily Bronte conceives a situation in order to have the satisfaction of a disciplined imaginative exercise . . . The marks of the imaginative self-projection that is insufficiently informed by experience are there in the poem and (especially with the aid of the contrast with Hardy) a duly perceptive reader could discern and describe them, without knowing the biographical fact. They are in the noble . . . declamation, and in the accompanying generality, the absence of any convincing concreteness of a presented situation that speaks for itself. (pp. 93–4)

One may have reservations about the apparent implication that an artist would have to live through an experience in order to be able to express it sincerely in his art. Yet there is undoubtedly something in the contention that the most profound works of art can be created only by a man or woman with considerable experience of and sensitivity to life. Moreover, readers of the poems could not adequately appreciate them without similar experience.

Hardy offers 'a precise account of the highly specific situation defined by the poem' — 'precisions of concrete realization, specificities, complexities'. By contrast to the 'declamatory generality' of Emily Bronte's poem, Hardy offers a 'quiet presentment of specific fact and concrete circumstance'. Thus 'to say that Hardy's poem has an advantage in reality is to say . . . that it represents a profounder and completer sincerity'.

This is, of course, an inadequate sketch of Leavis's perceptive analysis, but I hope it is sufficient to illustrate how a deeper insight into a concept which is primarily grounded in ordinary language can be gained through reflecting on its use in the arts.

Learning to Experience Feelings

There are important implications for the education of emotional feelings. For, as the Leavis example shows, perceptive reasoning can give not just a richer under-standing of feelings, but richer feelings. Without that rational understanding, one could not experience the feelings. One can come to recognize in a poem the criteria of sincere feelings, and one can involve oneself by imaginatively projecting oneself into the poet's situation. To involve oneself with his form of expression is, in that sense, to experience that feeling.

Writing of Hardy's poem, Leavis uses such phrases as 'the opposite of the rhetorical'; 'it is tenderly familiar and matter-of-fact'; 'No alchemy of idealization, no suggestion of the transcendental, no nobly imaginative self-deceiving attends on this devotion to the memory of a woman'; 'matter-of-fact precision and im-mediacy (there is no plangency about the resonance)'. Qualities such as these are what we should recognize as criteria of integrity of feeling in a relevantly similar life situation — even the apparent clumsiness of Hardy's opening line: 'Hereto I come to view a voiceless ghost'. Sincerity in people in such circumstances consists in such clumsiness, control, playing-down and lack of extrovert emotionalism. Leavis points out the precise features of the poems which constitute the criteria for sincere feelings. This again brings out clearly the rational, cognitive character of the emotional feelings involved. A clearer *understanding* of the poetic criteria of feeling is inseparably related to the possibility of deeper and more discriminating feelings. In this case, we may learn that certain forms of expression, and feelings, amount to the sentimentalism and self-dramatization which obscure and vitiate the capacity for genuine feeling — hence Leavis's insight that sincerity is insepa-rable from reality. For sentimentalism involves escape into the fantasy of self-indulgence, by contrast to the rigorous courage to recognize and respond to the truth.

This example brings out very clearly the parallel between life and art. It also indicates something of the immensely rich and varied possibilities of learning from emotional involvement in the arts, in ways which can enrich our under-standing and feelings in life. Simone Weil, castigating the dishonest romanticism of most literature, writes (1968, p. 161):

> But it is not only in literature that fiction generates immorality. It does so in life itself. For the substance of our life is composed of fiction. We fictionalize our future; and unless we are heroically devoted to truth, we fictionalize our past, refashioning it to our taste. We do not study other people; we invent what they are thinking, saying, and doing.

It is important to recognize the contrast between (a) 'fiction' in the sense of 'fantasy' or 'escapism', and (b) 'fiction' as opposed to 'fact' or 'history'. Simone Weil is exposing the immorality of fiction, in life and art, in the sense of escapist fantasy. Her comment underlines a principal theme of this chapter, which is concerned emphatically to *reject* the common assumption that the arts are fictional in *that* sense . Thus, for instance, Shakespeare's *Measure for Measure* is certainly *not* fiction in the sense that it is an escape from reality into fantasy, since, on the contrary, it brings sharply home to us important *truths* about the human condition. For instance, it includes penetrating insights, from which we can learn truths about ourselves, into the power and danger of self-deception. The situation against which Simone Weil was inveighing is now far worse, since television has turned fantasy into what many people take for reality, and other people become cliché images, passing by as background noise on a blurred screen.

Yet, to deepen integrity of feeling incurs the penalty of increasing vulnerability. Leavis sees the 'rare integrity' of Hardy's poem in its saying, in effect, that 'the *real* for me, the focus of my affirmation is the remembered realest thing, though to remember vividly is at the same time, inescapably, to embrace the utterness of loss' (p. 96). Although the price is very great, it has to be paid for that depth and integrity of feeling, since 'Hardy, with the subtlest and completest integrity is intent on recapturing what *can* be recaptured of that which, with all his being, he judges to have been the supreme experience of life, the realest thing, the centre of value and meaning'. By reflection on and involvement with such a poem one can learn more about what it is to experience profoundly sincere feelings in life. And this may open the possibility of *experiencing* more profoundly sincere feelings.

The meaning and values which govern one's life are expressed not just in words but in how one lives. A work of art can reveal a *Weltanschauung*, a conception of life, in its details, perhaps in previously unrecognized or only partly recognized failures of integrity manifested in self-deception, and self-indulgent sentimentalism. As Coleridge has put it: 'We know a man for a poet by the fact that he makes us poets'. Moreover, one of the criteria for the depth and sincerity of a person is the kind of art which engages him, and, perhaps, above all, the kind of *involvement* with the arts which he evinces. Involvement with the arts can give increasing depth and sensitivity to one's understanding of and experiences in life.

If faced with integrity, experiences in life are perplexingly heterogeneous, and serious involvement with the arts can help one to appreciate this. Criticizing the ordered artificiality of traditional novels, Virginia Woolf (1945) asks us to examine an ordinary mind on an ordinary day:

> The mind receives a myriad impressions . . . Life is not a series of gig lamps symmetrically arranged . . . Let us record the atoms as they fall upon the mind in the order in which they fall, let us trace the pattern however disconnected and incoherent in appearance, which each sight or incident scores upon the consciousness. Let us not take it for granted that life exists more fully in what is commonly thought big than in what is commonly thought small. (pp. 189–90)

Progressively, an educated appreciation of the arts can help to remove the oversimple, misleading conceptual/emotional props of childhood and early youth: it can help to encourage the integrity and emotional sensitivity to explore the reality of the immense variety of the human condition. When we recognize that emotions are not just a matter of 'natural' instinctive or subjective responses, but that emotional feelings are *rational in character*, and thus can be indefinitely learned and refined, as one extends and deepens one's understanding, we can begin to recognize the enormously important contribution which the arts can make to personality development.

Conclusion

It should, perhaps, be repeated that to emphasize the crucial importance of understanding and rational learning to the feelings involved in the arts is not in the least to oppose spontaneous response. In Chapter 2 it was pointed out that the *roots* of the arts are to be found in immediate reactions. The ability to respond with feeling should not be lost as more sophisticated understanding is achieved. Not all feelings will be immediate, since it may require reflection to understand a work and thus to respond appropriately. But some feelings will be immediate — or if not, one has lost touch with the roots and spirit of the arts. My thesis is not primarily concerned with whether responses are or are not spontaneous, but with showing that the kinds of feeling which are central to involvement with the arts are necessarily rational and cognitive in kind. To put it briefly, they are inseparable from *understanding*. That is, without such understanding an individual would be *incapable* of such feelings, whether spontaneous or not. Martha Graham once said that it takes at least five years of rigorous training in the discipline to be spontaneous in dance.

This reveals the incoherence of purported psychological explanations of intentional action solely in terms of the stimulus-response causation model. As we saw in Chapter 9, an artistic intention cannot be characterized independently of the concept of art. Thus any account of such an intention in purely physical terms is inevitably deficient. A physical movement of limbs, unlike an intentional action, cannot express a moral view, or reveal a vision of life. Similarly, an exclusively psychoanalytic account of the artist's intention or the spectator's response, for instance, in terms of the working out of repression, would inevitably be inadequate since it would omit the *art* aspect of the emotion. It would ignore the artistic medium in which, uniquely, the intention is formulated, and which is inseparable from it. Thus it would fail to distinguish artistic from non-artistic experiences. As we have seen, the feeling is inseparable from the possibility of its expression in the *arts*. Lucian Freud has said about his portraits: 'As far as I am concerned the paint is the person'.

The point, which is a major theme of this chapter and of this book, can be illustrated by Wilfrid Owen's insistence about his own work that it was *not* that the pity was in the poetry, but that the poetry was in the pity. The poignant sense of pity which he felt for the appalling tragedies and agonies of the soldiers of the First World War was inseparable from the poetry in which *alone*, he could express it. The pity could not otherwise be identified; without that poetry it could not exist: it was *that* pity — the pity of the poetry.

One's experience on reading such poetry can be a powerful analogue of the experience of those who were in the trenches. Through such an artistic experience one can come to understand, in a sense which one did not understand before, just what it feels like to have such an experience in life. Indeed, that is a serious understatement of the understanding which can be gained through the arts, for it is quite possible for someone actually to have been in the trenches yet never to have felt just what that situation amounted to until he read the poem. Simone Weil (1978, p. 59) writes: 'It is due to feeling alone that a thing becomes freed from abstraction and becomes something individual and concrete.'

A work of art, and through it a perceptive teacher or critic, can reveal the character of sincere feelings, and give the possibility of deeper and more finely discriminated emotional experience. As Leavis puts it (1952–3, p. 92): 'the superiority can be *demonstrated*'. That is, perceptive reasons can demonstrate the character and quality of the expression of feelings, and thus the character and quality of feelings themselves. In this way reasoning in the arts can give a richer possibility of feeling, not only in the arts, but in life.

Note

1 I am indebted to my former teacher at Cambridge, Professor John Wisdom, for suggesting this example, at a meeting of the Welsh Philosophical Society where I read a version of part of this chapter as a paper.

References

ANSCOMBE, G.E.M. (1965) 'The intentionality of sensation', in R. BUTLER (Ed.), *Analytical Philosophy*, Vol. II, London, OUP, pp. 158–80.

ARGYLE, M. (1975) *Bodily Communication*, London, Methuen.

BAMBROUGH, J.R. (1973), 'To reason is to generalize', *The Listener*, Vol. 89, No. 2285, 11 January, pp. 42–3.

BAMBROUGH, J.R. (1979) *Moral Scepticism and Moral Knowledge* (London: Routledge & Kegan Paul).

BAMBROUGH, J.R. (1984) 'The roots of moral reason', in EDWARD REGIS, Jr (Ed.), *Gewirth's Ethical Rationalism*, Chicago, Chicago University Press.

BEARDSMORE, R.W. (1971) *Art and Morality*, London, Macmillan.

BEARDSMORE, R.W. (1973) Two trends in contemporary aesthetics, *British Journal of Aesthetics*, Vol. 12, No. 4.

BEARDSLEY, MONROE C. (1979) 'In defense of aesthetic value', Presidential Address at the American Philosophical Association, *Proceedings*, Vol. 52, No. 6, pp. 728.

BECKETT, S. (1963) *Watt*, London, Calder & Boyars.

BENNETT, J.F. (1964) *Rationality*, London, Routledge & Kegan Paul.

BEST, D. (1974) *Expression in Movement and the Arts*, London, Lepus.

BEST, D. (1978) Physical education and the aesthetic, *Bulletin of Physical Education*, Vol. 14, No. 3, pp. 12–15 Co-published in the *Journal of the Australian Association of Health, Physical Education, and Recreation*, No. 82, December.

BEST, D. (1978) *Philosophy and Human Movement*, London, Allen and Unwin.

BEST, D. (1984) The aesthetic and the artistic, *Philosophy*, 54.

BEST, D. (1985) *Feeling and Reason in the Arts*, London, George Allen and Unwin.

BEST, D. (1988) 'Sport is not Art', and 'The Aesthetic in Sport', in *Philosophical Inquiry in Sport*, Eds. WILLIAM J. MORGAN/KLAUS V. MEIER. Champaign, Illinois. Herman Kinetics Publishers Inc.

BEST, D. (1990) The Arts in Schools: A Critical Time. (Monograph), Corsham, Wiltshire; Birmingham Institute of Art and Design, and National Society for Education in Art and Design.

BEST, D. (1991) 'Creativity: Education in the Spirit of Enquiry', *British Journal of Educational Studies*.

BEST, D. (1992) 'Generic Arts: An Expedient Myth', *Journal of Art and Design Education*.

BEST, D. (1992) 'Generic Arts in Education: An Expedient Myth', *Times Higher Education Supplement*, 31 January.

BOLTON, G. (1984) *Drama as Education*, Harlow, Essex; Longman Group.

BONDI, H. (1972) 'The achievements of Karl Popper', *The Listener*, Vol. 88, No. 2265, pp. 225–9.

BOSANQUET, B. (1915) *Three Lectures on Aesthetic*, London, Macmillan.
BRITTON, K. (1972–3) 'Concepts of action and concepts of approach', *Proceedings of the Aristotelian Society*, pp. 105–18.
BRONOWSKI, J. (1973) 'Knowledge and certainty', *The Listener*, 19 July, pp. 79–83.
CARRITT, E.F. (1953) 'Croce and his aesthetic', *Mind*, p. 456.
COLLINGWOOD, R. (1938) *The Principles of Art*, Oxford, Clarendon.
DILMAN, I. (1987) *Love and Human Separateness*, Oxford, Blackwell.
DUCASSE, C.J. (1929) *The Philosophy of Art*, New York, Oskar Piest.
EISNER, E. (1981) 'The role of the arts in cognition and curriculum', *Report of INSEA World Congress, Rotterdam*, Amsterdam, De Trommel, pp. 17–23.
GOODMAN, N. (1969) *Languages of Art*, London, OUP.
HAMPSHIRE, S. (1954) 'Logic and appreciation', in W.R. ELTON (Ed.), *Aesthetics and Language*, Oxford: Blackwell, pp. 161–9.
HART-DAVIES, R. (1962) *The Letters of Oscar Wilde*, London, Hart-Davies.
HEPBURN, R.W. (1965) 'Emotions and emotional qualities', in C. BARRETT (Ed.), *Collected Papers on Aesthetics*, Oxford, Blackwell, pp. 185–198.
HEPBURN, R.W. (1966) 'Contemporary aesthetics and the neglect of natural beauty', in B.A.O. WILLIAMS and A. MONTEFIORE (Eds), *British Analytic Philosophy*, London, Routledge & Kegan Paul.
HIRST, P.H. (1974) *Knowledge and the Curriculum*, London, Routledge & Kegan Paul.
HIRST, P.H. (1980) Transcript of a symposium 'Education with the arts in mind', Bretton Hall.
HOLLAND, R.F. (1980) *Against Empiricism*, Oxford, Blackwell.
JAMES, W. (Ed.) (1966) *Virginia Woolf: Selections from Her Essays*, London, Chatto & Windus.
KERR, F. (1986) *Theology After Wittgenstein*, Oxford, Blackwell.
KANT, I. (1929) *Critique of Pure Reason*, trans. N. Kemp Smith, London, Macmillan.
KUHN, T.S. (1975) *The Structure of Scientific Revolutions*, Chicago, University of Chicago Press.
LANGER, S. (1957) *Problems of Art*, London, Routledge & Kegan Paul.
LAWRENCE, D.H. (1936) *Phoenix: The Posthumous Papers*, Ed. E.D. McDonald, London, Heinemann.
LAWRENCC, D.H. (1962) *Collected Letters*, Vol. 1, London, Heinemann.
LEAVIS, F.R. (1952–3) 'Reality and sincerity', *Scrutiny*, Vol. 19, No. 2, pp. 90–98.
McADOO, N. (1987) 'Aesthetic education and the antimony of taste', *British Journal of Aesthetics*, Vol. 27, No. 4.
McADOO, N. (1987) *Review of Feeling and Reason in the Arts,* in *Journal of Philosophy of Education*, Vol. 21, No. 1.
MACDONALD, M. (1952–3) 'Art and imagination', *Proceedings of the Aristotelian Society*, pp. 205–2.
McFEE, G. (1992) Chapter 2, *Understanding Dance*, London, Routledge.
MACINTYRE, A. (Ed.) (1965) *Hume's Ethical Writings*, New York, Macmillan.
MACINTYRE, A. (1967) *Secularization and Moral Change*, London, OUP.
MANGAN, M. (1991) *Settling with the Indians*, BBC Radio 4 Thursday Play. Directed by David Sheasby, BBC Manchester.
MEAGER, R. (1965) 'The uniqueness of a work of art', in C. BARRETT (Ed.), *Collected Papers on Aesthetics*, Oxford, Blackwell.
MOUNCE, H.O. (1980) 'Art and real life', *Philosophy*, Vol. 55, April, pp. 183–.
NEWTH, M. (1989) *The Abduction*, London, Simon and Schuster.
NUSSBAUM, M. (1985) 'Finely aware and richly responsible: Moral attention and the moral task of literature', *The Journal of Philosophy*.
PERRY, R.B. (1926) *General Theory of Value*, New York, Longman.
PHENIX, P. (1964) *Realms of Meaning*, New York, McGraw Hill.
PHILLIPS, D.Z. (1970) *Death and Immortality*, London, Macmillan.

RADFORD, C. (1975) 'How can we be moved by the fate of Anna Karenina?', *Proceedings of the Aristotelian Society*, Suppl. Vol. 49 (July), pp. 67–80.

REID, L.A. (1931, pp. 62–3) *A Study in Aesthetics*, New York, Macmillan.

REID, L.A. (1969) *Meaning in the Arts*, London, Allen & Unwin.

REID, L.A. (Spring 1980) 'Human Movement, the Aesthetic and Art', *British Journal of Aesthetics*, Vol. 20, No. 2.

RHEES, R. (1969) *Without Answers*, London, Routledge & Kegan Paul.

ROBINSON, I. (1973) *The Survival of English*, Cambridge, CUP.

Robinson, K. (1989) *The Future of the Arts in Schools*, Edited by WORSDALE, A., London, National Foundation for Arts Education.

RYLE, G. (1949) *The Concept of Mind*, London, Hutchinson & Co. Ltd.

SAW, R. (1972) 'What is a work of art?', in her *Aesthetics: An Introduction* (London: Macmillan); first published in *Philosophy*, Vol. 36, 1961.

SCRUTON, R. (1974) *Art and Imagination*, London, Methuen.

SHAHN, B. (1957) *The Shape of Content*, Cambridge, Mass., Harvard University Press.

SIBLEY, F.N., and TANNER, M. (1968) 'Objectivity and aesthetics', *Proceedings of the Aristotelian Society*, Suppl. Vol. 42, pp. 31–72.

SPENCER, L., and WHITE, W. (1972) 'Empirical examination of dance', *British Journal of Physical Education*, Vol. 3, No. 1, pp. 4–5.

STANISLAVSKY, K. (1961) *Chekov and the Theatre*, originally from *My Life in Art* (Moscow).

STRAWSON, P.F. (1968) 'Freedom and resentment', in P. F. STRAWSON (Ed.), *Studies in the Philosophy of Thought and Action*, London, OUP.

SWIFT, J. (1726) *Gulliver's Travels*, Oxford, OUP.

TAYLOR, R. (1992) *The Visual Arts in Education*, London, Falmer Press.

TOLSTOY, L. (1930) *What is Art?*, trans. A. MAUDE, London, OUP.

THE ARTS IN SCHOOLS. (1982) London, Calouste Gulbenkian Foundation.

'Towards a Policy for Expressive Arts in the Primary School'. (1984), Scottish Committee on Expressive Arts in the Primary School.

URMSON, J.O. (1957) 'What makes a situation aesthetic?', *Proceedings of the Aristotelian Society*, Suppl. Vol. 31. pp. 75–99.

WEIL, S. (1951) *Waiting on God* (London: Routledge & Kegan Paul).

WEIL, S. (1952) *Gravity and Grace* (London: Routledge & Kegan Paul).

WEIL, S. (1962) *Selected Essays 1934–43*, chosen and trans. Richard Rees (London: OUP).

WEIL, SIMONE (1968) Morality and literature, *On Science, Necessity and the Love of God*, Ed. RICHARD REES, OUP, pp. 160–165.

WEIL, S. (1978) *Lectures on Philosophy*, trans. H. Price, Cambridge, CUP.

WILSON, R. (1967) 'The aerial view of Parnassus', *Oxford Review of Education*, Vol. 3, No. 2, pp. 123–34.

WIMSATT, W.K., and BEARDSLEY, M. (1960) 'The affective fallacy', in W.K. WIMSATT (Ed.), *The Verbal Icon*, New York, Noonday Press, pp. 21–39.

WIMSATT, W.K., and BEARDSLEY, M. (1962) 'The intentional fallacy', in J. MARGOLIS (Ed.), *Philosophy Looks at the Arts*, New York, Scribner, pp. 91–105.

WINCH, P. (1958) *The Idea of a Social Science*, London, Routledge & Kegan Paul.

WINCH, P. (1972) *Ethics and Action*, London, Routledge & Kegan Paul.

WISDOM, J. (1952) *Other Minds*, Oxford, Blackwell.

WITKIN, R. (1980) 'Art in mind — reflections on *The Intelligence of Feeling*', in J. CONDOUS, J. HOWLETT and J. SKULL (Eds), *Arts in Cultural Diversity*, Sydney, Holt, Rinehart & Winston, pp. 89–95.

WITTGENSTEIN, L. (1958) *Philosophical Investigations*, 2nd Ed., Oxford, Blackwell.

WITTGENSTEIN, L. (1967) *Zettel*, Oxford: Blackwell.

WITTGENSTEIN, L. (1969) *On Certainty*, Oxford, Blackwell.

WITTGENSTEIN, L. (1976) 'Cause and effect: intuitive awareness', *Philosophia*, Vol. 6, Nos. 3–4, p. 410.

WITTGENSTEIN, L. (1980) *Remarks on the Philosophy of Psychology*, Vol. 11, Ed. G.H. VON WRIGHT AND HEIKKI NYMAN, Trans. C.G. LUCKHARDT and M.A.E. AVE, Blackwell, Oxford.

WOLLHEIM, R. (1970) *Art and its Objects*, Harmondsworth, Penguin. p. 112.

WOOLF, V. (1945) 'Modern fiction', in *The Common Reader*, 5th Ed., London, The Hogarth Press, pp. 184–95.

Index